AF515499

English Language Teaching

English Language Teaching

Editors

Dr. A.A. Khan

Dr. Anil Saxena

SHREE PUBLISHERS & DISTRIBUTORS

NEW DELHI-110 002

© Publisher

This book, or any part thereof must not be reproduced or reprinted in any form, whatsoever, without the written permission of the publisher, except for the purpose of references and review.

Edition : 2012

Published by :
SHREE PUBLISHERS & DISTRIBUTORS
22/4735 Prakash Deep Building,
Ansari Road, Darya Ganj,
New Delhi–110 002

ISBN : 978–81–8329–487–4

Printed by :
D.G. Printers
Delhi–110 094

Preface

English for Indians, is not an alien language now. This international language is essential for all the students in universities and for others, who may be aspiring for different competitions and various positions, in the corporate and government setup. Beyond the learning of the language, a thorough study of English Literature is helpful in understanding life better and knowing society, further, in a rational manner. Hence, there is always a need for good books to attain knowledge in this regard. Notably, English literature is the literature, written in the English language, including the literature, composed in English by writers, not necessarily from England.

English literature is as diverse as the varieties and dialects of English, spoken around the world. For instance, Robert Burns was Scottish, James Joyce was Irish, Joseph Conrad was Ukrainian, Dylan Thomas was Welsh, Edgar Allan Poe was American, Vladimir Nabokov was Russian and V.S. Naipaul has been born in Trinidad and Salman Rushdi is of Indian origin. Mulk Raj Anand and R.K. Narayan are from India, but all of them are considered significant writers in the history of English literature.

These books have been designed and prepared, within the parameters of the courses for the post-graduate students in various universities of the country. These books, on different topics, are in accordance with the requirements of various courses for the M.A. Examination. All these books have very strictly been shaped as per the prescribed syllabus, on a point to point basis. Therefore, it can be ascertained that these books would be able to fulfil all needs of the students, who are, in fact, our targeted readers. These books would expectedly be accepted by students and acknowledged by teachers, who in turn may recommend these reader-friendly books to their pupils.

We are indebted to all scholars, authors and compilers, whose valuable contributions, we have benefited from, while preparing these books. We are also thankful to the publishers and website operators, whose works, we have referred to, during the compilation of these books. And last but not the least, the undersigned express a wholehearted gratitude to all the associates, who extended their full cooperation in shaping and finalising these books.

These books have covered the whole gamut of English Literature, from the earliest era, through medieval and modern periods to the current age. This particular book is on: ***English Language Teaching.*** Enlightening advisory notes and esteemed remarks are solicited from all concerned circles.

— Dr. A.A. Khan
Dr. Anil Saxena

Contents

1 Applied Linguistics

Linguistics has a significant role in teaching of a certain language. Applied linguistics is an interdisciplinary field of study that identifies, investigates, and offers solutions to language-related real-life problems. Some of the academic fields related to applied linguistics are education, linguistics, psychology, computer science, anthropology, and sociology.

Definition

The use of language-related research in a wide variety of fields, including language acquisition, language teaching, literacy, literary studies, speech therapy, discourse analysis, censorship, workplace communication, media studies, translation studies, lexicography, and forensic linguistics come under applied linguistics.

Observations

"Applied linguistics began life in the 1950s as a post-graduate qualification. Its initial target, largely language teaching, has always been practical, policy-oriented. Its preparation at post-graduate level has been multidisciplinary and, as in mathematics, there is a continuing tension between pure (general, theoretical) linguistics and applied linguistics. It does not expect its conclusions to be buttressed with certainty (and it is unclear whether theoretical linguistics or any other social science can expect that, either). For applied linguistics, there is no finality: the problems such as how to assess language proficiency, what is the optimum age to begin a second language, what distinguishes native and non-native speakers, how we can treat memory loss, these problems may find local and temporary solutions but the problems recur. No doubt, once again, the same may be said of theoretical linguistics: whether all grammars are fundamentally one grammar; what the relation is between the sign and the referent; answers are partial, never final—the problems remain."

The Backdrop

The tradition of applied linguistics established itself in part as a response to the narrowing of focus in linguistics with the advent in the late 1950s of generative linguistics, and has always maintained a socially accountable role, demonstrated by its central interest in language problems. Although the field of applied linguistics started from Europe and the United States, the field rapidly flourished in the international context.

Applied linguistics first concerned itself with principles and practices on the basis of linguistics. In the early days, applied linguistics was thought as "linguistics-applied" at least from the outside of the field. In the 1960s, however, applied linguistics was expanded to include language assessment, language policy, and second language acquisition. As early as the 1970s, applied linguistics became a problem-driven field rather than theoretical linguistics. Applied linguistics also included solution of language-related problems in the real world. By the 1990s, applied linguistics has broadened including critical studies and multilingualism. Research of applied linguistics was shifted to "the theoretical and empirical investigation of real world problems in which language is a central issue."

The Domains

Major branches of applied linguistics include bilingualism and multilingualism, computer-mediated communication (CMC), conversation analysis, contrastive linguistics, sign linguistics, language assessment, literacies, discourse analysis, language pedagogy, second language acquisition, lexicography, language planning and policies, stylistics, pragmatics, forensic linguistics, and translation.

Major journals of the field include *Annual Review of Applied Linguistics, Applied Linguistics, International Review of Applied Linguistics, International Journal of Applied Linguistics, Issues in Applied Linguistics,* and *Language Learning.*

United States

In the United States, applied linguistics also began narrowly as the application of insights from structural linguistics—first to the teaching of English in schools and subsequently to second and foreign language teaching. The *linguistics applied* approach to language teaching was promulgated most strenuously by Leonard Bloomfield, who developed the foundation for the Army Specialised Training Programme, and by Charles C. Fries, who established the English Language Institute (ELI) at the University of Michigan in 1941. In 1948, the Research Club at Michigan established *Language Learning: A Journal of Applied Linguistics,* the first journal to bear the term *applied linguistics.* In the late 1960s, applied linguistics began to establish its own identity as an interdisciplinary field concerned with real-world language issues. The new identity was solidified by the creation of the American Association for Applied Linguistics in 1977.

United Kingdom

The British Association of Applied Linguistics (BAAL) was established in 1967. Its mission is "the advancement of education by fostering and promoting, by any lawful charitable means, the study of language use, language acquisition and language teaching and the fostering of interdisciplinary collaboration in this study".

Australia

Australian applied linguistics took as its target the applied linguistics of mother tongue teaching and teaching English to immigrants. The Australia tradition shows a strong influence of continental Europe and of the USA, rather than of Britain. Applied Linguistics Association of Australia (ALAA) was established at a national congress of applied linguists held in August 1976.

Japan

In 1982, the Japan Association of Applied Linguistics (JAAL) was established in the Japan Association of College English Teachers

(JACET) in order to engage in activities on a more international scale. In 1984, JAAL became an affiliate of the International Association of Applied Linguistics (AILA).

Contrastive Linguistics

Contrastive linguistics is a practice-oriented linguistic approach that seeks to describe the differences and similarities between a pair of languages (hence it is occasionally called "*differential* linguistics").

The Backdrop

While traditional linguistic studies had developed comparative methods (comparative linguistics), chiefly to demonstrate family relations between cognate languages, or to illustrate the historical developments of one or more languages, modern contrastive linguistics intends to show in what ways the two respective languages differ, in order to help in the solution of practical problems. (Sometimes the terms diachronic linguistics and synchronic linguistics are used to refer to these two perspectives.)

Contrastive linguistics, since its inception by Robert Lado in the 1950s, has often been linked to aspects of applied linguistics, e.g., to avoid interference errors in foreign-language learning, as advocated by Di Pietro (1971), to assist interlingual transfer in the process of translating texts from one language into another, as demonstrated by Vinay & Darbelnet (1958) and more recently by Hatim (1997), and to find lexical equivalents in the process of compiling bilingual dictionaries, as illustrated by Heltai (1988) and Hartmann (1991).

Contrastive descriptions can be made at every level of linguistic structure: speech sounds (phonology), written symbols (graphology), word-formation (morphology), word meaning (lexicology), collocation (phraseology), sentence structure (syntax) and complete discourse (textology). Various techniques used in corpus linguistics have been shown to be relevant in intralingual and interlingual contrastive studies, e.g. by 'parallel-text' analysis (Hartmann 1997).

Contrastive linguistic studies can also be applied to the differential description of one or more varieties within a language, such as styles (contrastive rhetoric), dialects, registers or terminologies of technical genres.

Major Branches of Applied Linguistics

Cognitive Approaches

Much modern research in second language acquisition has taken a cognitive approach. Cognitive research is concerned with the mental processes involved in language acquisition, and how they can explain the nature of learners' language knowledge. This area of research is based in the more general area of cognitive science, and uses many concepts and models used in more general cognitive theories of learning. As such, cognitive theories view second language acquisition as a special case of more general learning mechanisms in the brain. This puts them in direct contrast with linguistic theories, which posit that language acquisition uses a unique process different from other types of learning.

The dominant model in cognitive approaches to second language acquisition, and indeed in all second language acquisition research, is the computational model. The computational model involves three stages. In the first stage, learners retain certain features of the language input in short-term memory. (This retained input is known as *intake.*) Then, learners convert some of this intake into second language knowledge, which is stored in long-term memory. Finally, learners use this second language knowledge to produce spoken output. Cognitive theories attempt to codify both the nature of the mental representations of intake and language knowledge, and the mental processes which underly these stages.

In the early days of second language acquisition research *interlanguage* was seen as the basic representation of second language knowledge; however, more recent research has taken a number of different approaches in characterising the mental representation of language knowledge. There are theories that hypothesise that learner language is inherently variable, and there is the functionalist perspective that sees acquisition of language as intimately tied to the function it provides. Some researchers make the distinction between *implicit* and *explicit* language knowledge, and some between *declarative* and *procedural* language knowledge. There have also been approaches that argue for a *dual-mode system* in which some language knowledge is stored as rules, and other language knowledge as items.

The mental processes that underly second language acquisition can be broken down into micro-processes and macro-processes. Micro-processes include attention; working memory; integration and restructuring, the process by which learners change their interlanguage systems; and *monitoring*, the conscious attending of learners to their own language output. Macro-processes include the distinction between intentional learning and incidental learning; and also the distinction between explicit and implicit learning. Some of the notable cognitive theories of second language acquisition include the nativisation model, the multidimensional model and processability theory, emergentist models, the competition model, and skill-acquisition theories.

Other cognitive approaches have looked at learners' speech production, particularly learners' speech planning and communication strategies. Speech planning can have an effect on learners' spoken output, and research in this area has focused on how planning affects three aspects of speech: complexity, accuracy, and fluency. Of these three, planning effects on fluency has had the most research attention. Communication strategies are conscious strategies that learners employ to get around any instances of communication breakdown they may experience. Their effect on second language acquisition is unclear, with some researchers claiming they help it, and others claiming the opposite.

Sociocultural Approaches

While still essentially being based in the cognitive tradition, sociocultural theory has a fundamentally different set of assumptions to approaches to second language acquisition based on the computational model. Furthermore, although it is closely affiliated with other social approaches, it is a theory of mind and not of general social explanations of language acquisition. According to Ellis, "It is important to recognise ...that this paradigm, despite the label 'sociocultural' does not seek to explain how learners acquire the cultural values of the L2 but rather how knowledge of an L2 is internalised through experiences of a sociocultural nature." The origins of sociocultural theory lie in the work of Lev Vygotsky, a Russian psychologist.

Linguistic Approaches

Linguistic approaches to explaining second language acquisition spring from the wider study of linguistics. They differ from cognitive approaches and sociocultural approaches in that they consider language knowledge to be unique and distinct from any other type of knowledge. The linguistic research tradition in second language acquisition has developed in relative isolation from the cognitive and sociocultural research traditions, and as of 2010 the influence from the wider field of linguistics was still strong. Two main strands of research can be identified in the linguistic tradition: approaches informed by universal grammar, and typological approaches.

Typological universals are principles that hold for all the world's languages. They are found empirically, by surveying different languages and deducing which aspects of them could be universal; these aspects are then checked against other languages to verify the findings. The interlanguages of second language learners have been shown to obey typological universals, and some researchers have suggested that typological universals may constrain interlanguage development.

The theory of universal grammar was proposed by Noam Chomsky in the 1950s, and has enjoyed considerable popularity in the field of linguistics. It is a narrowly-focused theory that only concentrates on describing the linguistic competence of an individual, as opposed to mechanisms of learning. It consists of a set of *principles*, which are universal and constant, and a set of *parameters*, which can be set differently for different languages.

The "universals" in universal grammar differ from typological universals in that they are a mental construct derived by researchers, whereas typological universals are readily verifiable by data from world languages. It is widely accepted among researchers in the universal grammar framework that all first-language learners have access to universal grammar; this is not the case for second-language learners, however, and much research in the context of second language acquisition has focused on what level of access learners may have.

Individual Variations

There is considerable variation in the rate at which people learn second languages, and in the language level that they ultimately reach. Some learners learn quickly and reach a near-native level of competence, but others learn slowly and get stuck at relatively early stages of acquisition, despite living in the country where the language is spoken for several years. The reason for this disparity was first addressed with the study of language learning aptitude in the 1950s, and later with the *good language learner studies* in the 1970s. More recently research has focused on a number of different factors that affect individuals' language learning, in particular strategy use, social and societal influences, personality, motivation, and anxiety. The relationship between age and the ability to learn languages has also been a subject of long-standing debate.

The issue of age was first addressed with the critical period hypothesis. The strict version of this hypothesis states that there is a cut off age at about 12, after which learners lose the ability to fully learn a language. This strict version has since been rejected for second language acquisition, as adult learners have been observed who reach native-like levels of pronunciation and general fluency. However, in general, adult learners of a second language rarely achieve the native-like fluency that children display, despite often progressing faster in the initial stages. This has led to speculation that age is indirectly related to other, more central factors that affect language learning.

There has been considerable attention paid to the strategies which learners use when learning a second language. Strategies have been found to be of critical importance, so much so that *strategic competence* has been suggested as a major component of communicative competence. Strategies are commonly divided into *learning strategies* and *communicative strategies*, although there are other ways of categorising them. Learning strategies are techniques used to improve learning, such as mnemonics or using a dictionary. Communicative strategies are strategies a learner uses to convey meaning even when she doesn't have access to the correct form, such as using pro-forms like *thing*, or using non-verbal means such as gestures.

Effective Factors

The learner's attitude to the learning process has also been identified as being critically important to second language acquisition. Anxiety in language-learning situations has been almost unanimously shown to be detrimental to successful learning. A related factor, personality, has also received attention, with studies showing that extroverts are better language learners than introverts.

Social attitudes such as gender roles and community views towards language learning have also proven critical. Language learning can be severely hampered by cultural attitudes, with a frequently cited example being the difficulty of Navajo children in learning English. Also, the motivation of the individual learner is of vital importance to the success of language learning. Studies have consistently shown that *intrinsic motivation*, or a genuine interest in the language itself, is more effective over the long-term than *extrinsic motivation*, as in learning a language for a reward such as high grades or praise.

In the Classroom

While the majority of SLA research has been devoted to language learning in a natural setting, there have also been efforts made to investigate second language acquisition in the classroom. This kind of research has a significant overlap with language education, but it is always empirical, based on data and statistics, and it is mainly concerned with the effect that instruction has on the learner, rather than what the teacher does.

The research has been wide-ranging. There have been attempts made to systematically measure the effectiveness of language teaching practices for every level of language, from phonetics to pragmatics, and for almost every current teaching methodology. This research has indicated that many traditional language-teaching techniques are extremely inefficient. It is generally agreed that pedagogy restricted to teaching grammar rules and vocabulary lists does not give students the ability to use the L2 with accuracy and fluency. Rather, to become proficient in the second language, the learner must be given opportunities to use it for communicative purposes.

Another area of research has been on the effects of corrective feedback in assisting learners. This has been shown to vary depending on the technique used to make the correction, and the overall focus of the classroom, whether on formal accuracy or on communication of meaningful content. There is also considerable interest in supplementing published research with approaches that engage language teachers in action research on learner language in their own classrooms. As teachers become aware of the features of learner language produced by their students, they can refine their pedagogical intervention to maximise interlanguage development.

Multilingualism: Multilingualism is the act of using, or promoting the use of, multiple languages, either by an individual speaker or by a community of speakers. Multilingual speakers outnumber monolingual speakers in the world's population. Multilingualism is becoming a social phenomenon governed by the needs of globalisation and cultural openness. Thanks to the ease of access to information facilitated by the Internet, individuals' exposure to multiple languages is getting more and more frequent, and triggering therefore the need to acquire more and more languages. People who speak more than one language are also called polyglots.

Computer-mediated Communication

Computer-mediated communication (CMC) is defined as any communicative transaction that occurs through the use of two or more networked computers. While the term has traditionally referred to those communications that occur via computer-mediated formats (e.g., instant messages, *e*-mails, chat rooms), it has also been applied to other forms of text-based interaction such as text massaging. Research on CMC focuses largely on the social effects of different computer-supported communication technologies. Many recent studies involve Internet-based social networking supported by social software.

Scope of the Field

Scholars from a variety of fields study phenomena that can be described under the umbrella term of CMC. For example, many take a sociopsychological approach to CMC by examining how humans use "computers" (or digital media) to manage interpersonal interaction, form impressions and form and maintain relationships. These studies have often focused on the differences between on-line and off-line interactions, though contemporary research is moving towards the view that CMC should be studied as embedded in everyday life. Another branch of CMC research examines the use of paralinguistic features such as emoticons, pragmatic rules such as turn-taking and the sequential analysis and organisation of talk, and the various sociolects, styles, registers or sets of terminology specific to these environments. The study of language in these contexts is typically based on text-based forms of CMC, and is sometimes referred to as "computer-mediated discourse analysis".

The way humans communicate in professional, social, and educational settings varies widely, depending upon not only the environment but also the method of communication in which the communication occurs, which in this case is through computers or other information and computer technologies (ICTs). The study of communication to achieve collaboration—common work products—is termed computer-supported collaboration and includes only some of the concerns of other forms of CMC research.

Popular forms of CMC include *e*-mail, video, audio or text chat (text conferencing including "instant massaging"), bulletin boards, listservs and MMOs. These settings are changing rapidly with the development of new technologies. Weblogs (blogs) have also become popular, and the exchange of RSS data has better enabled users to each "become their own publisher".

Conversation Analysis

Conversation analysis (commonly abbreviated as CA) is the study of talk in interaction (both verbal and non-verbal in situations of everyday life). CA generally attempts to describe the orderliness, structure and sequential patterns of interaction, whether institutional (in school, a doctor's surgery, court or elsewhere) or in casual conversation.

Inspired by ethnomethodology (e.g. Harold Garfinkel) and Erving Goffman, CA was developed in the late 1960s and early 1970s principally by the sociologist Harvey Sacks and his close associates Emanuel Schegloff and Gail Jefferson. Today CA is an established method used in sociology, anthropology, linguistics, speech-communication and psychology. It is particularly influential in interactional sociolinguistics, discourse analysis and discursive psychology, as well as being a coherent discipline in its own right. Recently CA techniques of sequential analysis have been employed for instance by phoneticians to explore the fine phonetic detail of speech (Kelly and Local 1989).

The use of the term "conversation" to label this disciplinary movement is sometimes considered to be misleading. For instance, one of CA's principal practitioners, Emanuel Schegloff, has more recently identified "talk-in-interaction" as CA's topic. Perhaps for this same reason, others (e.g., Jonathan Potter) who use CA methods identify themselves as discourse analysts (DA), though that term was first used to identify researchers using methods different from CA (cf., Levinson, 1983), and still identifies a group of scholars larger than those who use only CA methods.

Language Assessment

Language assessment or language testing is a field of study under the umbrella of applied linguistics. Its main focus is the assessment of first, second or other language in the school, college, or university context; assessment of language use in the workplace; and assessment of language in the immigration, citizenship, and asylum contexts. The assessment may include listening, speaking, reading, writing or cultural understanding. Equal weightage may be placed on knowledge (understanding how the language works theoretically) and proficiency (ability to use the language practically), or greater weightage may be given to one aspect or the other.

Literacy

Literacy has traditionally been described as the ability to read for knowledge, write coherently and think critically about printed material. Literacy represents the lifelong, intellectual process of gaining meaning from print. Key to all literacy is reading development, which involves a progression of skills that begins with the ability to understand spoken words and decode written words, and culminates in the deep understanding of text.

Reading development involves a range of complex language underpinnings including awareness of speech sounds (phonology), spelling patterns (orthography), word meaning (semantics), grammar (syntax) and patterns of word formation (morphology), all of which provide a necessary platform for reading fluency and comprehension. Once these skills are acquired the reader can attain full English literacy, which includes the abilities to approach printed material with critical analysis, inference and synthesis; to write with accuracy and coherence; and to use information and insights from text as the basis for informed decisions and creative thought.

The United Nations Educational, Scientific and Cultural Organisation (UNESCO) defines literacy as the "ability to identify, understand, interpret, create, communicate, compute and use printed and written materials associated with varying contexts. Literacy involves a continuum of learning in enabling individuals to achieve their goals, to develop their knowledge and potential, and to participate fully in their community and wider society."

Discourse Analysis

Discourse analysis (DA), or discourse studies, is a general term for a number of approaches to analysing written, spoken, signed language use or any significant semiotic event.

The objects of discourse analysis—discourse, writing, talk, conversation, communicative event, etc.—are variously defined in terms of coherent sequences of sentences, propositions, speech acts or turns-at-talk. Contrary to much of traditional linguistics, discourse analysts not only study language use 'beyond the sentence boundary', but also prefer to analyse 'naturally occurring' language use, and not invented examples. This is known as corpus linguistics; text linguistics is related. The essential difference between discourse analysis and text linguistics is that it aims at revealing socio-psychological characteristics of a person/persons rather than text structure.

Discourse analysis has been taken up in a variety of social science disciplines, including linguistics, sociology, anthropology, social work, cognitive psychology, social psychology, international relations, human geography, communication studies and translation studies, each of which is subject to its own assumptions, dimensions of analysis, and methodologies.

Pedagogy

Pedagogy is the study of being a teacher or the process of teaching. The term generally refers to strategies of instruction, or a style of instruction. Pedagogy is also occasionally referred to as the correct use of instructive strategies. For example, Paulo Freire referred to his method of teaching adult humans as "critical pedagogy". In correlation with those instructive strategies the instructor's own philosophical beliefs of instruction are harboured and governed by the pupil's background knowledge and experience, situation, and environment, as well as learning goals set by the student and teacher. One example would be the Socratic schools of thought.

Second Language Acquisition

Second language acquisition or second language learning is the process by which people learn a second language. Second language acquisition (often capitalised as Second Language Acquisition or abbreviated to SLA) is also the name of the scientific discipline devoted to studying that process. *Second language* refers to any language learned in addition to a person's first language; although the concept is named *second* language acquisition, it can also incorporate the learning of third, fourth or subsequent languages. Second language acquisition refers to what learners do; it does not refer to practices in language teaching.

The academic discipline of second language acquisition is a sub-discipline of applied linguistics. It is broad-based and relatively new. As well as the various branches of linguistics, second language acquisition is also closely related to psychology, cognitive psychology, and education. To separate the academic discipline from the learning process itself, the terms *second language acquisition research, second language studies*, and *second language acquisition studies* are also used. SLA research began as an interdisciplinary field, and because of this it is difficult to identify a precise starting date. However, it does appear to have developed a great deal since the mid-1960s. The term *acquisition* was originally used to emphasise the subconscious nature of the learning process, but in recent years *learning* and *acquisition* have become largely synonymous.

Second language acquisition can incorporate heritage language learning, but it does not usually incorporate bilingualism. Most SLA researchers see bilingualism as being the end result of learning a language, not the process itself, and see the term as referring to native-like fluency. Writers in fields such as education and psychology, however, often use bilingualism loosely to refer to all forms of multilingualism. Second language acquisition is also not to be contrasted with the acquisition of a foreign language; rather, the learning of second languages and the learning of foreign languages involve the same fundamental processes in different situations.

There has been much debate about exactly how language is learned, and many issues are still unresolved. There have been many theories of second language acquisition that have been proposed, but none has been accepted as an overarching theory by all SLA researchers. Due to the interdisciplinary nature of the field of second language acquisition, this is not expected to happen in the foreseeable future.

2 Importance of Applied Linguistics

Second Language Acquisition

Second language acquisition or second language learning is the process by which people learn a second language. Second language acquisition (often capitalised as Second Language Acquisition or abbreviated to SLA) is also the name of the scientific discipline devoted to studying that process. *Second language* refers to any language learned in addition to a person's first language; although the concept is named *second* language acquisition, it can also incorporate the learning of third, fourth or subsequent languages. Second language acquisition refers to what learners do; it does not refer to practices in language teaching.

The academic discipline of second language acquisition is a sub-discipline of applied linguistics. It is broad-based and relatively new. As well as the various branches of linguistics, second language acquisition is also closely related to psychology, cognitive psychology, and education. To separate the academic discipline from the learning process itself, the terms *second language acquisition research, second language studies,* and *second language acquisition studies* are also used. SLA research began as an interdisciplinary field, and because of this it is difficult to identify a precise starting date. However, it does appear to have developed a great deal since the mid-1960s. The term *acquisition* was originally used to emphasise the subconscious nature of the learning process, but in recent years *learning* and *acquisition* have become largely synonymous.

Second language acquisition can incorporate heritage language learning, but it does not usually incorporate bilingualism. Most SLA researchers see bilingualism as being the end result of learning a language, not the process itself, and see the term as referring to native-like fluency. Writers in fields such as education and psychology, however, often use bilingualism loosely to refer to all forms of multilingualism. Second language acquisition is also not to be contrasted with the acquisition of a foreign language; rather, the learning of second languages and the learning of foreign languages involve the same fundamental processes in different situations.

There has been much debate about exactly how language is learned, and many issues are still unresolved. There have been many theories of second language acquisition that have been proposed, but none has been accepted as an overarching theory by all SLA researchers. Due to the interdisciplinary nature of the field of second language acquisition, this is not expected to happen in the foreseeable future.

The Backdrop

As SLA began as an interdisciplinary field, it is hard to pin down a precise starting date. However, there are two publications in particular that are seen as instrumental to the development of the modern study of SLA: Pitt Corder's 1967 essay *The Significance of Learners' Errors*, and Larry Selinker's 1972 article *Interlanguage*. Corder's essay rejected a behaviourist account of SLA and suggested that learners made use of intrinsic internal linguistic processes; Selinker's article argued that second language learners possess their own individual linguistic systems that are independent from both the first and second languages.

In the 1970s the general trend in SLA was for research exploring the ideas of Corder and Selinker, and refuting behaviourist theories of language acquisition. Examples include research into error analysis, studies in transitional stages of second-language ability, and the "morpheme studies" investigating the order in which learners acquired linguistic features. The 70s were dominated by naturalistic studies of people learning English as a second language.

By the 1980s, the theories of Stephen Krashen had become the prominent paradigm in SLA. In his theories, often collectively known as the Input Hypothesis, Krashen suggested that language acquisition is driven solely by comprehensible input, language input that learners can understand. Krashen's model was influential in the field of SLA and also had a large influence on language teaching, but it left some important processes in SLA unexplained.

Research in the 1980s was characterised by the attempt to fill in these gaps. Some approaches included Lydia White's descriptions of learner competence, and Manfred Pienemann's use of speech processing models and lexical functional grammar to explain learner output. This period also saw the beginning of approaches based in other disciplines, such as the psychological approach of connectionism.

The 1990s saw a host of new theories introduced to the field, such as Michael Long's interaction hypothesis, Merrill Swain's output hypothesis, and Richard Schmidt's noticing hypothesis. However, the two main areas of research interest were linguistic theories of SLA based upon Noam Chomsky's universal grammar, and psychological approaches such as skill acquisition theory and connectionism. The latter category also saw the new theories of processability and input processing in this time period. The 1990s also saw the introduction of sociocultural theory, an approach to explain second language acquisition in terms of the social environment of the learner.

In the 2000s research was focused on much the same areas as in the 1990s, with research split into two main camps of linguistic and psychological approaches. VanPatten and Benati do not see this state of affairs as changing in the near future, pointing to the support both areas of research have in the wider fields of linguistics and psychology, respectively.

Comparisons with First Language Acquisition

People who learn a second language differ from children learning their first language in a number of ways. Perhaps the most striking of these is that very few adult second language learners reach the same competence as native speakers of that language. Children learning a second language are more likely to achieve native-like fluency than adults, but in general it is very rare for someone speaking a second language to pass completely for a native speaker. When a learner's speech plateaus in this way it is known as fossilisation.

In addition, some errors that second language learners make in their speech originate in their first language. For example, Spanish speakers learning English may say "Is raining" rather than "It is raining", leaving out the subject of the sentence. French speakers learning English, however, do not usually make the same mistake. This is because sentence subjects can be left out in Spanish, but not in French. This influence of the first language on the second is known as language transfer.

Also, when people learn a second language, the way they speak their first language changes in subtle ways. These changes can be with any aspect of language, from pronunciation and syntax to gestures the learner makes and the things they tend to notice. For example, French speakers who spoke English as a second language pronounced the /t/ sound in French differently from monolingual French speakers. When shown a fish tank, Chinese speakers of English tend to remember more fish and fewer plants than Chinese monolinguals. This effect of the second language on the first led Vivian Cook to propose the idea of multi-competence, which sees the different languages a person speaks not as separate systems, but as related systems in their mind.

Learner Language

Learner language is the written or spoken language produced by a learner. It is also the main type of data used in second language acquisition research. Much research in second language acquisition is concerned with the internal representations of a language in the mind of the learner, and in how those representations change over time. It is not yet possible to inspect these representations directly with brain scans or similar techniques, so SLA researchers are forced to make inferences about these rules from learners' speech or writing.

Item and System Learning

There are two types of learning that second language learners engage in. The first is item learning, or the learning of formulaic chunks of language. These chunks can be individual words, set phrases, or formulas like *Can I have a ___?* The second kind of learning is system learning, or the learning of systematic rules.

Interlanguage Exercise

Originally attempts to describe learner language were based on comparing different languages and on analysing learners' errors. However, these approaches weren't able to predict all the errors that learners made when in the process of learning a second language. For example, Serbo-Croat speakers learning English may say "What does Pat doing now?", although this is not a valid sentence in either language.

To explain these kind of systematic errors, the idea of the *interlanguage* was developed. An interlanguage is an emerging language system in the mind of a second language learner. A learner's interlanguage is not a deficient version of the language being learned filled with random errors, nor is it a language purely based on errors introduced from the learner's first language. Rather, it is a language in its own right, with its own systematic rules. It is possible to view most aspects of language from an interlanguage perspective, including grammar, phonology, lexicon, and pragmatics.

There are three different processes that influence the creation of interlanguages:

Language Transfer: Learners fall back on their mother tongue to help create their language system. This is now recognised not as a mistake, but as a process that all learners go through.

Overgeneralisation: Learners use rules from the second language in a way that native speakers would not. For example, a learner may say "I goed home", overgeneralising the English rule of adding *-ed* to create past tense verb forms.

Simplification: Learners use a highly simplified form of language, similar to speech by children or in pidgins. This may be related to linguistic universals.

The concept of interlanguage has become very widespread in SLA research, and is often a basic assumption made by researchers.

Social Aspects

Although the dominant perspective in second language research is a cognitive one, from the early days of the discipline researchers have also acknowledged that social aspects play an important role. There have been many different approaches to sociolinguistic study of second language acquisition, and indeed, according to Rod Ellis, this plurality has meant that "sociolinguistic SLA is replete with a bewildering set of terms referring to the social aspects of L2 acquisition". Common to each of these approaches, however, is a rejection of language as a purely psychological phenomenon; instead, sociolinguistic research views the social context in which language is learned as essential for a proper understanding of the acquisition process.

Ellis identifies three types of social structure which can affect the acquisition of second languages: socialinguistic setting, specific social factors, and situational factors. Socialinguistic setting refers to the role of the second language in society, such as whether it is spoken by a majority or a minority of the population, whether its use is widespread or restricted to a few functional roles, or whether the society is pre-dominantly bilingual or monolingual. Ellis also includes the distinction of whether the second language is learned in a natural or an educational setting. Specific social factors that can affect second language acquisition include age, gender, social class, and ethnic identity, with ethnic identity being the one that has received most research attention. Situational factors are those which vary between each social interaction. For example, a learner may use more polite language when talking to someone of higher social status, but more informal language when talking with friends.

There have been several models developed to explain social effects on language acquisition. Schumann's acculturation model proposes that learners' rate of development and ultimate level of language achievement is a function of the "social distance" and the "psychological distance" between learners and the second language community. In Schumann's model the social factors are most important, but the degree to which learners are comfortable with learning the second language also plays a role. Another sociolinguistic model is Gardner's socio-educational model, which was designed to explain classroom language acquisition. The inter-group model proposes "ethnolinguistic vitality" as a key construct for second language acquisition. Language socialisation is an approach with the premise that "linguistic and cultural knowledge are *constructed* through each other", and saw increased attention after the year 2000. Finally, Norton's theory of social identity is an attempt to codify the relationship between power, identity, and language acquisition.

External Factors

Input and Interaction: The primary factor affecting language acquisition appears to be the input that the learner receives. Stephen Krashen took a very strong position on the importance of input, asserting that comprehensible input is all that is necessary for second language acquisition. Krashen pointed to studies showing that the length of time a person stays in a foreign country is closely linked with his level of language acquisition. Further evidence for input comes from studies on reading: large amounts of free voluntary reading have a significant positive effect on learners' vocabulary, grammar, and writing. Input is also the mechanism by which people learn languages according to the universal grammar model.

The type of input may also be important. One tenet of Krashen's theory is that input should not be grammatically sequenced. He claims that such sequencing, as found in language classrooms where lessons involve practising a "structure of the day", is not necessary, and may even be harmful.

While input is of vital importance, Krashen's assertion that *only* input matters in second language acquisition has been contradicted by more recent research. For example, students enrolled in French language immersion programmes in Canada still produced non-native-like grammar when they spoke, even though they had years of meaning-focused lessons and their listening skills were statistically native-level.

Output appears to play an important role, and among other things, can help provide learners with feedback, make them concentrate on the form of what they are saying, and help them to automatise their language knowledge. These processes have been codified in the theory of comprehensible output.

Researchers have also pointed to interaction in the second language as being important for acquisition. According to Long's interaction hypothesis the conditions for acquisition are especially good when interacting in the second language; specifically, conditions are good when a breakdown in communication occurs and learners must negotiate for meaning. The modifications to speech arising from interactions like this help make input more comprehensible, provide feedback to the learner, and push learners to modify their speech.

Internal Factors

Internal factors affecting second language acquisition are those which stem from the learner's own mind. Attempts to account for the internal mechanisms of second language acquisition can be divided into three general strands: cognitive, sociocultural, and linguistic. These explanations are not all compatible, and often differ significantly.

Lexicography

Lexicography is divided into two related disciplines:

- Practical lexicography is the art or craft of compiling, writing and editing dictionaries.
- Theoretical lexicography is the scholarly discipline of analysing and describing the semantic, syntagmatic and paradigmatic relationships within the lexicon (vocabulary) of a language, developing theories of dictionary components and structures linking the data in dictionaries, the needs for information by users in specific types of situation, and how users may best access the data incorporated in printed and electronic dictionaries. This is sometimes referred to as 'metalexicography'.

A person devoted to lexicography is called a lexicographer. General lexicography focuses on the design, compilation, use and evaluation of general dictionaries, i.e. dictionaries that provide a description of the language in general use. Such a dictionary is usually called a general dictionary or LGP dictionary (Language for General Purpose). Specialised lexicography focuses on the design, compilation, use and evaluation of specialised dictionaries, i.e. dictionaries that are devoted to a (relatively restricted) set of linguistic and factual elements of one or more specialist subject fields, e.g. legal lexicography. Such a dictionary is usually called a specialised dictionary or LSP dictionary and following Nielsen 1994, specialised dictionaries are either multi-field, single-field or sub-field dictionaries.

There is some disagreement on the definition of lexicology, as distinct from lexicography. Some use "lexicology" as a synonym for theoretical lexicography; others use it to mean a branch of linguistics pertaining to the inventory of words in a particular language. It is now widely accepted that lexicography is a scholarly discipline in its own right and not a sub-branch of applied linguistics, as the chief object of study in lexicography is the dictionary.

Language Planning

Language planning is a deliberate effort to influence the function, structure, or acquisition of languages or language variety within a speech community. It is often associated with government planning, but is also used by a variety of non-governmental organisations, such as grassroots organisations and even individuals. The goals of language planning differ depending on the nation or organisation, but generally include making planning decisions and possibly changes for the benefit of communication. Planning or improving effective communication can also lead to other social changes such as language shift or assimilation, thereby providing another motivation to plan the structure, function and acquisition of languages.

Language engineering involves the creation of natural language processing systems whose cost and outputs are measurable and predictable as well as establishment of language regulators, such as formal or informal agencies, committees, societies or academies as language regulators to design or develop new structures to meet contemporary needs. It is a distinct field contrasted to natural language processing and computational linguistics. A recent trend of language engineering is the use of Semantic Web technologies for the creation, archival, processing, and retrieval of machine processable language data.

Pragmatics

Pragmatics is a subfield of linguistics which studies the ways in which context contributes to meaning. Pragmatics encompasses speech act theory, conversational implicature, talk in interaction and other approaches to language behaviour in philosophy, sociology, and linguistics. It studies how the transmission of meaning depends not only on the linguistic knowledge (e.g. grammar, lexicon etc.) of the speaker and listener, but also on the context of the utterance, knowledge about the status of those involved, the inferred intent of the speaker, and so on. In this respect, pragmatics explains how language users are able to overcome apparent ambiguity, since meaning relies on the manner, place, time etc. of an utterance. The ability to understand another speaker's intended meaning is called *pragmatic competence.* So an utterance describing pragmatic function is described as metapragmatic. Pragmatic awareness is regarded as one of the most challenging aspects of language learning, and comes only through experience.

Forensic Linguistics

Forensic linguistics is the application of linguistic knowledge, methods and insights to the forensic context of law, language, crime investigation, trial, and judicial procedure. It is a branch of applied linguistics. There are principally three areas of application for linguists working in forensic contexts - understanding language of the written law, understanding language use in forensic and judicial processes and the provision of linguistic evidence. The discipline of forensic linguistics is not homogenous; it involves a range of experts and researchers in different areas of the field.

Translation

Translation is the communication of the meaning of a source-language text by means of an equivalent target-language text. Whereas interpreting undoubtedly antedates writing, translation began only after the appearance of written literature; there exist partial translations of the Sumerian *Epic of Gilgamesh* (ca. 2000 BCE) into Southwest Asian languages of the second millennium BCE.

Translators always risk inappropriate spill-over of source-language idiom and usage into the target-language translation. On the other hand, spillovers have imported useful source-language calques and loanwords that have enriched the target languages. Indeed, translators have helped substantially to shape the languages into which they have translated.

Due to the demands of business documentation consequent to the Industrial Revolution that began in the mid-18th century, some translation specialities have become formalised, with dedicated schools and professional associations.

Because of the laboriousness of translation, since the 1940s engineers have sought to automate translation (machine translation) or to mechanically aid the human translator (computer-assisted translation). The rise of the Internet has fostered a worldwide market for translation services and has facilitated language localisation.

Sequences of Acquisition

In the 1970s there were several studies that investigated the order in which learners acquired different grammatical structures. These studies showed that there was little change in this order among learners with different first languages. Furthermore, it showed that the order was the same for adults as well as children, and that it did not even change if the learner had language lessons. This proved that there were factors other than language transfer involved in learning second languages, and was a strong confirmation of the concept of interlanguage.

However, the studies did not find that the orders were exactly the same. Although there were remarkable similarities in the order in which all learners learned second language grammar, there were still some differences among individuals and among learners with different first languages. It is also difficult to tell when exactly a grammatical structure has been learned, as learners may use structures correctly in some situations but not in others. Thus it is more accurate to speak of *sequences* of acquisition, where particular grammatical features in a language have a fixed sequence of development, but the overall order of acquisition is less rigid.

Second Language Acquisition Theories

Second language acquisition theories are various theories and hypotheses in the field of second language acquisition about how people learn a second language. Second language acquisition research is closely related to several disciplines including linguistics, sociolinguistics, psychology, neuroscience, and education, and consequently most theories of second language acquisition can be identified as having roots in one of them. Each of these theories can be thought of as shedding light on one part of the language learning process; however, no one overarching theory of second language acquisition has yet been widely accepted by researchers.

Universal Grammar

From the field of linguistics, the most influential theory by far has been Chomsky's theory of Universal Grammar (UG). The UG model of principles, basic properties which all languages share, and parameters, properties which can vary between languages, has been the basis for much second language research.

From a UG perspective, learning the grammar of a second language is simply a matter of setting the correct parameters. Take the *pro-drop* parameter, which dictates whether or not sentences must have a subject in order to be grammatically correct. This parameter can have two values: *positive*, in which case sentences do not necessarily need a subject, and *negative*, in which case subjects must be present. In German the sentence "*Er spricht*" (he speaks) is grammatical, but the sentence "*Spricht*" (speaks) is ungrammatical. In Italian, however, the sentence "*Parla*" (speaks) is perfectly normal and grammatically correct. A German speaker learning Italian would only need to deduce that subjects are optional from the language he hears, and then set his *pro-drop* parameter for Italian accordingly. Once he has set all the parameters in the language correctly, then from a UG perspective he can be said to have learned Italian, i.e. he will always produce perfectly correct Italian sentences.

Universal Grammar also provides a succinct explanation for much of the phenomenon of language transfer. Spanish learners of English who make the mistake "Is raining" instead of "It is raining" have not yet set their *pro-drop* parameters correctly and are still using the same setting as in Spanish.

The main shortcoming of Universal Grammar in describing second language acquisition is that it does not deal at all with the psychological processes involved with learning a language. UG scholarship is only concerned with whether parameters are set or not, not with *how* they are set.

Acquisition-learning Hypothesis

Stephen Krashen introduced the acquisition-learning hypothesis, which makes a distinction between conscious language learning and subconscious language acquisition. Krashen argues that only subconscious acquisition can lead to fluency.

A distinction closely related to that made by Krashen (1982) between acquisition and learning is one between implicit and explicit linguistic knowledge. Learners gain implicit knowledge by processing target-language input without consciously giving attention to acquiring the forms and structures of the language. On the other hand, learners get explicit knowledge of a language when they process language input with the conscious intention of discovering the structural rules of the language. A distinction between the implicit learning involved in acquiring a first language (L1) and the mix of implicit and explicit learning that takes place in L2 acquisition has been one analytic route for understanding the virtually universal success of L1 acquisition versus the more limited success of L2 acquisition among adult learners (Hulstijn, 2005). Ellis has found empirical confirmation for the distinct constructs of implicit and explicit language knowledge.

Input Hypothesis

Learners' most direct source of information about the target language is the target language itself. When they come into direct contact with the target language, this is referred to as "input." When learners process that language in a way that can contribute to learning, this is referred to as "intake."

Generally speaking, the amount of input learners take in is one of the most important factors affecting their learning. However, it must be at a level that is comprehensible to them. In his Monitor Theory, Krashen advanced the concept that language input should be at the "i+1" level, just beyond what the learner can fully understand; this input is comprehensible, but contains structures that are not yet fully understood. This has been criticised on the basis that there is no clear definition of i+1, and that factors other than structural difficulty (such as interest or presentation) can affect whether input is actually turned into intake. The concept has been quantified, however, in vocabulary acquisition research; Nation reviews various studies which indicate that about 98% of the words in running text should be previously known in order for extensive reading to be effective.

In his Input Hypothesis, Krashen proposes that language acquisition takes place only when learners receive input just beyond their current level of L2 competence. He termed this level of input "i+1." However, in contrast to emergentist and connectionist theories, he follows the innate approach by applying Chomsky's Government and binding theory and concept of Universal grammar (UG) to second language acquisition. He does so by proposing a Language Acquisition Device that uses L2 input to define the parameters of the L2, within the constraints of UG, and to increase the L2 proficiency of the learner. In addition, Krashen (1982s) Affective Filter Hypothesis holds that the acquisition of a second language is halted if the leaner has a high degree of anxiety when receiving input. According to this concept, a part of the mind filters out L2 input and prevents uptake by the learner, if the learner feels that the process of SLA is threatening. As mentioned earlier, since input is essential in Krashen's model, this filtering action prevents acquisition from progressing.

A great deal of research has taken place on input enhancement, the ways in which input may be altered so as to direct learners' attention to linguistically important areas. Input enhancement might include bold-faced vocabulary words or marginal glosses in a reading text. Research here is closely linked to research on pedagogical effects, and comparably diverse.

Monitor Model

Other concepts have also been influential in the speculation about the processes of building internal systems of second language information. Some thinkers hold that language processing handles distinct types of knowledge. For instance, one component of the Monitor Model, propounded by Krashen, posits a distinction between "acquisition" and "learning." According to Krashen, L2 acquisition is a subconscious process of incidentally "picking up" a language, as children do when becoming proficient in their first languages. Language learning, on the other hand, is studying, consciously and intentionally, the features of a language, as is common in traditional classrooms. Krashen sees these two processes as fundamentally different, with little or no interface between them. In common with connectionism, Krashen sees input as essential to language acquisition.

Further, Bialystok and Smith make another distinction in explaining how learners build and use L2 and interlanguage knowledge structures. They argue that the concept of interlanguage should include a distinction between two specific kinds of language processing ability. On one hand is learners' knowledge of L2 grammatical structure and ability to analyse the target language objectively using that knowledge, which they term "representation," and, on the other hand is the ability to use their L2 linguistic knowledge, under time constraints, to accurately comprehend input and produce output in the L2, which they call "control." They point out that often non-native speakers of a language have higher levels of representation than their native-speaking counterparts have, yet have a lower level of control. Finally,

Bialystok has framed the acquisition of language in terms of the interaction between what she calls "analysis" and "control." Analysis is what learners do when they attempt to understand the rules of the target language. Through this process, they acquire these rules and can use them to gain greater control over their own production.

Monitoring is another important concept in some theoretical models of learner use of L2 knowledge. According to Krashen, the Monitor is a component of an L2 learner's language processing device that uses knowledge gained from language learning to observe and regulate the learner's own L2 production, checking for accuracy and adjusting language production when necessary.

Interaction Hypothesis

Long's interaction hypothesis proposes that language acquisition is strongly facilitated by the use of the target language in interaction. Similarly to Krashen's Input Hypothesis, the Interaction Hypothesis claims that comprehensible input is important for language learning. In addition, it claims that the effectiveness of comprehensible input is greatly increased when learners have to negotiate for meaning.

Interactions often result in learners receiving negative evidence. That is, if learners say something that their interlocutors do not understand, after negotiation the interlocutors may model the correct language form. In doing this, learners can receive feedback on their production and on grammar that they have not yet mastered. The process of interaction may also result in learners receiving more input from their interlocutors than they would otherwise.

Furthermore, if learners stop to clarify things that they do not understand, they may have more time to process the input they receive. This can lead to better understanding and possibly the acquisition of new language forms. Finally, interactions may serve as a way of focusing learners' attention on a difference between their knowledge of the target language and the reality of what they are hearing; it may also focus their attention on a part of the target language of which they are not yet aware.

Output Hypothesis

In the 1980s, Canadian SLA researcher Merrill Swain advanced the output hypothesis, that meaningful output is as necessary to language learning as meaningful input. However, most studies have shown little if any correlation between learning and quantity of output. Today, most scholars contend that small amounts of meaningful output are important to language learning, but primarily because the experience of producing language leads to more effective processing of input.

Competition Model

Some of the major cognitive theories of how learners organise language knowledge are based on analyses of how speakers of various languages analyse sentences for meaning. MacWhinney, Bates, and Kliegl found that speakers of English, German, and Italian showed varying patterns in identifying the subjects of transitive sentences containing more than one noun. English speakers relied heavily on word order; German speakers used morphological agreement, the animacy status of noun referents, and stress; and speakers of Italian relied on agreement and stress. MacWhinney et al. interpreted these results as supporting the Competition Model, which states that individuals use linguistic cues to get meaning from language, rather than relying on linguistic universals. According to this theory, when acquiring an L2, learners sometimes receive competing cues and must decide which cue(s) is most relevant for determining meaning.

Connectionism and Second Language Acquisition

These findings also relate to Connectionism. Connectionism attempts to model the cognitive language processing of the human brain, using computer architectures that make associations between elements of language, based on frequency of co-occurrence in the language input. Frequency has been found to be a factor in various linguistic domains of language learning.

Connectionism posits that learners form mental connections between items that co-occur, using exemplars found in language input. From this input, learners extract the rules of the language through cognitive processes common to other areas of cognitive skill acquisition. Since connectionism denies both innate rules and the existence of any innate language-learning module, L2 input is of greater importance than it is in processing models based on innate approaches, since, in connectionism, input is the source of both the units and the rules of language.

Noticing Hypothesis

Attention is another characteristic that some believe to have a role in determining the success or failure of language processing. Schmidt states that although explicit metalinguistic knowledge of a language is not always essential for acquisition, the learner must be aware of L2 input in order to gain from it.

In his "noticing hypothesis," Schmidt posits that learners must notice the ways in which their interlanguage structures differ from target norms. This noticing of the gap allows the learner's internal language processing to restructure the learner's internal representation of the rules of the L2 in order to bring the learner's production closer to the target. In this respect, Schmidt's understanding is consistent with the ongoing process of rule formation found in emergentism and connectionism.

Processability

Some theorists and researchers have contributed to the cognitive approach to second language acquisition by increasing understanding of the ways L2 learners restructure their interlanguage knowledge systems to be in greater conformity to L2 structures. Processability theory states that learners restructure their L2 knowledge systems in an order of which they are capable at their stage of development.

For instance, In order to acquire the correct morphological and syntactic forms for English questions, learners must transform declarative English sentences. They do so by a series of stages, consistent across learners. Clahsen proposed that certain processing principles determine this order of restructuring. Specifically, he stated that learners first, maintain declarative word order while changing other aspects of the utterances, second, move words to the beginning and end of sentences, and third, move element's within main clauses before subordinate clauses.

Automaticity

Thinkers have produced several theories concerning how learners use their internal L2 knowledge structures to comprehend L2 input and produce L2 output. One idea is that learners acquire proficiency in an L2 in the same way that people acquire other complex cognitive skills. Automaticity is the performance of a skill without conscious control. It results from the gradated process of proceduralisation. In the field of cognitive psychology, Anderson expounds a model of skill acquisition, according to which persons use procedures to apply their declarative knowledge about a subject in order to solve problems. On repeated practice, these procedures develop into production rules that the individual can use to solve the problem, without accessing long-term declarative memory.

Performance speed and accuracy improve as the learner implements these production rules. DeKeyser tested the application of this model to L2 language automaticity. He found that subjects developed increasing proficiency in performing tasks related to the morphosyntax of an artificial language, Autopractan, and performed on a learning curve typical of the acquisition of non-language cognitive skills. This evidence conforms to Anderson's general model of cognitive skill acquisition, supports the idea that declarative knowledge can be transformed into procedural knowledge, and tends to undermine the idea of Krashen that knowledge gained through language "learning" cannot be used to initiate speech production.

Declarative/Procedural Model

Michael T. Ullman has used a declarative/procedural model to understand how language information is stored. This model is consistent with a distinction made in general cognitive science between the storage and retrieval of facts, on the one hand, and understanding of how to carry out operations, on the other.

It states that declarative knowledge consists of arbitrary linguistic information, such as irregular verb forms, that are stored in the brain's declarative memory. In contrast, knowledge about the rules of a language, such as grammatical word order is procedural knowledge and is stored in procedural memory. Ullman reviews several psycholinguistic and neurolinguistic studies that support the declarative/procedural model.

Memory and Second Language Acquisition

Perhaps certain psychological characteristics constrain language processing. One area of research is the role of memory. Williams conducted a study in which he found some positive correlation between verbatim memory functioning and grammar learning success for his subjects. This suggests that individuals with less short-term memory capacity might have a limitation in performing cognitive processes for organisation and use of linguistic knowledge.

Individual Variation in Second Language Acquisition

Individual variation in second language acquisition is a general term for studies in second language acquisition that seek to address the question: *Why do some learners do better than others?* Unlike child language acquisition, people learning a second language rarely reach the same level of competence as native speakers of that language. Some may stop studying a language before they have fully internalised it, and others may stop improving despite living in a country where a language is spoken for many years. It also appears that children are more likely than adults to reach native-like competence in a second language. There have been many studies that have attempted to explain these phenomena.

A flurry of studies in the 1970s, often labelled the "good language learner studies", sought to identify the distinctive factors of successful learners. Although those studies are now widely regarded as simplistic, they did serve to identify a number of factors affecting language acquisition. More detailed research on many of these specific factors continues today. For this reason, *individual variation in second language acquisition* is not generally considered a single area of research. Rather, it is simply a convenient way to categorise studies about language aptitude, age and language learning, strategy use, and affective factors that affect language acquisition.

Language Aptitude

Tests of language aptitude have proven extremely effective in predicting which learners will be successful in learning. However, considerable controversy remains about whether language aptitude is properly regarded as a unitary concept, an organic property of the brain, or as a complex of factors including motivation and short-term memory. Research has generally shown that language aptitude is quite distinct from general aptitude or intelligence, as measured by various tests, and is itself fairly consistently measurable by different tests.

Language aptitude research is often criticised for being irrelevant to the problems of language learners, who must attempt to learn a language regardless of whether they are gifted for the task or not. This claim is reinforced by research findings that aptitude is largely unchangeable.

In addition, traditional language aptitude measures such as the Modern Language Aptitude Test strongly favour decontextualised knowledge of the sort used in taking tests, rather than the sort used in conversation. For this reason little research is carried out on aptitude today. However, operators of selective language programmes such as the United States Defence Language Institute continue to use language aptitude testing as part of applicant screening.

Age: How children acquire native language (L1) and the relevance of this to foreign language L2 learning has long been debated. Although evidence for L2 learning ability declining with age is controversial, a common notion is that children learn L2s easily and older learners rarely achieve fluency. This assumption stems from 'critical period' (CP) ideas. A CP was popularised by Eric Lenneberg in 1967 for L1 acquisition, but considerable interest now surrounds age effects on second language acquisition (SLA).

SLA theories explain learning processes and suggest causal factors for a possible CP for SLA, mainly attempting to explain apparent differences in language aptitudes of children and adults by distinct learning routes, and clarifying them through psychological mechanisms. Research explores these ideas and hypotheses, but results are varied: some demonstrate pre-pubescent children acquire language easily, and some that older learners have the advantage, and yet others focus on existence of a CP for SLA. Recent studies have recognised that certain aspects of SLA may be affected by age, though others remain intact.

Strategic Use

The effective use of strategies has been shown to be critical to successful language learning, so much so that Canale and Swain (1980) included "strategic competence" among the four components of communicative competence. Research here has also shown significant pedagogical effects. This has given rise to "strategies-based instruction."

Strategies are commonly divided into learning strategies and communicative strategies, although there are other ways of categorising them. Learning strategies are techniques used to improve learning, such as mnemonics or using a dictionary. Learners (and native speakers) use communicative strategies to get meaning across even when they lack access to the correct language: for example, by using pro-forms like "thing", or non-spoken means such as mime. Communicative strategies may not have any direct bearing on learning, and some strategies such as avoidance (not using a form with which one is uncomfortable) may actually hinder learning.

Learners from different cultures use strategies in different ways, as a research tradition led by Rebecca Oxford has demonstrated. Related to this are differences in strategy use between male and female learners. Numerous studies have shown that female learners typically use strategies more widely and intensively than males; this may be related to the statistical advantage which female learners enjoy in language learning.

Effective Factors

Affective factors relate to the learner's emotional state and attitude towards the target language. Research on affect in language learning is still strongly influenced by Bloom's taxonomy, which describes the affective levels of receiving, responding, valuing, organisation, and self-characterisation through one's value system. It has also been informed in recent years by research in neurobiology and neurolinguistics.

Effective Filter

Furthermore, researchers believe that language learners all possess an affective filter which affects language acquisition. If a student possesses a high filter they are less likely to engage in language learning because of shyness, concern for grammar or other factors. Students possessing a lower affective filter will be more likely to engage in learning because they are less likely to be impeded by other factors. The affective filter is an important component of second language learning.

Anxiety

Although some continue to propose that a low level of anxiety may be helpful, studies have almost unanimously shown that anxiety damages students' prospects for successful learning. Anxiety is often related to a sense of threat to the learner's self-concept in the learning situation, for example if a learner fears being ridiculed for a mistake.

Personality Factors

Second language acquisition is defined as the learning and adopting of a language that is not your native language. Studies have shown that extraverts (or unreserved and outgoing people) acquire a second language better than introverts (or shy people).

One particular study done by Naiman reflected this point. The subjects were 72 Canadian high school students from grades 8, 10 and 12 who were studying French as a second language.

Naiman gave them all questionnaires to establish their psychological profiles, which also included a French listening test and imitation test. He found that approximately 70% of the students with the higher grades (B or higher) would consider themselves extroverts.

Extroverts will be willing to try to communicate even if they are not sure they will succeed. Two scientists, Kinginger and Farrell, conducted interviews with US students after their study abroad programme in France in 2003. They found that many of the students would avoid interaction with the native speakers at all costs, while others jumped at the opportunity to speak the language. Those who avoided interaction were typically quiet, reserved people, (or introverts).

Logically, anxiety will cause students not to try and advance their skills, especially when they feel they are under pressure. Just the lack of practice will make introverts less likely to fully acquire the second language.

Social Effects

The process of language learning can be very stressful, and the impact of positive or negative attitudes from the surrounding society can be critical. One aspect that has received particular attention is the relationship of gender roles to language achievement. Studies across numerous cultures have shown that women, on the whole, enjoy an advantage over men.

Some have proposed that this is linked to gender roles. Doman notes in a journal devoted to issues of Cultural affects on SLA, "Questions abound about what defines SLA, how far its borders extend, and what the attributions and contributions of its research are. Thus, there is a great amount of heterogeneity in the entire conceptualisation of SLA. Some researchers tend to ignore certain aspects of the field, while others scrutinise those same aspects piece by piece."

Community attitudes towards the language being learned can also have a profound impact on SLA. Where the community has a broadly negative view of the target language and its speakers, or a negative view of its relation to them, learning is typically much more difficult. This finding has been confirmed by research in numerous contexts. A widely-cited example is the difficulty faced by Navajo children in learning English as a second language.

Other common social factors include the attitude of parents towards language study, and the nature of group dynamics in the language classroom. Additionally, early attitudes may strengthen motivation and facility with language in general, particularly with early exposure to the language. All these sum up to affect learners' acquisition of the target language and learners' language/ code choice when multiple varieties of a (second) language are involved.

Motivation

The role of motivation in SLA has been the subject of extensive scholarship, closely influenced by work in motivational psychology. Motivation is internally complex, and Dornyei begins his work by stating that "strictly speaking, *there is no such thing as motivation.*" There are many different kinds of motivation; these are often divided into types such as integrative or instrumental, intrinsic or extrinsic. Intrinsic motivation refers to the desire to do something for an internal reward. Most studies have shown it to be substantially more effective in long-term language learning than extrinsic motivation, for an external reward such as high grades or praise.

Integrative and instrumental orientations refer to the degree that a language is learned "for its own sake" (integratively) or for instrumental purposes. Studies have not consistently shown either form of motivation to be more effective than the other, and the role of each is probably conditioned by various personality and cultural factors.

Some research has shown that motivation correlates strongly with proficiency, indicating both that successful learners are motivated and that success improves motivation. Thus motivation is not fixed, but is strongly affected by feedback from the environment. Accordingly, the study of motivation in SLA has also examined many of the external factors discussed above, such as the effect of instructional techniques on motivation. An accessible summary of this research can be found in Dornyei (2001a).

In their research on Willingness to communicate, MacIntyre et al. have shown that motivation is not the final construct before learners engage in communication. In fact, learners may be highly motivated yet remain unwilling to communicate.

The European Union Lifelong learning programme has funded a project to research and build a set of best practices to motivate adult language learners, called Don't Give Up.

3 Approaches and Studies in Sociocultural Perspectives

Approaches to Learning and Development

Sociocultural approaches emphasise the interdependence of social and individual processes in the co-construction of knowledge. This article uses three central tenets of a Vygotskian framework to examine the relationship between learning and development: (a) social sources of individual development, (b) semiotic (signs and symbols, including language) mediation in human development, and (c) genetic (developmental) analysis. The role played by culture and language in human development is an essential aspect of the Vygotskian framework and provides an overarching theme for this article. The methodological foundation of this framework is examined, particularly as it contrasts with other perspectives on the process of internalisation of social interaction in the construction of knowledge. The article concludes by surveying sociocultural research on and applications to classroom learning and teaching, particularly that which examines the role of collaboration. It is significant that this special issue of *Educational*

Psychologist contains an article on sociocultural theory on the centenary of the birth of its founder, the Russian psychologist Lev Vygotsky. In the last few decades there has been increasing interest in this theory and its implications for research on classroom learning and teaching. There is a range of interpretations and applications of sociocultural approaches, reflecting the vitality of this perspective. Nevertheless, some common assumptions of the sociocultural community have been refined and clarified by contemporary scholars based on Vygotsky's original writings. A number of sources provide overviews of these approaches and reflect the varied interpretations of Vygotsky's theory (van der Veer & Valsiner, 1991; Wertsch, 1985, 1991; Cole & Scribner, 1978; John-Steiner & Souberman, 1978).

To examine the central concepts of sociocultural theory the methodological foundations should be analysed. The dialectical method Vygotsky used differentiates it from other perspectives presented in this issue. We focus on the differences between social constructivist and sociocultural approaches since these two perspectives are often associated, resulting in confusion about their similarities and differences.

This article consists of three main sections: 1) a brief overview of sociocultural approaches; 2) an examination of sociocultural methodology; and 3) an overview of sociocultural contributions to research and applications to classroom learning and teaching. An overarching focus is the interdependence of social and individual processes in the co-construction of knowledge. This focus clarifies the differences between sociocultural theories based on Vygotsky's contributions and other perspectives reviewed in this issue.

Sociocultural Theory

Sociocultural approaches to learning and development were first systematised and applied by L. S. Vygotsky and his collaborators in Russia in the nineteen-twenties and thirties. They are based on the concept that human activities take place in cultural contexts, are mediated by language and other symbol systems, and can be best understood when investigated in their historical development. At a time when psychologists were intent on developing simple explanations of human behaviour, Vygotsky developed a rich, multifaceted theory through which he examined a range of subjects including the psychology of art; language and thought; and learning and development, including a focus on the education of students with special needs. However, his work was suppressed for 20 years and did not become accessible again until the late fifties and early sixties. Since then, sociocultural approaches have gained increasing recognition and have been further developed by scholars in over a dozen countries. Contemporary interpretations and reinterpretations of Vygotsky's and his collaborators' work reflect the visibility and obscurity of this theory's sixty-year existence. The expansions and interpretations in the last 25 years have led to diverse perspectives on sociocultural theory.

The dissemination of Vygotsky's ideas and the application of his work in diverse national contexts have contributed to "a complex of related but heterogeneous proposals" (Rogoff, Radziszewska, & Masiello, 1995, p. 125). Vygotsky's ideas are condensed, and at times not fully developed as he died at a young age of tuberculosis. Much of his work remains untranslated into English. In spite of these difficulties, his theories are increasingly influential in Western countries. The impact of Vygotsky's ideas has grown substantially in the United States, particularly since the publication of a selection of his writings in *Mind in Society* in 1978.

The power of Vygotsky's ideas lies in his explanation of the dynamic interdependence of social and individual processes. He arrived at his views by analysing the crisis in psychology he saw in the two predominant schools in the field, "each of which claimed to possess an explanatory system adequate to become the basis of general psychology" (Kozulin, 1990, p. 87). In contrast to those approaches which focused on internal or subjective experience and behaviourist approaches which focused on the external, *Vygotsky conceptualised development as the transformation of socially shared activities into internalised processes.* In this way he rejected the Cartesian dichotomy between the internal and the external.

The nature of the interdependence between individual and social processes in the construction of knowledge can be clarified by examining three major themes in Vygotsky's writings highlighted by Wertsch (1991): 1) individual development, including higher mental functioning, has its origins in social sources; 2) human action, on both the social and individual planes, is mediated by tools and signs; and 3) the first two themes are best examined through genetic, or developmental, analysis. In developing these themes, we will rely on

Vygotsky's writings as well as the elaborations of his ideas by his coworkers and scholars influenced by his work.

Social Sources of Development

Human development starts with dependence on caregivers. The developing individual relies on the vast pool of transmitted experiences of others. Vygotsky in his well-known "genetic law of development" emphasises this primacy of social interaction in human development:

> Every function in the cultural development of the child comes on the stage twice, in two respects; first in the social, later in the psychological, first in relations between people as an interpsychological category, afterwards within the child as an intrapsychological category....All higher psychological functions are internalised relationships of the social kind, and constitute the social structure of personality. *(In Valsiner, 1987, p. 67)*

This principle describes a process situated in, but not limited to, social interaction. When beginning an activity, learners depend on others with more experience. Over time, they take on increasing responsibility for their own learning and participation in joint activity (Lave & Wenger, 1991). Expanding Vygotsky's genetic law of development, Rogoff characterises this process as *guided participation*. In her cross-cultural studies, she documents children's varying forms of participation with parents and peers. Rogoff (1990) found that even when children were not conversational partners with adults, they were involved in the adult world as participants in adult agricultural and household work. She describes the supportive engagement of Mayan mothers with their children as an example of the non-verbal guidance adults give children.

> The routine arrangements and interactions between children and their caregivers and companions provide children with thousands of opportunities to observe and participate in the skilled activities of their culture. Through repeated and varied experience in supported routine and challenging situations, children become skilled practitioners in the specific cognitive activities in their communities. (1991)

Thus learners participate in a wide variety of joint activities which provide the opportunity for synthesising several influences into the learner's novel modes of understanding and participation. By internalising the effects of working together, the novice acquires useful strategies and crucial knowledge.

The acquisition of language provides another example of a social source of development. Zukow-Goldring and Ferko (1994) and other researchers have shown the close relationship between promoting shared attention between beginning speakers and their caregivers and the emergence of the lexicon. Contemporary research supports the sociocultural claim that the relationship between individuals forms a basis for cognitive and linguistic mastery. This process, whether in the classroom or elsewhere, includes transmission, construction, transaction, and transformation in a continuing, complex interplay.

Semiotic Mediation

Semiotic mediation is key to all aspects of knowledge co-construction. For Vygotsky, semiotic mechanisms (including psychological tools) mediate social and individual functioning, and connect the external and the internal, the social and the individual (Wertsch and Stone, 1985). Vygotsky (1981) listed a number of examples of semiotic means: "language; various systems of counting; mnemonic techniques; algebraic symbol systems; works of art; writing; schemes, diagrams, maps and mechanical drawings; all sorts of conventional signs and so on". Other tools, increasingly recognised in sociocultural discourse — the paint brush, the computer, calendars, and symbol systems — are central to the appropriation of knowledge through representational activity by the developing individual.

In the introduction to Vygotsky's *Thought and Language*, Jerome Bruner (1962) described Vygotsky's view of the role of semiotic mediation:

> He believed that in mastering nature we master ourselves. For it is the internalisation of overt action that makes thought, and particularly the internalisation of external dialogue that brings the powerful tool of language to bear on the stream of thought. Man, if you will, is shaped by the tools and instruments that he comes to use, and neither the mind nor the hand alone can amount to much....And if neither hand nor intellect alone prevails, the tools and aids that do are the developing streams of internalised language and conceptual thought that

> sometimes run parallel and sometimes merge, each affecting the other.

Wertsch (1991) adopts Wittgenstein's metaphor of a socially provided tool kit of semiotic means. Those means and practices, which become internalised and available for independent activity, are critical in supporting and transforming mental functioning. Physical tools are directed towards the external world; psychological tools are directed internally and are appropriated during activity.

Knowledge is not internalised directly, but through the use of psychological tools. Vygotsky's colleague Leontiev (1981) used the term *appropriation* to describe the adoption by an individual of one of these socially available psychological tools and wrote that children cannot and need not reinvent the artifacts that have taken millennia to evolve in order to appropriate such objects into their own system of activity. The child has only come to an understanding that is adequate for using the culturally elaborated object in the novel life circumstances he encounters. (Quoted in Newman, Griffin, & Cole, 1989)

Leinhardt (1996) in her discussion of teaching—instructional explanations of mathematical concepts provides another example of semiotic mediation. In describing the role of representations, she illustrates the concept of "per cent" by discussing various representations, such as number lines, circles and squares. Representational activities, whether in the form of inner speech, imagery, or kinetic concepts are linked to culturally shared systems, such as language, and to developmental activities including scaffolding (John-Steiner, 1995).

Thus, psychological tools are not invented by the individual in isolation. They are products of sociocultural evolution to which individuals have access by being actively engaged in the practices of their communities. In a recent article, Wertsch (1994) elaborates on the centrality of mediation in understanding Vygotsky's contributions to psychology and education.

Mediation is the key in his approach to understanding how human mental functioning is tied to cultural, institutional, and historical settings since these settings shape and provide the cultural tools that are mastered by individuals to form this functioning. In this approach, the mediational means are what might be termed the "carriers" of sociocultural patterns and knowledge.

Cognitive Pluralism

Although the importance of semiotic mediation in thinking is recognised by most members of the sociocultural thought community, interpretations of it differ. Almost all sociocultural researchers place language in a central position; however, some consider that other semiotic means are of little theoretical interest (Kozulin, 1990). We claim a pluralistic rather than a monistic theory of semiotic mediation (John-Steiner, 1991; 1995) and have coined the term *cognitive pluralism* for this stance. Evidence for cognitive pluralism includes the planning notes of experienced thinkers which incorporate words, drawings, musical notes, and scientific diagrams (John-Steiner, 1985).

The diversity of these means and the psychological tools that they represent are of special interest to educators who work in multicultural settings and with children who have special needs. In an issue of the *Educational Psychologist* devoted to Vygotsky's ideas, Boris Gindis (1995) describes the emphasis Vygotsky placed on the variety of psychological tools in approaching the study of children who had special physical or mental circumstances. "Vygotsky pointed out that our civilization has already developed different means (e.g. Braille system, sign language, lip-reading, finger spelling, etc.) to accommodate a handicapped child's unique way of acculturation through acquiring various symbol systems".

These acts of representation are embedded in social practice and rely on socially developed semiotic means. Ecology, history, culture, and family organisation play roles in patterning experience and events in the creation of knowledge (John-Steiner, 1995). For example, the tasks confronting children, such as learning to talk, to walk, and to attach meaning to their experiences are reflected in cognitive strategies, derived in part from the culturally patterned environment into which they are born. Their thought is shaped by the prevalent methods of physical and economic survival, by the language and visual symbols used by their people, and by socially ordered ways of parenting. Some children who are born into tribal or agricultural communities spend many hours strapped to the back of their mothers and other caregivers. In this position, they observe and represent the life of their community in a way that is not possible to children who are placed in cribs and playpens (John-Steiner, 1985)

Representational activities and the sociocultural theory of semiotic mediation are fundamental to Vygotsky's concept of internalisation and the transformation of interpersonal processes into intrapersonal ones. Vygotsky used the concept of semiotic mediation to explain qualitative transformations in the human mind historically, ontogenetically, and microgenetically. The role played by semiotic mediation in the development of higher psychological processes provided a central focus for Vygotsky's research. The concept of semiotic mediation is essential to the sociocultural view that the process of internalisation is transformative rather than transmissive.

Genetic Analysis

Vygotsky used genetic analysis which examines the origins and the history of phenomena, focusing on their *interconnectedness*, to develop his theoretical framework and guide his research. In describing this approach he emphasised the need to concentrate not on the

> *product* of development but on the very *process* by which higher forms are established....To study something historically means to study it in the process of change; that is the dialectical method's basic demand. To encompass in research the process of a given thing's development in all its phases and changes —from birth to death — fundamentally means to discover its nature, its essence, for "it is only in movement that a body shows what it is." Thus, the historical (that is in the broadest sense of history) study of behaviour is not an auxiliary aspect of theoretical study, but rather forms its very base. (Vygotsky, 1978)

According to this perspective, learning and development take place in socially and culturally shaped contexts. Historical conditions are constantly changing, resulting in changed contexts and opportunities for learning. For that reason, there can be no universal schema that adequately represents the dynamic relation between external and internal aspects of development (John-Steiner & Souberman, 1978).

Vygotsky argued that psychological systems that unite separate functions into new combinations and complexes arise in the process of development. An example of this unification is the linking of spoken and written language into a new and broader semiotic system. When it was discovered that it was "possible to represent the sounds of language using marks in clay just as it is possible to represent objects" (Cole, 1990, p. 95), a qualitative transformation in the development of humanity occurred. The unification of separate functions represented in literacy also provides insights into the relationships between individual and social processes.

In his studies of disabilities, Vygotsky analysed the unification of separate physiological (anatomical, biochemical, and evolving neural) and psychological processes. His collaborator, neuropsychologist Alexander Luria (1973, 1979) examined cognitive functions in brain damage at different levels of analysis. This led to the concept of *functional systems* which is particularly useful in the examination of phenomena at the interface of neural and cognitive processes. Functional systems are dynamic psychological systems in which diverse internal and external processes are coordinated and integrated. These systems reveal a variety of characteristics including the use of variable means or mechanisms by individuals to perform particular tasks. In order to succeed when faced with new learning challenges, these individuals reorganise their cognitive strategies. Cole and Scribner (1974) used the concept of functional systems extensively in their cross-cultural research, as did Newman, Griffin, & Cole (1989), who found that "External devices like talk and charts and writing are windows in the evolution and appearance of cognitive constructs. They are an essential part of the functional system that gives the actors as well as the analysts access to the changes occurring".

Functional system analysis captures the dynamic relationship between changing and stable features of phenomena and the ways in which these are integrated in different contexts. In work with Native American children, John-Steiner and Osterreich (1975) found it particularly useful in examining the children's use of various learning styles and modalities to accomplish similar goals and tasks. A functional systems approach helped analyse Native American children's learning approaches, viewing them as part of a dynamic system instead of splitting them into visual and verbal approaches.

Within genetic analysis the use of functional systems provides a framework for representing the complex interrelationships between external devices, psychological tools, the individual, and the social world. Vygotsky used the sociocultural framework based on the three central tenets described above — social sources of development, semiotic mediation, and genetic analysis — to develop his concept of internalisation.

Vygotsky's Methodological Approach

An understanding of Vygotsky's methodological approach helps to clarify the concept of internalisation and to differentiate it from other theoretical perspectives. Vygotsky approached methodological issues on two interrelated levels — the theoretical and the psychological. On the theoretical level he examined complex systems in the process of change, using dialectical logic to understand the interrelationships between components of the systems.

On the psychological level he chose research methods to capture the dynamics of process consistent with his theoretical approach. On both levels his emphasis was on the examination of cognitive change in diverse contexts. "Any psychological process, whether the development of thought or voluntary behaviour, is a process undergoing changes right before one's eyes" (Vygotsky, 1978, p. 61) To capture the processes at play, Vygotsky used the experimental-developmental method in which developmental changes are provoked in laboratory settings. Through intervention, the experimenter is able to record participants' initial efforts to solve a problem beyond their existing means or strategies.

One of the intervention methods was providing auxiliary means through which the problem could be solved. This type of mediated assistance was of theoretical and methodological interest to Vygotsky. In studying memory in complex choice responses, he focused on the developmental changes taking place in the course of one or several sessions during which the learner appropriates new psychological tools.

Contemporary Vygotskian scholars researching cognitive change in classroom learning rely on both experimental and qualitative methods to focus on developmental processes. Sociocultural researchers reject "the cause-effect, stimulus-response, explanatory science in favour of a science that emphasises the emergent nature of mind in activity and that acknowledges a central role for interpretation in its explanatory framework" (Cole, 1996).

Vygotskian researchers use this theoretical and methodological approach to study and describe the concept of internalisation. This is germane to the discussion on classroom learning and teaching in this issue of the *Educational Psychologist.* There is a vigorous discussion among sociocultural theorists and proponents of differing theoretical perspectives about the way that concepts are learned and the processes through which they are acquired, appropriated, or internalised. These processes cannot be adequately understood, we believe, without comprehending the dialectical method Vygotsky used to examine them. This section presents Vygotsky's use of the dialectical method, explains the authors' conception of internalisation, and distinguishes sociocultural concepts of internalisation from other perspectives.

Dialectical Method

Vygotsky did not simply try to impose laws or principles of dialectics on existing psychological theories, rather he scientifically investigated and analysed concrete questions in specific areas of psychological enquiry. This approach was described by one of his collaborators, Leontiev (1977), who wrote that in science "dialectic logic does not amount to just the formalistic imposition of its principles on any particular scientific discipline. It itself develops as scientific enquiry proceeds; it is the result of empirical science". Vygotsky underscored the centrality of this method to all of his work. *"The search for method becomes one of the most important problems of the entire enterprise of understanding the uniquely human forms of psychological activity. In this case, the method is simultaneously prerequisite and product, the tool and the result of the study..." (Vygotsky, 1978, p. 65).*

In contrast to Aristotelian logic which placed phenomena, such as mind and matter, into fixed, unchanging categories, Vygotsky analysed higher mental functions as developmental processes in a constant state of dialectical change. He examined mind and matter in their interconnectedness and included a "scientific explanation of both external manifestations and the process under study" (1978).

A central concept of dialectics, the unification of contradictions, distinguishes it from traditional approaches. "Whereas, within the standard view, conceptual unity among objects relies on the commonality of elements, it is the interrelatedness of diverse elements and the integration of opposites that creates unity within dialectics" (Falmagne, 1995, p. 207). Dialectics surmounts dichotomies by looking at phenomena as syntheses of contradictions. In twentieth century physics, it was the unified vision of light as both wave and particle that led to a broader theoretical understanding. In nature, qualitative transformations unify contradictions — water, for example, as unification of hydrogen and oxygen will go through transformations from gas to liquid to solid with quantitative changes in temperature. Additionally, physical tools can unify contradictory functions — the claw hammer is used to both pound in and pull out nails; the pencil is used to create and erase (Weber, 1992).

Vygotsky (1986) used the dialectical notion of synthesis to analyse a central psychological tool — verbal thought. He examined the way that thought and speech, which initially have separate planes or levels of development in children in a "pre-linguistic period in thought and a pre-intellectual period of speech," become inextricably intertwined. Throughout his work Vygotsky uses the dialectical method to analyse, explain, and describe interrelationships fundamental to human development where others posited dichotomies — for example, mind and matter, language and thought, external and inner speech, nature and culture, and social and individual processes in the construction of knowledge.

Our concept of development implies a rejection of the frequently held view that cognitive development results from the gradual accumulation of separate changes. We believe that child development is a complex dialectical process characterised by periodicity, unevenness in the development of different functions, metamorphosis or qualitative transformation of one form into the other, intertwining of external and internal factors, and adaptive processes which overcome impediments that the child encounters. *(Vygotsky, 1978)*

Using this approach, sociocultural theorists analyse internalisation and individual and social processes as interrelated parts of neurophysiological, psychological, educational, political, and cultural systems *(Tobach, 1995)*.

Internalisation

Our concept of internalisation recognises unique human minds which owe their existence to and are inextricably intertwined with social, historical, cultural, and material processes (including brain activities). Internalisation is conceived of as a representational activity, a process that occurs simultaneously in social practice and in the human brain/mind. Sociocultural researchers include the learners' appropriation of socially elaborated symbol systems as a critical aspect of learning-driven development. This appropriation of symbol systems was a central focus of Vygotsky's work, particularly as applied to educational pedagogy, and led to his most fully elaborated application of the concept of internalisation — the transformation of communicative language into inner speech and further into verbal thinking (*Vygotsky, 1986, Ch. 7*).

Although "cognitive constructivist research and practise...is mostly oriented towards understanding the individual learner" (Derry, 1996, this issue) and separates individual processes of knowledge construction from social processes of joint understanding, we think of them as connected and interdependent. The development of the mind of the child is both individual and social at the same time and is the result of a long process of developmental events (Vygotsky, 1978). A focus of sociocultural research is the study of the way that the co-construction of knowledge is internalised, appropriated, transmitted, or transformed in formal and informal learning settings.

Vygotsky examined and explained the processes through which humans construct minds in interaction with the external world of nature and with other humans, changing in the process both themselves and nature.

The dialectical approach, while admitting the influence of nature on man, asserts that man, in turn, affects nature and creates through his changes in nature new natural conditions for his existence. This position is the keystone of our approach to the study and interpretation of man's higher psychological functions and serves as the basis for the new methods of experimentation and analysis we advocate. *(Vygotsky, 1978)*

The Russian philosopher, E. V. Ilyenkov adds that "the socio-historical environment, the world of things, created by human labour, and the system of human relations, formed in the process of labour" must also be considered, and that "outside the individual lies not only nature as such ('in itself'), but also *humanised* nature, nature remade by human labour" *(Bakhurst, 1995)*.

In a psychological framework the unification of nature and culture is powerfully embodied in early development. For example, a human embryo is both a material and a conceptual reality for the mother, but its own consciousness is dependent upon the full (prenatal and post-natal) development of the infant's own nervous system and his or her subsequent internalisation of culturally developed sign systems. Bakhurst (1995) writes that "the nature and content of an individual's mental life cannot be understood independently of the culture of which that individual is part". He further suggests that there are two intuitions which lie behind the claims of "strong cultural theories of the mind":

> The first is that meaning is the medium of the mental, and meaning is (in some sense) socially constructed; the second is that the human mind, and the forms of talk in which human beings explain and predict the operations of minds, should be understood on the model of tools, and like all artifacts, we cannot make sense of them independently of the social processes which make them what they are.

Lemke (1995) poses the contradictory character of the relationship between individual and social processes in the making of meaning: "how to have an active, creative human subject which constructs social meanings, at the same time that this subject itself must be a social construction". Vygotsky's use of dialectics to unravel this contradictory relationship between individual and social processes in which the individual constructs the social and at the same time is constructed by the social distinguishes the sociocultural perspective from others presented in this issue.

We favour the view of Penuel and Wertsch (1995) that "sociocultural processes on the one hand and individual functioning on the other exist in a dynamic, irreducible tension rather than a static notion of social determination. A sociocultural approach...considers these poles of sociocultural processes and individual functioning as interacting moments in human action, rather than as static processes that exist in isolation from one another".

Distinctions from other Perspectives

The way in which internalisation has been interpreted by a variety of critics highlights the distinctions between sociocultural and other approaches. For example, social constructivist critics of the Vygotskian framework such as Cobb & Yackel (1996) characterise it in this issue of *Educational Psychologist* as a transmission model through which students inherit the cultural meanings that constitute their intellectual bequest from prior generations. Their position is both linked to and differentiated from a Vygotskian stand when they question the metaphor "of students and teachers being embedded or included in social practice" (Cobb, Wood, & Yackel, 1993). Although their emergent approach has many commonalities with sociocultural theory, Cobb and Yackel repeatedly criticise the latter as a transfer-of-knowledge model where students imitate "established mathematical practices" (1996,). This interpretation of sociocultural theory reduces and simplifies the mutuality of learning, and its interpersonal and intergenerational dynamic. In attempting to differentiate their approaches from sociocultural theory, social constructivists misinterpret the transformative character of internalisation as described by sociocultural researchers *(John-Steiner, 1996).*

The conceptualisation of internalisation as unidirectional transmission freezes the debate, in part, by distorting sociocultural theorists' views of the roles of both teacher and student. It does not recognise that the sociocultural theory of internalisation analyses the complex process of transmission, transformation, and synthesis in the co-construction of knowledge. As Leontiev wrote, "the process of internalisation is not the *transferal* of an external activity to a pre-existing internal 'plane of consciousness': it is the process in which this plane is formed" (Wertsch & Stone, 1985). In classroom learning the student plays an active role and constantly informs the teacher as their mutual negotiation and collaboration build knowledge.

As well as the presentation of new information, there needs to be extended opportunity for discussion and problem-solving in the context of shared activities, in which meaning and action are collaboratively constructed and negotiated. In other words, education must be thought of in terms not of the transmission of knowledge but of transaction and transformation. (Chang-Wells & Wells, 1993) We will explore other studies of classroom collaboration exhibiting transformative knowledge co-construction later in this article.

There are different modes of internalisation, reflecting different teaching/interaction strategies. A continuum with direct instruction on one end to creative and collaborative learning on the other could describe the wide range of teaching/learning situations in which internalisation occurs. Whether in the learning of a young child or in the activities of experienced thinkers, internalisation is a fundamental part of the lifelong process of the co-construction of knowledge and the creation of the new.

Other critics warn that using the concept of internalisation to explain the learning processes creates the danger of focusing on just the *individual* mental construction of knowledge. For example, Martin Packer's (1993) analysis, which is linked to an hermeneutic, interpretive approach, suggests that "Descartes' ghost may still be with us", because he sees elements of dualism in sociocultural concepts of internalisation. While he appreciates the work of Vygotskian scholars, Packer is concerned that "the processes and mechanisms being examined keep creeping back inside the head". In contrasting the view of learning as mental change with an alternative which focuses on participatory activities, his analysis is similar to that of Barbara Rogoff (1994) who writes that "learning is a process of transforming participation in shared sociocultural endeavours".

In our view, internalisation is simultaneously a social and an individual process. In working with, through, and beyond what they have appropriated in social participation and then internalised, individuals co-construct new knowledge. In contrast to facile internalisation which leads to a limited combination of ideas, internalisation that involves sustained social and individual endeavours becomes a constituent part of the interaction with what is known and leads to the creation of new knowledge.

Chang-Wells & Wells (1993) in their study of the role of instructional conversations in classroom learning describe this interdependent and transformative view of internalisation: "...It is at points of negotiation of meaning in conversation that learning and development occur, as each learner's individual psychological processes mediate (and at the same time are mediated by) the constitutive intermental processes of the group".

Sociocultural approaches are also distinguished from other perspectives by the importance they place on cultural variation and its interrelationship with development (John-Steiner & Panofsky, 1992). This distinction is particularly relevant in contrasting sociocultural approaches with those derived from a Piagetian framework. The emphasis on culture has resulted in the broad use by sociocultural researchers of approaches which examine the ways in which learning and teaching take place under differing cultural circumstances and in differing historical contexts, contributing to a *contextualised* rather than a universalistic theory of development. And while social constructivists do engage in an analysis of cultural norms, they maintain a conceptual dichotomy between the individual's constructive activity on the one hand and social processes on the other. For example, Cobb and Yackel (1996) view the individual through one lens and the social through another without making explicit the dialectical interdependence of social and individual processes. To study these processes interdependently requires a reliance on cross-cultural comparisons and active collaboration between researchers drawn from varied backgrounds examining teachers and children in diverse settings.

The significant role of cross-cultural comparisons in theory construction and the development of educational practice is illustrated by the work of Tharp and Gallimore (1988) and their collaborators who developed a highly effective, culturally sensitive approach to teaching Hawaiian children. In their well-known Kamehameha Early Education Programme (KEEP) instructional conversations are designed to resemble the talk story format — overlapping speech, joint performance, and informal turn taking — favoured in the native Hawaiian community.

However, when this highly successful programme was implemented among Navajo children, the results were mixed (Jordan, Tharp, & Vogt, 1985). The researchers became aware of the difficulties in applying a promising culturally sensitive approach from one indigenous context to another. They found that for Hawaiian children groups of four to five students of mixed sex and ability produce the maximum peer interaction and learning cooperation.

However, Navajo children were uncomfortable in the larger mixed groups and worked best in dyads of the same sex. These studies illustrate the importance to sociocultural approaches of inclusion of anthropologists, Native teachers, and the learners themselves as educational activity planners whose joint efforts help educators understand the culturally-patterned learning styles children bring to school. This emphasis upon interdisciplinary action research by Vygotskian educators contrasts with other approaches in educational psychology.

Sociocultural researchers emphasise methods which document cognitive and social change. Rather than seeing a dichotomy between quantitative and qualitative research, approaches are chosen that emphasise process and development and the multiple ways in which both can be revealed. They include experimental research such as Frauenglass and Diaz's (1985) work on private speech which studied Vygotsky's hypotheses on the universality and self-regulatory significance of private speech.

In a laboratory setting they "compared the frequencies of preschoolers' private speech in perceptual versus semantic tasks, with or without instructions that permitted and encouraged the use of overt verbalisations....And found that researchers who choose to study private speech in laboratory settings must pay close attention to task and setting variables that may increase or inhibit the amount of private speech produced by children in their samples" (Diaz, 1992, p. 57).

Other sociocultural approaches combine experimental and ethnographic research as illustrated by Scribner and Cole's (1981) work in Liberia. In their studies of literacy they include observational and ethnographic methods and combined them with tasks first developed in laboratory settings. Examples of sociocultural methods of research on cognitive change in the classroom are described in the next section.

Sociocultural, Educational Research and Practice

This section briefly examines Vygotsky's analysis of the relationship between learning and development, his concept of the zone of proximal development, and implications drawn from them for research on collaborative learning. Vygotsky's analysis of spontaneous and scientific concepts is then examined, focusing on the central roles in concept formation played by language and culture. The integrated influences of culture and language are then examined in practical applications of sociocultural approaches to classroom learning and teaching in literacy instruction. An additional and related theme highlighted in this section is the way sociocultural theory helps educators provide instruction which recognises and empowers linguistically and culturally diverse students.

Learning and Development and the Zone of Proximal Development

In contrast to prevailing theories of his time which dichotomised learning and development viewing one as an external and the other as an internal process, Vygotsky (1978) looked at their unity and interdependence starting from a child's birth.

Our hypothesis establishes the unity but not the identity of learning processes and internal developmental processes. It presupposes that the one is converted into the other. Therefore, it becomes an important concern of psychological research to show how external knowledge and abilities in children become internalised.

He thus criticised theories such as Piaget's, in which "maturation is viewed as a pre-condition of learning but never the result of it" and developed the following position:

> ...Learning awakens a variety of internal developmental processes that are able to operate only when the child is interacting with people in his environment and in cooperation with his peers....Learning is not development; however, properly organised learning results in mental development and sets in motion a variety of developmental processes that would be impossible apart from learning. Thus learning is a necessary and universal aspect of the process of developing culturally organised, specifically human, psychological functions.

To help explain the way that this social and participatory learning took place, Vygotsky (1978) developed the concept of the zone of proximal development (ZPD), which he defined as "...the distance between the actual developmental level as determined through independent problem solving and the level of potential development as determined through problem solving under adult guidance or in collaboration with more capable peers". Sociocultural theorists, expanding the concept of the zone of proximal development, increasingly conceptualise learning as *distributed* (Cole & Engestrom, 1993), *interactive* (Chang-Wells & Wells, 1993), *contextual* (John-Steiner, Panofsky, & Smith, 1994), and the result of the *learners' participation in a community of practice* (Rogoff, 1994).

Ann Brown and her collaborators (1992, 1993) have developed and implemented educational programmes based on this concept of learning. They suggest that the active agents within the zone of proximal development "can include people, adults and children, with various degrees of expertise, but it can also include artifacts, such as books, videos, wall displays, scientific equipment and a computer environment intended to support intentional learning" (1993). In expanding the zone of proximal development to include artifacts in addition to people, Brown integrates Vygotsky's analyses of tools and symbols with the roles played by the participants in the learning process.

One of the important features of Brown and her collaborators' work is the examination of the way "divergent classrooms can become learning communities — communities in which each participant makes significant contributions to the emergent understandings of all members, despite having unequal knowledge concerning the topic under study" (Palincsar, Brown, & Campione, 1993). They examine the role of "reciprocal teaching," an approach in which "students and teachers take turns leading discussions about shared text", to see whether structured dialogues foster a learning community. The teachers in these studies have a changing role. They share with the students the well-defined tasks of questioning, clarifying, summarising, and predicting in order to construct text-based knowledge. These studies exemplify two themes in sociocultural approaches to classroom learning and teaching — (1) the implementation of an educational programme that allows for or encourages the co-construction of knowledge and (2) the analysis of this learning that contributes to our understanding of classroom learning from a sociocultural perspective. Collaborative learning plays an increasing role in these as well as many other innovative classrooms.

Collaboration Research

In current applications of sociocultural theory with emphases on co-participation, cooperative learning, and joint discovery, teachers bring existing knowledge to students by co-constructing it with them. These applications have made clear the need to examine patterns of interaction and collaboration in this type of classroom. A major goal of our current research is to produce a theoretical model of the collaboration process and to identify collaborator's values, roles, working methods, and conflict-resolution strategies. Through the analysis of selected project documents and transcribed discourse from group meetings, as well as through focused interviews, our initial work has revealed four patterns - *distributed, complementary, family,* and *integrative* — among individual, small groups, and larger complex collaborations. We use a circle and dotted lines to show that collaborative efforts are dynamic, changing processes. While the corresponding characteristics of values, working methods, and roles for each pattern are depicted in the bands around the wheel, there is no rigidity in the divisions. The order of the patterns is not hierarchical, and a collaboration can be initiated at any level and be transformed over time. A goal is to examine how the resolutions of tensions inherent in collaborations transform the character of the collaboration and determine whether it continues.

In the move from the outer edge of the wheel in to the centre, collaborations tend to be longer term and are characterised by the increasing importance of negotiated and common values. In distributed collaborations, such as collective e-mail discussions where the exchange of information is featured, values need not extend beyond similar interests; whereas in integrated collaborations — long-term, often dyadic and intimate — values are reflected in the development of shared ideologies. Complementary collaborations, such as those found in the organisation of teams in classrooms and in the business world, are distinguished by clear divisions of labour and discipline-based approaches. In contrast, family collaborations, often centred on providing social services including education, are characterised by the fluidity of roles and the integration of expertise.

The conceptualisation of the patterns of collaboration is use in the study of classrooms engaged in collaborative learning. Complex social relationships and differing cultural values will shape the intellectual interdependence in the co-construction of knowledge in classes which are not based on the traditional teacher-centred transmission model of education.

The way that cultural and linguistic factors shape learning and development and the impact that these factors have on pedagogical approaches provide a theoretical foundation for sociocultural research of collaboration in the classroom. There is a growing literature on cooperative learning and peer collaboration of interest to both Piagetian and Vygotskian researchers (Damon & Phelps, 1989; Slavin, 1983, 1987; Tudge & Rogoff, 1989) which can inform classroom practice.

In differentiating their approach from others Forman and McPhail (1993) highlight three features of a sociocultural perspective on the study of collaboration in education. First, rather than locating the source of individual motivation and understanding within or between individuals, they locate it in sociocultural practices in which children have the opportunity "to observe and participate in essential economic, religious, legal, political, instructional, or recreational activities."

Through guided participation "children internalise or appropriate their affective, social, and intellectual significance". Second, Forman and McPhail write:

> For Vygotsky, cognitive, social, and motivational factors were interrelated in development. Thus it makes no sense to evaluate the benefits of peer collaboration in purely intellectual terms, e.g., via individual achievement testing. A Vygotskian perspective also implies that the outcomes of peer collaboration must be evaluated in context and over time.

The third feature of Forman and McPhail's approach is that discourse analysis can be used to examine participants' "epistemological and affective dispositions towards collaborative problem solving. Their discourse should reflect their individual and shared understandings and feelings about the task setting, as well as the definitions of the activity that are provided by their particular cultural and historical situation".

Using this framework, Forman and McPhail (1993) examine the ways in which learners assist each other. Their work, which focuses on dyads engaged in problem-solving activities, illustrates the *complementary* pattern of collaboration. The two students in the study, after initial differences on task definition, developed a division of labour based on areas of expertise reflected in specialised forms of discourse — scientific and mathematical. This study highlights the need to develop joint perspectives over time to achieve shared goals. Forman and McPhail (1993) emphasise the role of mutuality and the use of specialised forms of discourse "to engage in logical arguments, to share ideas, and to work together in the pursuit of common goals". (This finding corresponds to our own, where we have found the importance of trust in the development of working methods in sustained collaboration.)

A different pattern of collaboration was revealed in Moll & Whitmore's (1993) study of a bilingual classroom in the Southwestern United States in which reading and writing in two languages were integrated in project-oriented literacy activities. This study, using a sociocultural approach, examined the interactive and contextual character of cognitive change as students created and participated in communities of learners. The collaboration described by Moll and Whitmore (1993) exemplified the *family* pattern, with a fluidity of roles and a reliance on various areas of expertise from the students and the teacher in the joint construction of knowledge. Because the teachers and children were actively and mutually creating learning situations, the roles of both were flexible. The children often took the lead in shaping text-related discussions.

The teacher's roles include those of *guide* and *supporter* whose "guidance is purposely mediated, almost hidden, embedded in the activities;" *participant* in thematic research activities; *evaluator* of the students' development; and *facilitator* and *planner* who organises "the environment, curriculum, and materials to provide functional and purposeful uses for language, literacy, and learning processes". At the same time the "children have considerable control of virtually all aspects of their own learning experiences. They select groups, reading materials, writing topics, theme topics, and language to use for each". Moll and Whitmore (1993) describe a pattern of collaboration where the development of trust among the participants is of central concern. These patterns of shared responsibilities in teaching and learning have contributed to a broadened understanding of the zone of proximal development and help illustrate the emerging patterns of collaboration.

Another example of the family pattern of collaboration is the after-school programme known as the "Fifth Dimension," developed by Michael Cole, Peg Griffin, and their collaborators at the University of California, San Diego, which brings together children and adolescents, community institutions, undergraduate students, and researchers. It relies upon computer technology, collaborative learning, play, and imagination "within the framework of a shared and voluntarily accepted system of impersonal rules" (Nicolopoulou & Cole, 1993, p. 293). Cole (1995) and his colleagues have extended Vygotskian analyses of learning beyond the dyadic and small group level to include an examination of different sites as institutional and cultural contexts for these activities. The success of the Fifth Dimension is based, in part, on the character of the collaboration which includes a fluidity of roles across ages and areas of expertise. The integration of play and learning helps meet the shared goals and objectives of the programme. This innovative, collaborative programme contrasts with traditional models of education which isolate teachers in their classrooms.

Sociocultural research on collaboration also includes examination of the mutual dependence of teachers engaged in collective activity and dialogue in the process of curriculum innovation. Yjro Engestrom (1994) in his study of teachers found an additional benefit of collaboration research:

> One of the most persistent methodological difficulties of studying thinking has to do with access to on-line data from thought processes. When thinking is defined as a private, individual phenomenon only indirect data is accessible. Thinking embedded in collaborative practical activity must to a significant degree take the form of talk, gesture, use of artifacts, or some other publicly accessible mediational instrumentality; otherwise mutual formation of ideas would be rendered impossible. Collaborative thinking opens up access to direct data on thought processes.

Teachers in traditional schools often don't have the opportunity to interact with colleagues as in the Engestrom study and thus have "limited opportunities for receiving assistance through modelling and feedback, two means of assistance crucial to acquisition of complex social repertoires....necessary to meet the criterion of teaching-as-assisted-performance in the zone of proximal development" *(Gallimore & Tharp, 1990).*

A particularly powerful example of collaboration, and one that can inform our efforts at educational reform, is provided by Brazilian teachers who worked together with community activists to educate previously excluded populations (Souza Lima, 1995). Their local initiatives, broadened and strengthened through the use of the sociocultural theories of Vygotsky, Wallon, and Freire, are being applied to citywide and broader reform efforts. Studies of teachers in dynamic interactions with other teachers, students, researchers, and reformers will be important in the ongoing sociocultural research into collaboration and educational change.

Spontaneous and Scientific Concepts

In classrooms in which there is co-participation, cooperative learning, and joint discovery, environments are created in which students are able to build upon the culturally-shaped knowledge and value systems they bring to school. Vygotsky's analysis of spontaneous and scientific concepts provides a foundation for examining how children learn before they enter school and how this knowledge relates to concepts learned at school.

> By spontaneous concepts Vygotsky meant concepts that are acquired by the child outside of the context of explicit instruction. In themselves these concepts are mostly taken from adults, but they never have been introduced to the child in a systematic fashion and no attempts have been made to connect them with other related concepts. Because Vygotsky explicitly acknowledged the role of adults in the formation of these so-called spontaneous concepts he preferred to call them "everyday" concepts, thus avoiding the idea that they had been spontaneously invented by the child....By "scientific" concepts Vygotsky meant concepts that had been explicitly introduced by a teacher at school. Ideally such concepts would cover the essential aspects of an area of knowledge and would be presented as a system of interrelated ideas. (van der Veer & Vlasiner, 1991)

Even though Vygotsky discusses spontaneous and scientific concepts by highlighting their distinguishing characteristics, he still recognised their interdependence. "We believe that the two processes — the development of spontaneous and of non-spontaneous concepts — are related and constantly influence each other. They are parts of a single process: the development of concept formation which is affected by varying external and internal conditions but is essentially a unitary process, not a conflict of antagonistic, mutually exclusive forms of thinking" *(Vygotsky, 1986).*

The social situatedness of concept formation is studied by Moll (1992) who uses Vygotsky's analysis to gain insight into providing effective education for linguistically and culturally diverse students:

> One advantage of a sociocultural approach is that in studying human beings dynamically, within their social circumstances, in their full complexity, we gain a much more complete and...a much more valid understanding of them. We also gain, particularly in the case of minority children, a more positive view of their capabilities and how our pedagogy often constrains, and just as often distorts, what they do and what they are capable of doing.

Analysing how students learn, as well as acknowledging and attempting to understand the culturally-conditioned knowledge they bring to the classroom, can help lead to effective teaching. In an ethnographic study looking at how the knowledge that existed in Mexican American students' households could be used to bring about innovative instructional practice, Moll & Greenberg (1990) found a variety of "funds of knowledge" ranging from knowledge "about different soils, the cultivation of plants, and water management...animal husbandry, veterinary medicine, ranch economy, and mechanics as well as carpentry, masonry, electrical wiring...". They also found that this knowledge was socially distributed and that a reciprocal relationship existed between everyday knowledge used to understand school material and classroom activities used to help students understand social reality.

To facilitate this interaction an after-school lab was created "...within which researchers, teachers, and students meet to experiment with the teaching of literacy. We think of this lab setting, following Vygotsky, as a 'mediating' structure that facilitates strategic connections, multiple paths, between classrooms and household". Without such mediating structures, investigations into discourse practices in school and home have found that the variations between the two can lead to problems as students adjust to the requirements of formal education.

In order to understand children in school settings, sociocultural approaches examine the development of language and the ways that culturally different modes of discourse, both within and between cultures, shape children's development and impact their educational experiences.

From birth, the social forms of child-caretaker interactions, the tools used by humans in society to manipulate the environment, the culturally institutionalised patterns of social relations, and language, operating together as a socio-semiotic system, are used by the child in cooperation with adults to organise behaviour, perception, memory, and complex mental processes. For children, the development of language is a development of social existence into individuated persons and into culture. (John-Steiner & Tatter, 1983)

The linguist, James Gee (1989) argues that "discourses are intimately related to the distribution of social power and hierarchical structure in society". The impact of different, culturally-patterned modes of discourse is felt from the primary grades through higher education. Michele Minnis (1994) examines the ways in which linguistically and culturally diverse students are at a disadvantage in law school when faced with the norms of a legal community indifferent to their culture, discourse, and values. She quotes a Chicana law student:

> The game is alien to your upbringing. It is a manipulation of words in a foreign tongue — words which mystify, manipulation which obscures your search for justice. You will feel as if you don't belong....Group learning was almost impossible. Most of my classmates were heartlessly competitive....If I were to call someone ambitious in English, it would be a compliment. If I were to say the same in Spanish, it would be an insult.

Studies of schooled discourses are of particular interest to contemporary students of education and development. Some of these discourses are empowering as in the bilingual classroom studied by Moll and Whitmore (1993); others contribute to the oppression of the silenced (Belenky, Clinchy, Goldberger, & Tarule, 1986; Cazden, 1988, 1993; Freire, 1970). Gee (1991) drawing on research by Scribner and Cole (1981), Heath (1983) and others, identifies sociocultural explanations of school failure: 1) discontinuities between the culture (values, attitudes, and beliefs) of the home and school; 2) mismatches in communicative practices between non-mainstream children and mainstream teachers that lead to miscommunication and misjudgements; and 3) the internalisation of negative stereotypes by minority groups who have been marginalised and often see school as a site for opposition and resistance. Children whose mode of discourse is different from that used in school instruction find themselves at a disadvantage and often drop out, or are forced out, of school.

The ways in which children acquire language and construct knowledge in non-school environments and the dynamic relationship with what they are taught in school is maximally relevant to school learning. The conceptual and theoretical tool of spontaneous and scientific concepts provides particularly interesting applications and expansions in literacy acquisition.

Literacy Acquisition

Since the time when Vygotsky and the young Russian psychologists of the nineteen-twenties faced the social task of educating an overwhelmingly illiterate population following the tremendous upheavals that transformed the Soviet Union during the Russian revolution of 1917, literacy acquisition has been a central concern of sociocultural theory.

For example, Scribner and Cole (1981) built on Vygotsky's examination of the role of literacy in the transformation of children's learning when they enter school and analysed the relationship between literacy and cognitive development. They found that literacy can be acquired independently of schooling (particularly, schooling in the vast Western systems of education) and that literacy practices used in different contexts will have specific effects on cognitive competencies. Their findings contrast with more universal accounts of the relationship between literacy and formal modes of thought *(Olson, 1977).*

Chang-Wells & Wells (1993) use Vygotsky's work on both learning and development and spontaneous and scientific concepts to examine three dimensions of change in mental functioning that can be ascribed to formal learning: intellectualisation of mental functions, bringing them under conscious and voluntary control; decontextualisation, being able to detach a concept from the context in which it was first encountered; and a movement towards integration and systematisation.

They assert that all of these dimensions of cognitive change "are dependent on literacy, when it is understood not simply as the encoding and decoding of written language or the use of written texts for functional purposes but as engaging with texts of all kinds in ways that exploit the symbolic representation of meaning as a means of empowering intrapersonal mental activity". Using this theoretical foundation, they analyse the use of effective instructional discourse in two classrooms designed to present literacy instruction in the students' zones of proximal development.

To create an effective learning environment for literacy acquisition, Vygotsky (1978) wrote that "teaching should be organised in such a way that reading and writing are necessary for something....that writing should be meaningful....that writing be *taught* naturally....and that the natural methods of teaching reading and writing involve appropriate operations on the child's environment". These considerations have influenced recent sociocultural approaches to literacy instruction for children and adults in school, at workplaces, and in after-school, home, and day-care settings (Clay & Cazden, 1990; John-Steiner, Panofsky, & Smith, 1994; McNamee, 1990; Scribner & Cole, 1981; Zebroski, 1994).

Using a genetic approach to literacy acquisition, sociocultural theory examines the origins of both reading and writing. Panofsky (1994) studied the role of parent-child book reading in early literacy socialisation focusing on the functions and uses of language. She differentiated between representational and interactional functions of language, building upon Vygotsky's distinctions. Illustrating the roles of scaffolding and the zone of proximal development, she noted ...A shift in the use of functions from a pre-dominance of parent initiations to a pre-dominance of child initiations".

Vygotsky (1978) considered early literacy experiences important in the acquisition process. He saw the origin of writing in a child's gesture which "is the initial visual sign that contains the child's future writing as an acorn contains a future oak. Gestures, it has been correctly said, are writing in air, and written signs frequently are simply gestures that have been fixed".

In the child's development there are two other domains in which gestures are linked to the origins of written language — the first is in scribbling and the dramatisations that often accompany it; the second is in the area of symbolic play, where a child assigns meaning to an object through gesture. The varied sources of writing in children's early years intrigued Vygotsky, who wrote of drawing and play as preparation to literacy. In a related vein, McLane (1990) found in a study of writing by children in an after-school day-care programme that "children will, with adult involvement and support, use writing as a resource for extending their interests in drawing, in pretend and exploratory play, and as a means of exploring and conducting social relationships".

As a result of being read to and using a writing tool to inscribe a piece of paper, or often a wall, the child develops spontaneous concepts in the process of telling stories, acting out roles in imaginative play, or creating representations. When children begin formal schooling, they start with a foundation that is shaped by the nature of the interaction between caretaker and child, by literacy uses valued by a particular culture, by print in the environment, and by the child's own activity in literacy events. The challenge is to value and build on what the child brings to the classroom. "By broadening both teachers' and students' views of students' backgrounds and existing knowledge, the unique experiences that students bring to school make an important contribution to the process of literacy acquisition" (Hiebert, 1991, p. 3). In a study of Latino households in California, Gallimore and Goldenberg (1993) identified meaningful settings which provide literacy activities, such as letter writing, for novice learners of reading and writing. They focused on cultural experiences in everyday life and on the active participation of young learners in literacy events. If such a focus is not adopted, teachers will not be able to understand their students' attempts at literate ways of thinking (Langer, 1991) nor will they be able to provide the learning opportunities to facilitate literacy acquisition for all students.

Such differences in language use in ethnically mixed classes often result in differential access to literacy experiences....Teachers often unknowingly exclude or reduce the time minority students participate in literacy activities because features of their discourse do not conform to teachers' expectations or match their speaking style. *(McCullom, 1991)*

Understanding differences such as these are also important in teaching English to speakers of other languages. Sociocultural theory recognises the need for cultural, cognitive, and attitudinal bridges between English as a Second Language (ESL) students and their new environment. The use of dialogue journals with elementary and secondary students, as well as with adults, has been found to be an effective technique to co-construct knowledge by allowing ESL students to draw on their own experiences and develop their own voices in meaningful, interactive, written communication (Mahn, 1992; Staton, Shuy, Peyton, & Reed, 1988).

In recent years there has been a critical re-evaluation of the traditional methods of literacy instruction based on a single, universal time table and on cross-cultural universality. Vygotsky's advice about teaching literacy as a natural process is realised in whole language (Goodman, 1975; Goodman & Goodman, 1979) and process approaches to reading and writing (Emig, 1971; Calkins, 1986; Graves, 1983; Murray, 1985). These approaches view the interdependence of social and individual processes as a natural part of each student's development (Scinto, 1986). Reading and writing are not structured as solitary acts, but rather develop in collaborative efforts in a community of learners (Zebroski, 1994). The core elements of these innovative approaches to literacy instruction draw from and are supported by sociocultural theory and research.

The proponents and practitioners of such techniques and approaches, however, may not have ever heard of Vygotsky nor of sociocultural approaches. Increasingly though, teachers exposed to these ideas offer the sentiment that sociocultural theoretical perspectives provide the language for what they are doing in their classrooms. This shows both the limitations of and the promise for sociocultural approaches. Because this theory is complex and breaks radically from the traditional American educational model in which teachers have been schooled, it is hard to appropriate. The tendency is to abstract parts of the theory from the whole, which results in distorted understandings and applications. As more educators become aware of the broad scope of sociocultural theory, they will develop practical applications which will broaden and strengthen this theoretical framework. Such a perspective offers exciting opportunities for researchers and teachers as we face the challenges of educating youth for the twenty-first century.

Conclusion

A goal for sociocultural theorists is the sustained development of methodological approaches to educational and psychological research that focus on process and provide ways of documenting change and transformation. In this article we have presented a sociocultural approach to learning and development and implications for classroom learning and teaching. An emerging theme in both theory and practice is the collaborative and transformative way in which knowledge is co-constructed. We have focused on three central tenets from Vygotsky's complex legacy — social sources of individual development, semiotic mediation, and genetic analysis — and have presented an argument for viewing learning as distributed, interactive, contextual, and the result of the learners' participation in a community of practice.

Our aim has been to weave together some of Vygotsky's key ideas with pressing, contemporary concerns, particularly the need to shape educational institutions to deliver instruction which meets the needs of all students, especially the linguistically and culturally diverse who historically have been marginalised by traditional models of pedagogy. We believe a sociocultural point of view provides a deeper understanding of both the possibilities for and the problematic nature of educational reform.

Because educational institutions are a part of and reflect the larger social system in which they are situated, a proposal for substantial reform would have to consider economic, political, historical, social, and cultural factors. While such an analysis was not the intent in this article, we believe a concept it has presented — the socially structured interdependence of teaching and research, theory construction, and educational intervention — provides a starting point for local reform initiatives, such as the ones in Brazil described previously.

In the sociocultural framework notions of community and participation have been applied primarily to novice learners. The applications of these notions to adults to study the dynamics of collaboration and the interdependence of individual and social processes are areas for further practical and theoretical development.

Social constructivist frameworks, though not necessarily contradictory to sociocultural ones, focus more on the possibilities for change within the individual child, while sociocultural theoretical perspectives, as they develop and are applied to educational systems, look at change at different levels of analysis and organisation. Central to the task of educators and psychologists is conceiving of our work as a system rather than as a set of isolated activities. The sociocultural perspective can only thrive with the continued, and at times discordant, articulation of the many voices of this thought community.

4 Psychological Approaches to English Language Learning and Teaching

The amount of effort that is being expended in the teaching of foreign languages in this country has reached considerable proportions. According to various surveys conducted by the Modern Language Association of America, 80 per cent of public secondary schools offered FL courses in 1965 and more than one out of every four senior high school students were engaged in the study of a FL (Willbern, 1968). Some predictions estimate that by 1970 roughly half of all public school pupils will be engaged in the study of a language other than English. Most of the large universities in the country have either a college entrance requirement in their Liberal Arts and Sciences Schools or a college graduation requirement involving a FL.

There are powerful social pressures for the maintenance of such a large educational investment in the teaching of a second language which go beyond the traditional goals of FL study stated in terms of promoting the "cultured person." According to the 1966 Statistical Abstract of the United States there were in 1960 close to 24 million Americans in the category labelled "Native of foreign or mixed parentage," of which almost 10 million are foreign born. Over 18 million Americans claim that their mother tongue is not English (Fishman, 1966a). Considerable social effort is expended within a non-English medium of communication: over 500 periodicals are published regularly (including 61 daily newspapers); some 1,500 radio stations broadcast in a FL for several hours a week; there are approximately 2,000 ethnically affiliated schools of which more than half offer mother tongue (i.e., non-English) instruction; there exist at least 1,800 ethnic cultural organisations most of which favour maintenance of their FL (Fishman, 1966a).

An assessment of the present level of technology for teaching a second language is extremely difficult. Depending on the students involved, the available time for teaching, and the larger social context within which the instruction programme is embedded, variable results have been achieved. On the higher end of success the results are impressive: with pre-selected students for high motivation and high FL aptitude placed in an intensive programme of instruction involving anywhere from 6 to 14 hours of directed and individual study a day, day after day, meaningful levels of proficiency (e.g., fluent conversation with natives) can be insured within 30 to 40 days according to some lower estimates (Carroll, 1963) or six months according to some higher estimates (Mueller, 1967). Intermediate levels of success are achieved with FL majors in colleges (Carroll, 1967) where after several years of concentrated study audiolingual skills remain generally low. Much more modest levels of success are to be found in the massive educational effort of FL teaching in our high schools where the indications are that most of the students involved do not reach meaningful levels of proficiency.

In one sense the technology of teaching FL's has been solved. Given motivated and talented individuals we have the "know-how" to expose the individual to an instructional procedure that insures the learning of any FL within a matter of weeks or months. The fact that this success is limited to a pre-selected sample of individuals should not lead us to minimise this pedagogical achievement. It is far better than we knew how prior to the new techniques developed since World War II and it is comparable, and perhaps even superior, to most industrial training programmes designed to impart skills of a much lesser complexity.

On the other hand, and from a quite different perspective, our ability to train successfully the multitudes of students in our public schools in the use of a FL is considerably less and by all indications does not compare favourably to the pedagogical achievements of teaching the three "R's." This sobering assessment is apparently shared by members of society at large: parents, students, school administrators, legislators responsible for appropriating educational funds, educators not directly involved in the teaching of FL's, all are increasingly engaged in asking a persistent and disturbing question: Why should so much effort be spent on the teaching of FL's when the results appear to be so meagre? In a recent Gallup Poll Survey parents consistently expressed the opinion that FL courses represent the weakest part of the school curriculum and should be the first to go in any curtailment of efforts. There are signs that the largesse of federal grant assistance to the FL teaching effort is being tempered along with the general slow down of federal support for research and an increasing number of universities are "liberalising" their FL requirements, which is to say, reducing them at both the undergraduate and graduate levels. One might say that the FL instruction establishment has been put in a defensive position. It must come up with good answers to the baffling problem that besets it today: How is FL instruction to be made more successful and more relevant to the aspirations of the "New Student" in an educational setting that competes for his attention and time?

The responses to this challenge are likely to come along three levels. First, on the technological side, better trained teachers using more advanced techniques (including both "hardware" and "software") are to come on the scene. Second, FL's are to be taught increasingly earlier (cf., FLES efforts: Foreign Language for the Elementary School) affording more cumulative time for study. Third, increasing efforts are to be made to improve the motivation of students by recognising the social-psychological implications of FL study and taking into account the attitudinal and sociological matrix within which FL study and maintenance are embedded in the larger societal, national, and world contexts.

This chapter attempts to organise the main facts that have come to be known about the physiology and psychology of FL learning as they impinge upon the three-pronged attack of the problem just discussed. The main issues to be dealt with can be summarised as follows:

- Theory and Practice in FL Teaching: Out of Step. This section examines the problem of how research efforts come to influence teaching practices. Several statements by authoritative persons and organised bodies (e.g., The Modern Language Association or MLA) concerning the "state of the art" of FL teaching are to be summarised and reviewed. The conclusion that will be presented will stress the fact that most of what we know about teaching comes not from the experimental laboratory but from the teacher's experience in the classroom. Here, as in other areas of education, practical knowledge by far outstrips the specific contribution of organised research. Given the relatively backward condition of social science and educational research, this state of affairs is unavoidable and though it is pointless to criticise it, this situation should nevertheless be clearly and explicitly recognised.

- What is it to "Know a Language?" Everyone accepts the notion that language is a means of communication, but there is much less agreement about just what is involved in the ability to communicate. The distinction between "linguistic competence" and "communicative competence" is either not explicitly taken into account in the majority of FL courses or it is tacitly assumed that the former must precede the latter in such a way that a certain high level of linguistic competence must be achieved before attempting the functional use of the FL. Arguments will be presented which show the harmful consequences of this practice. "Liberated expression" and the practical use of a FL is both desirable and possible at even the very beginning stages of study. A new attitude to the assessment of communicative skills (rather than language skills) is long overdue in the language testing field.

- The Physiology of Second Language Learning. Current efforts at FLES are often justified on the grounds that there is a biological timetable for language learning which makes it increasingly difficult to learn a second language after puberty at which time the brain allegedly loses "plasticity." The discussion in this section will question the validity of this argument and will examine other grounds for both the advantages and disadvantages of early versus late FL teaching.

- Motivational Aspects of FL Study. The importance of the problem of knowing how to motivate the FL learner has been mentioned. This section will examine a number of issues relating to this pressing need: (a), the consequences of the fact that becoming bilingual entails becoming bicultural; (b), the attitude of the student towards FL study generally, the goals and purposes which he sees in it.
- Summary and Conclusions. This final section will attempt to summarise the major points that are discussed in this chapter and will offer some thoughts on some possible and desirable developments in the FL teaching field that may take place in the immediate future.

Learning a Language

It has been pointed out earlier in this chapter that disagreements about how best to teach a FL cannot be unequivocally resolved by experimental research methods. But the inability of research to solve these practical problems is not the only difficulty to be contended with. There are fundamental differences in what language teachers perceive to be the goals of a specific FL course.

Some of the differences pertain to esthetic considerations, such as for example whether or not to insist on correct speech, both in the grammatical and phonological areas. This is clearly an esthetic rather than a functional criterion as indicated by the fact that first, effective communication is possible without a high degree of accuracy in phonology and syntax, and second, native speakers of a language do not typically produce grammatical sentences in everyday speech (as a literal transcription of a tape recorded conversation would show).

Other differences pertain to conceptions about the correct order of development of language skills; thus, listening comprehension and speaking are considered to be primary skills and reading and writing secondary skills; paralinguistic features of speech and knowledge about the foreign culture are usually taught after the basic linguistic skills are already at a fairly advanced level, the assumption being that these constitute parallel knowledge rather than linguistic knowledge per se.

These various issues constitute basic and unresolved differences about the fundamental question of what it is to "know a language." Language tests that researchers devise and teachers use are interesting in this connection because they reflect the conceptions one has about what it is to know a language. And what are the constituent elements of most language tests currently used?

Vocabulary knowledge, recognition of correct grammatical structure, reading comprehension, dictation, translation, and so on: these may be termed knowledge about the mechanics of language and reflect what some linguists currently call linguistic competence. Linguists like Chomsky (cf., 1965) argue that the fact that native speakers do not typically speak grammatically is not an indication that their linguistic competence is wanting; he insists on a distinction to be made between linguistic competence and linguistic performance.

The latter is influenced by presumably non-linguistic factors such as inattention, limited memory, time pressure, emotional involvement, and so on, which interfere with the act of speaking and cause disfluencies, false starts, unfinished sentences, lack of grammatical accord, etc. He points out that when native speakers are presented with a written transcription of such sentences or an oral version presented piecemeal, they can recognise the ungrammatical elements and correct them thereby showing that linguistic performance is not a good measure of linguistic competence.

This argument is quite convincing and seems essentially correct as far as it goes. But it neglects certain crucial facts about how language is used for communicative purposes. An individual who has mastered the mechanics of a language, in short knows the meaning of so many words, knows the syntactic and phonological structure of the language, and nothing else, would be quite incapable of communicating in that language. Language teachers are well aware of this fact and have sometimes expressed it in no uncertain terms, as the following blunt quotation indicates: "The pedagogues supply ample anecdotal evidence not only that there are students who can perform beautifully on substitution drills, transformation drills, etc., yet with whom communication is virtually impossible; but also that there are students who 'do miserably on your tests, but, hell, we can talk about anything together' " (Upshur, 1968, p. 5). Spolsky (1968) has documented the fact that non-native speakers who have attained a certain sufficiently high level of proficiency can perform at almost native level on certain language tests, but as soon as they are presented with artificially mutilated speech (e.g., with background noise on a tape recorded conversation) they perform much lower than natives-indicating that they have not internalised certain fundamental knowledge about the language. Spolsky refers to this type of knowledge as the "redundancy aspect of language" and includes such things as knowledge of sequential probabilities of phonemes, letters, and lexical items in strings, knowledge about how words are organised semantically in lexical fields, cultural facts (e.g., what is appropriate to say under given situations) and psychological facts (e.g., what an individual is likely to say or think under given circumstances).

As Upshur points out, this principle of redundancy "suggests that it will not be possible to demonstrate that any given language item is essential to successful communication, nor to establish the functional load of any given item in communication. Consider the ease with which speakers of different dialects, dialects even with different number of phonemes manage to converse, or the ways in which speakers constantly handle their forgetting a specific word.

All of this suggests then that while a testing of specific linguistic items is likely to be valuable in the control of instruction, the assessment of proficiency in a language must rather be based on functioning in a much more linguistically complex situation than is provided by the one element test" (Upshur, 1968).

Belasco's (1967) call for the "total language experience" is motivated by a similar recognition of the independence of various aspects of knowing a language. He points out the following facts: "A student often has difficulty understanding a spoken sentence that he understands quite easily in print" (1967, p. 86); "We have shown elsewhere [Belasco, 196S] that it is possible to develop acceptable speaking ability without a concomitant development in listening comprehension" (1967, p. 86); "A student might control every structure and know the meaning of every word in a reading selection without understanding the selection" (1967).

None of the foregoing remarks are likely to contain any elements of surprise to the experienced language teacher. Yet many of them would insist that mechanical skills are logically to be taught separately and prior to communicative skills. But is this truly a logical requirement or an esthetic preference for which too high a price is being paid when students bored with practising mechanics end by giving up any real interest and motivation in FL study? And are teachers not placing such an emphasis on the acquisition of mechanical skills partly because currently used proficiency tests measure mechanical rather than communicative skills-thus allowing the curriculum to be guided by available tests rather than the reverse?

There is evidence that there is developing increasing awareness in the FL field of the importance of teaching communicative competence. Hayes (1964), being concerned with teaching "cross-cultural communication," has reviewed the pedagogical perspectives of paralinguistics and kinesics, these terms being defined as "the study of patterned tone-of-voice and body motion aspects of human communication, respectively" (1964, p. 152). "Pedagogically," he asserts, "we can expect the paralinguistic frame of reference to broaden considerably the scope of the descriptive component which underlies teaching materials" (Hayes, 1964, p. 155; see also Nostrand, 1966).

As soon as we raise the question of communicative, rather than linguistic, competence, it becomes clear that the traditional fourfold division of levels of skills-listening, speaking, reading, writing-becomes totally inadequate. Fishman has repeatedly emphasised that the FL teacher must make decisions about which communicative skills to teach within a much more complex framework.

For example, in a recent article (Fishman, 1966b) he reviews the "bilingual dominance configuration" in terms of the following factors: (a) What is the desirable level of proficiency in the second language to be encouraged in the various media such as listening, speaking, reading, writing? (b) What are the priorities the teacher wants to establish concerning the degree of proficiency to be encouraged in various roles such as comprehension, production, and inner speech (talking to oneself, thinking out loud)? (c) Which formality levels ought to be emphasised: intimate, casual, formal? "Each level of formality requires a vocabulary, a sentence structure, and a set of attitudes towards oneself and one's interlocutors quite different from those required by the others". (d) How shall the teacher treat the various domains of interaction: art, music, government, religion, business, home, school? As he points out, these are contextual factors, and the teacher must arrive at simultaneous decisions concerning all of these. 'In doing so, he will have determined the bilingual dominance configuration that he is seeking to create in his pupils".

This decision cannot be made by default by pretending to teach general language skills. "Foreign language teachers are producers of bilinguals" (Fishman, 1966b, p. 121) and the assessment of the success and relevance of the teaching process which creates "school-made bilinguals" must be made in no less complex and realistic terms than the description of "natural bilinguals" by such a communication framework as that suggested by Fishman (1966b) or Mackey (1966).

Current Theories and Practices

Two basic truths about the psychology of human learning are (a), that it is amazingly efficient and powerful-by such standards as the learning capacities of other living organisms or man-made automata and (b), that this learning goes on in ways that neither the individual learner nor the educator or social scientist can describe or explicate even in elementary and simplistic terms. Two outstanding instances which illustrate both truths are (i), the learning of a language and (ii), the learning of a culture during socialisation or acculturation. Concepts such as "stimulus," "response," "reinforcement," "habit," which social scientists have invented to account for these accomplishments of the individual have such weak explanatory power that even in much simpler learning situations, such as a rat running a maze, they allow for such inadequate and impotent descriptions that psychologists in a narrow field of specialisation disagree about them. The weakest aspect about these "scientific explanations" is that they attempt to describe the learning process through concepts that refer to external events (stimuli, responses, schedules of reinforcement, etc.), whereas what obviously accounts for the process is the internal mechanism of the brain, the capacities and workings of the human mind. (Jakobovits, 1968c).

Theories about the mind, theories about knowledge (as distinguished from theories about behaviour), theories about capacities, about Potentialities and competencies, have been proposed by many writers over the course of modern scientific history, but these occupy the back seat to the leading theories in the social sciences. The most influential and widespread approach to psychological explanation remains in the United States today, in education (cf., programmed instruction), in clinical psychology (cf., behaviour modification), in much of experimental psychology (cf., verbal conditioning), that of Skinnerian operant conditioning of behaviour. The latter is widely claimed as being sound and tough-minded in research, while theories of the mind are presented to graduate students and future researchers in a shadowy and not quite respectable light; they are soft, non-rigorous, wishy washy.

In the field of FL teaching the trend is notably the same. The recent book by Wilga Rivers (1964), The Psychologist and the Foreign-Language Teacher, is often cited as the most advanced scientific achievement in the field. While Dr. Rivers herself shows awareness of the theoretical shortcomings of the habit approach to language, many language teachers are not so cautious: they take the habit notion of the audiolingual approach quite literally, deriving much self-assurance from the scientific and rigorous pretentiousness of concepts such as stimulus, response, conditioning, and the automatic establishment of habits.

This is a strange situation, indeed. Teachers and therapists are practical people by necessity and they ought not to be castigated for adopting methods which seem to work. The two most notable and successful accomplishments achieved by the Skinnerians are programmed instruction and behavioural modification, yet the theoretical foundations from which they have sprung are simplistic and inadequate in the extreme. This is a curious paradox wherein surely lies the bankruptcy of the modern social scientific enterprise: what seems to work best on practical grounds, should not, it seems on theoretical grounds, and the theories that appear to be more sophisticated and more powerful do not enable us to develop effective practical approaches. It would seem to be a betrayal of the intellectual spirit to accept that which works when it should not, yet it would be folly to reject that which works merely because on theoretical grounds it ought not.

The resolution of this difficulty would seem to lie in a change of attitude on the part of both the theorist and the practitioner. On the one hand today's theorist should give up any claim that his speculations have the scientific authority whereby he can make infallible pronouncements about the solution of practical problems. On the other hand the practitioner should give up his attempt to justify his activities in the classroom and clinic by appealing to competing scientific theories often outdated by the time the practitioner gets hold of them. Careful thinkers have recognised the abyss that separates theory from practice. Skinner himself has consistently claimed for over a quarter of a century that his concern is with behaviour not with theory, and it is only when he strays into the morass of theoretical justification (as in some parts of his book on Verbal Behaviour, 1957) that the shortcomings of his system become so apparent. One of the most authoritative experts in the area of learning has recently stated that "thus far, there is little empirical evidence in support of the assumption that forgetting outside the laboratory is a function of the same variables and represents the same processes as are observed in formal studies on interserial interference" (Postman, 1961). In the area of language Chomsky (1968) stated that there is no evidence today in support of the view that the scientific endeavour will ever be successful in explicating the fundamental facts. Integrity dictates that we clearly recognise the inherent limitations of the social and behavioural sciences as we know them today and not to claim for them more than is reasonable.

When this limitation is accepted, as it surely must be, then the interplay between theoretical and practical concerns can become more honest and possibly more rewarding. Experimenters can tackle practical problems by relaxing their unrealistic insistence on experimental controls and statistically adequate designs. Practitioners such as the teacher and the therapist need not feel the need to take sides in theoretical controversies or to justify their practices by appealing to particular theories; instead, they can adopt a healthy functional attitude concerning the effects of their methods of approach, concentrating on developing and constantly using realistic evaluation criteria that would dictate maintaining or altering their activities in accord with the results they achieve. In subsequent sections of this chapter, such an attitude will be repeatedly advocated.

Audiolingual Method

The most widespread method of FL teaching today, the so-called "New Key" approach prevalent since the 1940's, is the audiolingual approach which claims to have largely displaced the earlier traditional method of grammar-translation. The proponents of the audiolingual approach base their claim of correctness on sound psychological theory as well as on efficient results. The purpose of this section is to show that both of these claims are questionable. In the following quotation an eminent figure in the FL field questions the first of these claims:

> "Let me point out that neither the audiolingual habit theory nor the cognitive code-learning theory is closely linked to any contemporary psychological theory of learning. The audiolingual habit theory has a vague resemblance to an early version of a Thorndikean association theory, while the cognitive code-learning theory is reminiscent of certain contemporary gestaltist movements in psychology which emphasise the importance of perceiving the "structure" of what is to be learned, without really relying on such movements. Actually, neither theory takes adequate account of an appreciable body of knowledge that has accumulated in the study of verbal learning. Among these facts are the following:
>
> - The frequency with which an item is practised per se is not so crucial as the frequency with which it is contrasted with other items with which it may be confused. Thus, the learning of items in pattern practice drills would be improved if instead of simple repetition there were a constant alternation among varied patterns.
> - The more meaningful the material to be learned, the greater the facility in learning and retention. The audiolingual habit theory tends to play down meaningfulness in favour of producing automaticity.
> - Other things being equal, materials presented visually are more easily learned than comparable materials presented aurally. Even though the objective of teaching may be the attainment of mastery over the auditory and spoken components of language learning, an adequate theory of language learning should take account of how the student handles visual counterparts of the auditory elements he is learning and help to prescribe the optimal utilisation of these counterparts, such as printed words, phonetic transcriptions, and other visual-symbol systems.

- In learning a skill it is often the case that conscious attention to its critical features and understanding of them will facilitate learning. This principle is largely ignored by the audiolingual habit theory; it is recognised by the cognitive code-learning theory. It would imply, for example, that in teaching pronunciation an explanation of necessary articulatory movements would be helpful.
- The more numerous kinds of association that are made to an item, the better are learning and retention. Again this principle seems to dictate against the use of systems of language teaching that employ mainly one sensory modality, namely, hearing. A recent experiment performed at the Defence Language Institute, West Coast Branch (Army Language School, Monterey, California) seems to show that dramatic facilitation of language learning occurs when words denoting concrete objects and physical actions are associated with actual motor performances involving those objects and actions. Thus, the student learns the meaning of the foreign language word for jump by actually jumping! Language teaching becomes a sort of physical exercise both for the students and for the instructor whose actions they imitate.

These then are a few examples of theory-derived principles that, if further examined and verified, could contribute to more effective ways of teaching foreign languages. It would be trite to say at this point that 'more research is needed,' although it is obviously the case. Actually, what is needed even more than research is a profound rethinking of current theories of foreign language teaching in the light of contemporary advances in psychological and psycholinguistic theory.

The audiolingual habit theory which is so prevalent in American foreign language teaching was, perhaps, fifteen years ago in step with the state of psychological thinking at that time, but it is no longer abreast of recent developments. It is ripe for major revision, particularly in the direction of joining with it some of the better elements of the cognitive code-learning theory. I would venture to predict that if this can be done, then teaching based on the revised theory will yield a dramatic change in effectiveness." (Carroll, 1966a).

Carroll's statement agrees with the assessment that theory and practice in FL teaching are out of step but he appears to believe that "contemporary advances in psychological and psycholinguistic theory" are necessarily relevant to FL teaching. As stated earlier, there are no good grounds for such optimism. Note that the five facts which he reviews and which he urges the FL teacher to consider are in the nature of empirical generalisations not theoretically derived principles. His call for "more research" can be welcomed as long as it is understood that this is to refer to efforts in the development of evaluation criteria of the effectiveness of teaching practices in terms of functional or terminal behaviours on the part of the learner (What can the learner do with the knowledge he has acquired?).

Experiments

There are two principal reasons for the weakness of currently known and practised experimental techniques: the difficulty (practical impossibility) of controlling a large number of simultaneously varying and interacting factors and the fact that the individual's learning strategy is largely independent of the teacher's manipulative efforts even though it is a factor that greatly influences the learning process.

With respect to the first difficulty we are confronted with a double bind which is this: carefully controlled small-scale laboratory experiments yield generalisations whose extrapolation to the real learning situation, where all things are not equal, is a dubious activity; large-scale experiments on contrasting teaching methods which have, at least potentially, direct relevance for classroom practices leave so many factors uncontrolled that the conclusions are either unconvincing on the strength of the data or the results are more often than not contradictory.

The second difficulty, the contribution of the individual himself to the learning process, is inherent to the nature of the mind as an information processing and storing device about which little of substance is known today. To the chagrin of many teachers the individual is not a habit forming automaton who can be conditioned by carefully arranging the presentation of stimuli and rewards contingent upon overt responses. Passive learning is immeasurably inferior to active learning and, although we have been able to measure general learning capacities with intelligence tests, these not only represent weak predictors in specific learning situations but are also unenlightening concerning the processes that underlie individual learning strategies and how to influence or manipulate them. The teacher may spend a lot of effort in arranging sequences of materials to be presented at various stages but he has no control over what in fact the individual does mentally with them: how well he remembers them, whether he focuses on just the intended distinction, whether he tries to assimilate the new material to the old, how much of it he will transfer to new situations, whether he inductively arrives at generalisations, and so on.

Computer based Programmes

Development of computer based programmed instruction in language (such as the PLATO system at the University of Illinois, Urbana) offers the possibility of a real alternative to the present inadequate policy of basing teaching practices on theoretical generalisations gained from laboratory experiments. Computer based individuated instruction, when fully developed, will not represent a teaching method as this is understood today. Rather it will consist of a conglomeration of many techniques and combinations thereof, fitted to the individual learner in terms of his own learning strategies, learning capacities, interests and goals.

Each student will be taught by a different method when one considers the total teaching process from beginning to end, that which is most effective for him and most consistent with the goals he has for learning the language. Until computer based programmed instruction is a reality for every pupil in the United States we must make do with the present less effective educational means at our disposal. There is much that can be done even during this stopgap interval to render the teaching of FL's more effective. The next section will review some such attempts which have been suggested by authoritative bodies in the FL teaching field.

Suggestions for Teachers and Learners

The Modern Language Association of America sponsored a conference in 1964 which resulted in a statement entitled "Advice to the Language Learner" (MLA, 1966). The 1964 statement was revised "in the light of comments from many teachers and linguists" and thus purports to represent the distillation of knowledge about the "state of the art." The following ten claims about the psychology of FL learning have been extracted from the 1966 revised statement:

- Learning a FL facilitates subsequent learning of another FL thanks to the acquisition of "techniques of FL study".
- "Any intelligent student" can learn a FL provided there are present "hard work," "a good teacher," and "a good textbook" (for a discussion on FL aptitude see the review by Carroll, 1965).
- A helpful strategy in learning a FL is to avoid making direct comparisons between it and English.
- "Learning a language means learning a whole new pattern of habits,"... "a little like learning to play the piano or the violin, except that it is easier." Therefore, it is important to practice, to practice, and to practice still more. Practice should be "intensive and enthusiastic," "in class and out," silently and out loud, to oneself while reading, and to fellow students. Involve "all your senses as you learn a language by using your ears, mouth, eyes, fingers. Use your imagination. Pretend that you are an actor whose lines you are learning".
- "There are three techniques in language learning: imitation, analogy, and analysis." Imitation consists of repeating "what you hear as closely as you can" by listening "carefully to your teacher and the other models." "Learning how to create by analogy is the purpose of pattern drills and other exercises." As one grows older, he begins "to lose the capacity for easy imitation" but he gains "the advantage of being able to reason: to analyse language." "Information of this sort given in grammatical explanations or rules can help you to learn the language faster."
- Memorising sessions should be broken up into several intense short periods of 15-20 minutes.
- Reading and writing are learned more easily if one first learns to speak the language. Even if one is not interested in the spoken language, one "can not learn to read it without using some kind of pronunciation, even if it is only a silent one you invent. So, it makes sense to learn the normal pronunciation." (No evidence available.)
- Practising to speak should be done right from the start.
- When reading a FL, one should at first read only what has been previously practised, and do so out loud (for a contrary

opinion, see Burling, 1968). Later, when reading new materials silently, one should underline new words, pronounce new phrases over and over, later returning to the underlined words.

- English translations of words or phrases should never be written on the page in the reading book. "Doing so puts the emphasis on the English equivalent and not on the foreign word, which is the word that you must learn" (Burling, 1968).

Physiology of Second Language Learning

Educators in this country and throughout the world have been concerned with the question of "What is the optimum age of beginning the study of a FL?" (e.g., Anderson, 1960, Kirsch, 1956, Larew, 1961). There has been in recent years a definite bias towards the view that FL's should be taught early in childhood, at least before puberty. This view is based on the observation that when children are exposed in a natural setting to two languages during their early childhood they achieve a mastery of both languages (sometimes even three or four languages) that is native-like in fluency and pronunciation and do so with natural ease and apparently without any special effort.

In fact, many people believe that true bilinguals are produced only under these conditions of childhood learning. This view was strongly reinforced by statements made by the eminent Canadian neurosurgeon, Dr. Wilder Penfield, who for many years has argued that the human brain loses "plasticity" after puberty and language learning after that age becomes increasingly difficult.

There are, however, opposing views to this argument. Many educators who have examined the effects of the early introduction of a second language in the elementary school curriculum caution against what has come to be known as the balance effect. This refers to the hypothesis that the more time is spent on the second language the less well one learns the first language, with consequent detrimental effects on the native language, on education, and on the intellectual development of the child.

The purpose of this section is to review the arguments for and against the early introduction of a FL in the school curriculum and to examine the physiological and educational implications that are involved in this topical and crucial question.

Evidence from Neurophysiology

The views of Penfield on the physiology of language learning have appeared principally in two places: in a speech given at the 134th meeting of the American Academy of Arts and Sciences in Boston (Penfield, 1953) and in the Epilogue of Speech and Brain Mechanisms (Penfield and Roberts, 1959), a chapter that has been reprinted by the Modern Language Association and widely circulated (also reprinted in Michel, 1967, pp. 192-214). A summary of his views is given by the following quotations:

> "In 1939 I was asked to give an address at Lower Canada College.... 'I have long wondered,' my talk began, 'about secondary education from the safe distance of a neurological clinic. I have wondered why the curriculum was not adjusted to the evolution of functional capacity in the brain...

Before the age of nine to twelve, a child is a specialist in learning to speak. At that age he can learn two or three languages as easily as one. It has been said that an Anglo-Saxon cannot learn other languages well. That is only because, as he grows up, he becomes a stiff and resistant individualist, like a tree-a sort of oak that cannot be bent in any graceful manner. But the Anglo-Saxon, if caught young enough, is as plastic and as good a linguist as the child of any other race.... when you enter the teaching profession, I beg you to arrange the curriculum according to the changing mental capacities of the boys and girls you have to teach.... Remember that for the purposes of learning languages the human brain becomes progressively stiff and rigid after the age of nine.

Again in 1953 I was called upon to address a lay audience. It was at a meeting of the American Academy of Arts and Sciences in Boston.... I chose as my subject: 'A Consideration of the Neurophysiological Mechanisms of Speech and some Educational Consequences.' . .

This aroused far more interest than I could have anticipated. The officers of the Modern Language Association of America heard of it, and, probably because it coincided with their own views, they had it reprinted. It was distributed then to the far flung membership of that Association.

...It may well be convenient, for those who must plan the curriculum, to postpone the teaching of secondary languages until the second decade of childhood. But if the plan does not succeed, as they would have it, let them consider whether they have consulted the timetable of the cerebral hemispheres. There is a biological clock of the brain as well as of the body glands of children.

...The learning of language in the home takes place in familiar stages which are dependent upon the evolution of the child's brain. The mother helps, but initiative comes from the growing youngster. The learning of the mother tongue is normally an inevitable process. No parent could prevent it unless he placed his child in solitary confinement!

The brain of the child is plastic. The brain of the adult, however effective it may be in other directions, is usually inferior to that of the child as far as language is concerned. This is borne out still further by the remarkable re-learning of a child after injury or disease destroys the speech areas in the dominant left cerebral hemisphere. Child and adult, alike, become speechless after such an injury, but the child will speak again, and does so, normally, after a period of months. The adult may or may not do so depending on the severity of the injury." (Penfield, in Penfield and Roberts, 1959).

It is clear from this extended quote, and from the rest of the article that Dr. Penfield does not claim any special expertise in FL teaching. One must therefore clearly separate what he says as an expert in neurophysiology from what he says as a concerned Canadian citizen interested in promoting bilingualism in that country. The FL teacher, not being an expert in neurophysiological matters may be quite justified to rely on the expertise of specialists such as Penfield and Roberts. The evidence and arguments they present on the neurophysiological bases of speech development in the infant appears convincing, at least to the non-specialist (but see the critique by Milner, 1960). This confidence in their argument is strengthened even more now that it has received further extensive confirmation by the recent comprehensive review of the subject given by Lenneberg (1967) in his book on the Biological Foundations of Language and elsewhere.

However, the crucial question which the FL teacher must carefully examine is just what is the relevance of the neurophysiological evidence for second language learning and teaching. It is clear that the learning of language, that is, first language, is dependent upon the child's biological mechanisms, that these brain mechanisms develop at crucial time periods, and that unless the child is exposed to human speech before the age of puberty he will most likely never speak a human language. Lenneberg presents the argument succinctly:

> "Primary language cannot be acquired with equal facility within the period from childhood to senescence. At the same time that cerebral lateralisation becomes firmly established (about puberty), the symptoms of acquired aphasia tend to become irreversible within about three to six months after their onset. Prognosis for complete recovery rapidly deteriorates with advancing age after the early teens. Limitation to the acquisition of primary language around puberty is further demonstrated by the mentally retarded who can frequently make slow and modest beginnings in the acquisition of language until their early teens, at which time their speech and language status becomes permanently consolidated.

... Thus we may speak of a critical period for language acquisition. At the beginning it is limited by lack of maturation. Its close seems to be related to a loss of adaptability and inability for reorganisation in the brain, particularly with respect to the topographical extent of neurophysiological processes. (Similar infantile plasticity with eventual irreversible topographical representation in the brain has been demonstrated for many higher mammals.) The limitations in man may well be connected with the peculiar phenomenon of cerebral lateralisation of function, which only becomes irreversible after cerebral growth phenomena have come to a conclusion" (Lenneberg, 1966; emphases supplied).

Here again it is clear that the neurophysiological evidence is restricted to primary or first language acquisition. However, Lenneberg too sometimes tends to overgeneralise the applicability of his evidence and to make certain claims about second language acquisition which are questionable. For instance, he presents a table of the process of language development throughout the life history of the individual which confounds at one point primary and secondary language acquisition. The table is presented here in a slightly altered form: (Lenneberg, 1966)

Age Usual Language Development

Months 0 to 3 Emergency of cooing

Months 4 to 20 From babbling to words

Months 21 to 36 Acquisition of language

Years 3 to 10 Some grammatical refinement; expansion of vocabulary

Years I 1 to 14 Foreign accents emerge

Mid teens to senium Acquisition of second language becomes increasingly difficult.

The first four entries in the table concern primary language acquisition while the last two deal with second language acquisition. None of the evidence considered throughout his book on "biological foundations" is directly relevant to the learning of a second language. Furthermore, both generalisations are questionable, especially the last. For instance, a recent study was designed to "examine some aspects of the commonly held view that young children are better able to learn the phonology of a second language than adults" (YeniKomshian, Zubin, and Afendras, 1968). The study used only two subjects (ages 5 and 21, respectively) and limited itself to seven hours of training two Arabic phoneme discriminations, and thus the results obtained are to be considered merely suggestive.

The authors concluded that their results "do not provide any evidence indicating that children are better than adults in acquiring novel speech sounds". Nevertheless, observation indicates that the children of immigrants who are exposed to a second language before their mid teens or thereabouts do seem to speak that language with closer native pronunciation than their parents or older siblings.

But this difference cannot be unequivocally (or even probably) attributed to neurophysiological factors since (a), children learning a second language in a school setting do not always (or even often) develop native pronunciation, and (b), some adults are capable of acquiring native-like pronunciation of a FL. The biological time table that Lenneberg speaks of and the correlated developmental stages of first language acquisition typically follow rigid patterns and do not permit variations of this sort.

Finally, concerning the last generalisation in the table, namely that the acquisition of a second language becomes increasingly difficult after the mid- teens, there is no evidence to support it. A number of known facts actually contradict it. For instance, a college level FL course of one semester is typically considered to be the equivalent of a whole year of study at the high school level. Also, some intensive FL courses for adults are capable of imparting a conversational knowledge of the language with native-like pronunciation in about one thousand hours with an active vocabulary of up to three thousand lexical items (Mueller, 1967). This rate of acquisition appears to be at least as good as that of the much younger immigrant child who is immersed in a foreign culture, and is probably superior to it. Again, although these intensive courses are for "gifted" adults, the number of such people is sufficiently large (up to 33 per cent of the population according to one estimate, see Carroll, 1965) that a neurophysiological explanation must be excluded.

Educational and Intellectual Evidence

The preceding section attempted to show that there is no neurophysiological evidence to the effect that children are more capable of learning a second language than adults. This section will briefly examine the evidence concerning the educational and intellectual consequences of the early teaching of a FL.

Macnamara's (1966) book on Bilingualism and Primary Education is the most extensive review on the subject to date. A large number of studies have been devoted to this question. Macnamara selected 77 of these for detailed analysis, those that seemed to him to have the most adequate experimental controls. The majority of these studies confirmed the balance effect indicating that on the whole children who were required to learn, use, or be educated in two languages had a weaker grasp of either language than monolingual children. Macnamara's own careful study of the "Irish experience" was consonant with this overall pattern. In his concluding chapter he states:

> "Yet despite the differences between Ireland and other countries in the conditions relating to the learning of languages the findings of our own study closely parallel those of the majority of papers which have been reviewed. Our own research adds to the already considerable

> evidence that there is a balance effect in language learning, at least where the time devoted to the second language is so extensive that the time available for the mother tongue is reduced. Native-speakers of English in Ireland who have spent 42 per cent of their school time learning Irish do not achieve the same standard in written English as British children who have not learned a second language (estimated difference in standard, 17 months of English age). Neither do they achieve the same standard in written Irish as native-speakers of Irish (estimated difference, 16 months of Irish age). Further the English attainments of native-speakers of Irish fall behind those of native-speakers of English born in Ireland (13 months of English age) and in Britain (30 months of English age).

Comparisons among groups of Irish children yield results which are also for the most part similar to results obtained in the majority of earlier researches. Teaching arithmetic in Irish to native English-speakers is associated with retardation in problem, but not in mechanical, arithmetic. The retardation in problem arithmetic is estimated as about 11 months of arithmetic age....

...The Irish findings relating to the teaching of other subjects through the medium of the second language are particularly discouraging. For it seems that the teaching of mathematics, at least, through the medium of the second language does not benefit the second language, while it has a detrimental effect on children's progress in mathematics" (Macnamara, 1966).

It ought to be kept in mind that there are a number of studies which, even if they are in the minority, do nevertheless provide a counterargument to the balance effect and to the alleged detrimental educational consequences of the early use of a second language. One recent study in particular carried out under the direction of Dr. Wallace Lambert, an eminent colleague of Macnamara at McGill University in Canada, shows that French-Canadian children in one bilingual setting in Montreal who have developed a good grasp of English are superior in both verbal and non-verbal intelligence to their French-speaking monolingual peers (Peal and Lambert, 1962). These authors hypothesise that early bilingualism "might affect the very structure of intellect . . .: . . . a large proportion of an individual's intellectual ability is acquired through experience and its transfer from one situation to another." They argue that bilingual children are exposed to "wider experiences in two cultures" and these will give them "advantages which a monolingual does not enjoy": "Intellectually the bilingual child's experience with two language systems seems to have left him with a mental flexibility, a superiority in concept formation, and a more diversified set of mental abilities..."

The educator and the FL teacher are likely to experience some confusion and frustration at such seemingly opposing views which these researchers hold, each buttressing their views with hard experimental data. A conclusion stated earlier in this chapter (Sections 2.1.1 and 2.1.8) once again comes to mind, namely that research by itself is incapable of providing ready answers to complex and perplexing social and educational problems.

It seems pointless to play the data game whereby an educator or a politician, having made up his mind in favour of bilingual education or the early teaching of a FL attempts to justify scientifically that his policy is a correct one by quoting those experimental reports which happen to agree with his bias. It would be too easy to find experimental reports that show just the opposite.

The serious educator must recognise the fact that in complex social and educational settings experimental findings are not easily generalisable: the conditions that hold for any particular setting are likely to be quite different, and significantly so, from any other setting, and his decisions must be made within a complex matrix of interacting factors, educational, social, political, philosophical, etc. Such decisions are always uncertain from the scientific point of view and the latter by itself can never provide a strict and sufficient justification.

This conclusion is supported by a report on an "International Meeting of Experts" presented by H. H. Stern. The report was published in 1963 by the UNESCO Institute for Education and has as its topic "The Teaching of Foreign or Second Languages to Younger Children":

> "It is not necessary to justify the teaching of languages in the primary years on the grounds that it is the optimum period. What is needed is (1) to show that it is socially and educationally desirable.... (2) It must be shown that it is sound from the point of view of the development of

> children, that, in fact, there are no contradictions on psychological grounds for teaching a language at this stage. (3) If, in addition, it can be demonstrated that the learning of languages in the early years has certain special merits this would add further weight. In other words, instead of searching for the optimum-age-in-general, it should be sufficient to show that the primary years are a good period for beginning a second language, offering certain special advantages . . . (Stern, 1963).

"Where no immediate urgency dictates a very early start the age to begin language instruction can therefore be decided on grounds of educational expediency. We conclude that the introduction of a language is not simply a matter of curriculum and method, nor one of correct psychological timing. It must also be viewed against the background of aspirations and social attitudes among the population served by the school system" (Stern. 1963. DD. 26 and 65).

Faced with the necessity of having to make a practical decision concerning the teaching of a second language, the educator must consider all the relevant aspects of the problem and weigh each of them according to the demands of the conditions that hold in his particular setting.

In some countries and communities the decision will be dictated by political factors, as was the case with the "Irish experience". In the United States there are powerful social forces in favour of language loyalty and maintenance by immigrant groups, significant political factors in favour of FL study as a means towards international cooperation and understanding, and there are also present traditional cultural views that favour the study of the major European languages.

These various motivations are usually primary and take precedence over the more specialised scientific concerns such as the neurophysiological underpinnings and psychological consequences of early or late FL study. A useful role that the latter concerns can play is to help implement whatever decisions were made on the basis of the more general social concerns by discovering the advantages and disadvantages of the policy being followed and showing ways of maximising the former and counteracting the latter by special or remedial training.

After reviewing the evidence on the relation between age and FL study, Stern (1963) presents a summary table of the pros and cons of the early teaching of a second language. The table is presented below in slightly modified form:

(1) Age of acquisition: before adolescence (ages 310):

(a) *Advantages:*

(i) Accords with the neurophysiology of the brain. (?)

(ii) Easiest and most effective. (?)

(iii) Natural good pronunciation.

(iv) Leaves richer linguistic memory traces for later expansion.

(v) Longer time for language can be allowed.

(b) *Disadvantages:*

(i) Possible confusion with first language habits.

(ii) No conscious acquisition of language learning process.

(iii) Time spent not commensurate with results.

(2) Age of acquisition: at adolescence (ages 11 to school leaving):

(a) *Advantages:*

(i) Increased capacity to appreciate many aspects of language and culture contacts.

(ii) Still sufficient time to attain high standard.

(iii) Improved memory and higher level of intellectual growth.

(iv) First language skills well established, hence no confusion.

(b) *Disadvantages:*

(i) More laborious than early learning.

(ii) Success demands tenacity.

(iii) Self-consciousness.

(iv) Possible refusal to memorise.

(v) Experience has shown poor results frequent.

(vi) Already crowded curricula and specialisation of studies.

(3) Age of acquisition: adulthood:

(a) *Advantages:*

(i) Specificity of purpose.

(ii) Good motivation added to reasons mentioned for adolescence.

(iii) Greatest amount of learning in least amount of time.

(b) *Disadvantages:*

(i) Not enough time.

(ii) Other preoccupation.

(iii) Irregularity of study.

Several of the listings above are either in error (e.g., 1.a.i.) or contradictory (e.g., 1.a.ii. with 3.a.iii.); others are at best highly controversial. No mention is made of the potential balance effect. Despite these shortcomings, however, the table is useful because it poses the problem of early FL teaching in terms of relative advantages and disadvantages rather than in terms of the pseudoquestion of which is the best time. (Note: the arguments listed above do not necessarily represent Dr. Stern's own views on the subject [Stern, 1970, personal communication]).

Motivational Aspects of Language Study

Bilingualism and multilingualism represent today a major problem in the world, as they have in the past and undoubtedly will remain to be in the foreseeable future. In the history of this planet there have been periods and situations where people have stood ready to die for maintaining the use of their language and resisting the attempt to impose upon them the use of a FL. In this decade of the 1960's there were times we could read in the daily newspaper of bloody riots and deaths, of terrorism's and civil strife associated with language conflicts in India, in Belgium, in Canada, and elsewhere. In all these situations much more was involved than the language question per se, questions of national identity, of cultural self-assertion, of social and economic competition, but the language question stood as a symbol for all these and was inextricably tied to them. The language of a people is a living, growing, changing reflection of that people's heart and mind. When we learn a FL we intermingle with a foreign people: language contact is inseparable from culture contact. In a real sense becoming bilingual entails becoming bicultural. When a person exposes himself to a FL he also exposes himself to a foreign culture. The latter kind of exposure can become for some individuals, we do not know for how many, a threatening experience. Professor Wallace Lambert of McGill University in Canada has for the last ten years explored the implications of such a threat. In one article he introduces the issue as follows:

> "This theory, in brief, holds that an individual successfully acquiring a second language gradually adopts various aspects of behaviour which characterise members of another linguistic-cultural group. The learner's ethnocentric tendencies and his attitudes towards the other group are believed to determine his success in learning the new language. His motivation to learn is thought to be determined by his attitudes and by his orientation towards learning a second language. The orientation is 'instrumental' in form if the purposes of language study reflect the more utilitarian value of linguistic achievement, such as getting ahead in one's occupation, and is 'integrative' if the student is oriented to learn more about the other cultural community as if he desired to become a potential member of the other group. It is also argued that some may be anxious to learn another language as a means of being accepted in another cultural group because of dissatisfactions experienced in their own culture while other individuals may be equally as interested in another culture as they are in their own. However, the more proficient one becomes in a second language the more he may find that his place in his original membership group is modified at the same time as the other linguistic-cultural group becomes something more than a reference group for him. It may in fact become a second membership group for him. Depending upon the compatibility of the two cultures, he may experience feelings of chagrin or regret as he loses ties

> in one group, mixed with the fearful anticipation of entering a relatively new group. The concept of 'anomie' ...refers to the feelings of social uncertainty which sometimes characterise not only the bilingual but also the serious student of a second language." (Lambert, 1963).

It is not known to what extent ethnocentrism and anomie might represent interfering factors in the study of FL's in the three school systems in the United States today. It is possible, however, that the change in instruction from reading and translation courses to audiolingual speaking courses may have increased the importance and effects of these social psychological factors. Some of Lambert's findings tend to show that students who are integratively oriented towards language study and those who show evidence of anomie are ultimately more successful than the instrumentally oriented students and the psychologically more detached learners, suggesting that the conflicts of anomie may seem as an internal drive and motivating factor. However, our knowledge on this is still very sketchy. Much may depend on how capable the individual is in handling and successfully resolving the conflicts of anomie. If these conflicts become unmanageable and psychologically too threatening a convenient defence reaction which serves as a protective device might be to slow down progress in the language or eliminate language study altogether. According to one estimate, up to 20 per cent of the student population in high schools and colleges are "beset by a frustrating lack of ability" in FL study (Pimsleur, Sundland, and Mclntyre, 1964).

These students have been labelled "underachievers" in FL study in view of the fact that their grades in FL courses are "at least one grade-point lower than their average grade in other major subjects." To what extent is this "lack of ability" attributable to motivational problems and conflicts involved specifically with FL study? It is significant for this question that two of the seven subparts of the FL Aptitude Battery developed by Pimsleur and his associates as a means of measuring ability to learn FL's consist of "Interest Tests" designed to assess the student's attitudes towards FL study. The FL teacher and the learner himself ought to be made more aware of the complex psychological issues that may be involved in the study of FL's. The teacher and the student may be aware of a lack of genuine interest in FL study, but to what extent are they aware of the reasons behind such a lack of interest? Teachers, educators, parents often ask the question "How can we infuse more motivation for FL study?" Part of the answer may lie in a recognition of the problems discussed in this section and in finding ways of helping the student manage feelings of anomie and transform it from a conflictual stumbling block into a positive driving force.

The management of anomie may be an important factor in the motivational problem of FL study, but there are undoubtedly additional factors that must be considered. Two of these will be discussed in this and the following section: the development of realistic self-evaluation criteria and the perceived relevance of specific instructional activities.

Self-evaluation Criteria

It is an interesting psychological observation, whose causes are not obvious, that the individual engaged in the study of a FL has some very definite ideas about the progress he believes he is making. Perhaps this pertains to the area of "folk linguistics" which Hoeningswald (1966) brought to our attention in a most interesting and perceptive article. People appear to have strong feelings about what constitutes knowing a language and who is or is not a bilingual.

A person who is capable of uttering a few mechanical and superficial sentences in a FL with good pronunciation and accurate syntax is a "good bilingual" and "knows the language well" while a person who is quite fluent and is capable of communicating over a wide range of situations, but whose pronunciation is foreign and whose syntax is inaccurate, but perhaps not more so than the conversational speech of the average native, is nevertheless not considered to be a "good bilingual." A student capable of reading advanced materials in a FL but who cannot understand the spoken language may minimise his actual achievement and knowledge of that FL. A student who speaks a FL with halting hesitations and uses stylistic circumlocutions to make up for a lack of vocabulary richness may grossly underestimate his actual knowledge of the language by a tendency to compare this performance to the effortless and automatic expressiveness he experiences in his mother tongue.

It is not known to what extent these kinds of self-generated presumptions affect the student's maintenance of motivation in FL study but it is not unreasonable to suppose that they may sometimes be a source of discouragement and a cause of loss of interest. The FL teacher can help the student develop more objective and more realistic evaluation criteria for assessing progress and achievement. Students can be given some insight into just how complex a system language is by pointing out the amount of knowledge they must have in order to be able to speak their mother tongue as they do and not be misled by the apparent effortlessness with which they speak it. They may thus gain a greater understanding about why it is that learning a FL requires so much effort and perhaps view with greater respect the "modest" achievements they attain at various stages.

The FL teacher could further carefully examine his own brand of "folk linguistics" to see whether he is rewarding meaningful achievement rather than superficialities. Does he insist on an inordinate degree of correct pronunciation and syntax too soon or even at any time? Does he appreciate the student's achievement in terms that are relevant to the latter's ability and effort rather than in terms of some general standard that may be unrealistic or irrelevant for this particular student? Does he have realistic expectations about how much progress can be made under the conditions he is teaching? These are important questions because the teacher is a source of feedback for the student whether this process is made explicit or remains unconscious and unstated.

Finally, the student's parents and their version of "folk linguistics" may be an influential source of encouragement or discouragement to him. In a recent national poll that was publicised over the news wire services, the majority of parents were reported to have said that they consider FL courses the weakest part of the school curriculum and should be the first to go if anything had to be cut.

In view of the widespread social, cultural, and political forces in favour of FL study which has traditionally existed in this country, this mounting negativism is both paradoxical and alarming. Much of it can undoubtedly be attributed to a gap between what the parents define as progress in a FL and what their judgement is about how close or how far their children approximate it. Again, are their expectations realistic? Are their evaluation criteria accurate and relevant? These are questions which the FL teacher and the school administrator may find it profitable to discuss at PTA meetings.

Student's Attitudes

To the student the purpose of the activities in the classroom and the laboratory or the assigned homework may often appear obscure and mysterious and sometimes even irrelevant and silly. Younger children and the more dull among the older children may not question these practices as much as the older and brighter students. But it is a sign of our times that students in our high schools and in our colleges are increasingly demanding that their studies be relevant to their goals and aspirations. The teacher and educator can view this age of the "New Student" with either alarm and worry or with excitement and confidence depending on whether he defines it as rebelliousness or maturity and involvement. Whatever the case may be, this new development in education is affecting the student's attitude towards and motivation for FL study. It must be dealt with.

What is the New Student's attitude towards FL study? A survey conducted at the University of Illinois (Urbana) in 1968 by a student committee of the Students Council of the College of Liberal Arts and Sciences provides some answers. The survey was planned, executed, and analysed by the student government representatives entirely on their own initiative. Five thousand questionnaires were distributed to the student body of which 863 were returned. The questionnaire consisted of 21 questions. The distribution of answers for 13 of these is presented below:

a. Were your grades in language lower than your grades in other courses outside your major field?

   Yes (444) No (374) Blank (20)

b. Did you start with a language, then find that you had difficulty with it and then switch to another language?

   Yes (53) No (785)

c. Do you prefer a language course oriented towards understanding of grammar and reading comprehension rather than a course oriented towards oral-aural comprehension?

   Yes (414) No (392) Blank (28)

d. Has the time spent in the language laboratory been beneficial to your study of a language?

   Yes (160) No (650) Blank (28)

e. Do you feel that you have to study more for a language course (per credit hour) than for other courses?

Yes (676) No (137) Blank (25)

e. If so, do you feel that this is unfair?

Yes (536) No or Blank (140)

f. Do you read any material voluntarily in the language you are taking or have taken?

Yes (233) No (598) Blank (7)

g. Has the language requirement for graduation in LAS at the University of Illinois prevented you from taking other courses in which you were very interested?

Yes (514) No (312) Blank (12)

h. Do you plan to be able to use the foreign language which you studied to meet graduate school requirements?

Yes (373) No (446) Blank (19)

i. Has foreign language helped you to develop discipline or learn better study habits?

Yes (145) No (679) Blank (14)

j. Do you approve of the present foreign language requirement in LAS?

Yes (199) No (634) Blank (5)

k. Do you think more language should be required, or less?

More (53) Less (674) Blank (111)

1. What is your attitude towards foreign language study?

Interested (306)

Study primarily for the grade (521)

Blank (11)

m. Would you prefer the alternative of taking a two-semester sequence on the literature (in English translation) of the language rather than 103 and 104 of that language?

Yes (561) No (261) Blank (16)

n. Overall do you think that your study of foreign language here has been beneficial or detrimental to you?
Beneficial (427) Detrimental (339) Blank (72)

If the opinions of students at the University of Illinois can be taken to be fairly representative of the national college population, then this survey shows that all is not well with the college FL curriculum. Several of the answers are in fact quite disturbing. While the LAS college curriculum forces everyone to take audiolingual courses, only 47 per cent of the students are actually interested in "oral-aural comprehension" and 50 per cent would prefer "grammar and reading comprehension."

The evidence for a lack of an intrinsic interest in FL study is clear: only 28 per cent read any material voluntarily in the language they are taking, 80 per cent feel that they have to work harder in FL courses-a situation which they consider unfair, and for 61 per cent of the students this extra work prevents them from taking other courses in which they are interested. Furthermore, 53 per cent don't even feel that they would be able to use the FL they studied for meeting graduate school requirements, and 80 per cent doubt that FL study is helpful in developing "discipline" or "better study habits." Finally, 76 per cent disapprove of the FL requirement and 40 per cent feel that FL study in college has actually been detrimental to them.

In considering the significance of these results two important questions pose themselves: Should the school curriculum be determined by a majority opinion of students or by the considered professional judgement of educators? and: Given a lack of intrinsic interest in FL study on the part of many students what should be done about it? Let us examine the implications of both questions.

Given the pedagogical philosophy that is prevalent in our society today very few educators would allow the school curriculum to be dictated by a student body vote, and in any event, the students themselves would be just as opposed to such a process. The real issue is not so much as who makes the specific decisions as whether the decisions made allow for sufficient flexibility to accommodate individual needs and interests. For instance, it would seem that the insistence on a single goal for FL study is open to question on both educational and philosophical grounds. If roughly half of the college student body is interested in a reading knowledge of a FL is it good educational policy to insist on everyone taking an audiolingual course?

Given the low degree of success attained by some students in speaking and reading a FL, would it not be more educationally profitable to allow these particular students to study a foreign culture through the medium of their mother tongue and thus still gain some, if not a completely adequate, knowledge of other peoples in the world? Just how useful is it to develop speaking and reading skills in a FL when the educational system fails to provide meaningful opportunities for the use of these skills?

It would seem that to make FL study more meaningful to the student it would be desirable to integrate the FL study with the rest of the educational curriculum. For instance, the student could be encouraged to use his FL skills in pursuing projects in other courses in the sciences and the humanities by reading relevant materials in a FL. Travel and study abroad, foreign films and plays, games and play-acting (Lee, 1965, Morgan, 1967), "The French Club", summer "language camps" (Haukebo, 1967), interaction with aliens in this country, are all activities which are encouraged and made increasingly available to the students in recognition of this principle, and the more we move in these directions the less we will encounter a motivational problem" in FL study.

Recent advances in self-instructional FL courses represent another promising development not only because of the efficiency associated with programmed instruction but also because these types of courses succeed in eliminating some of the motivational problems discussed in this section. Carroll (1966b) reports certain cases in which "well-developed programmes of instruction, particularly of the 'programmed' variety, yielded low correlation's between FL aptitude and performance suggesting that the obstacle of low aptitude may sometimes be surmounted by the use of small-step increment materials that do not challenge language aptitudes".

For instance Mueller and Harris (1966) attempted to reduce the high dropout rate in an audiolingual French course in college which a previous survey (Mueller and Leutenegger, 1964) had suggested is attributable to the students' disturbance over having to talk too soon and their feeling that too much emphasis was being put on sounds.

A reduction in dropout rate was achieved when a special French course called "Audio-Lingual Language Programme (ALLP)" was developed. The course uses programmed instruction techniques and states its terminal goal as the "native-like pronunciation and facility in speaking the language equivalent to that of a seven-year old."

The sounds of French are taught with "very little visual support" and sound drills are carried out sometimes without knowledge of the meaning of what is being said. These authors believe that the aversion to the sound emphasis which students often feel is overcome under conditions of programmed instruction where the students aren't being overwhelmed thanks to the step by step progression and immediate feedback.

The experienced FL teacher is well aware of the fact that the problem of student motivation is complex and multidimensional and cannot be solved by any one "trick." The solution attempted by Mueller and Harris just discussed seemed to work for them (dropout rate was reduced by 20 per cent at the end of the first year of study) but may not be equally successful in other situations and with different students. Its interesting feature was that it first determined what the students found objectionable then attempted to solve the problem by eliminating the source of dissatisfaction without changing the original goals of the course. The FL teacher ought to be aware of the possibility that the explicitly stated objections which students formulate merely represent their personal hypotheses about the dissatisfactions they feel and in these they may in fact be in error.

Thus when students state a preference for reading comprehension courses it may reflect either a genuine interest in reading over speaking or a reaction against boring drills in the laboratory or a demand for more "content" or a discouragement with a perceived (real or imagined) lack of progress, or several other possibilities. The solution is not necessarily to change the goals of the course, although that too ought to be considered, but to locate the real source of dissatisfaction and change it.

The numerous studies that have been carried out with the purpose of determining which method of instruction is most effective have m general led to disappointing results. It is clear that an important reason for this failure is that the concept of "a method of instruction" actually subsumes a very large number of separate and variable instructional activities in the classroom and laboratory. A much more realistic objective for comparison studies would be to examine the effects of such specific and limited instructional activities. Hayes, Lambert, and Tucker (1968) have recently published a check list of several hundred of such specific activities associated with FL instruction and efforts of this kind are more likely to yield real progress than the more traditional monolithic studies on "overall methods."

Summary and Conclusion

The major theme of this chapter has been the exposition of two curious paradoxes that beset the FL teaching field today. The first paradox consists of the widespread tendency on the part of FL teachers to seek justification for their practices in the classroom in originally weak and currently outdated scientific theories despite the fact that few experimentalists ever claim for their theories this kind of infallible generalizability to situations outside the laboratory.

The most unfortunate consequence of such an outlook has been that classroom practices have tended to become rigidified in the attempt to follow closely the dictates and prescriptions of so-called scientific principles. Thus, the New Key to FL instruction has turned into a mechanistic exercise of rote habit drills in which the original goal of liberated and sustained expression-that of communicative competence-has been in practice lost sight of and relegated to a supposedly utopian and unattainable status for the majority of students.

The second paradox lies in the fact that although we have achieved in the last twenty years a major breakthrough in the technology of teaching FL's the success of the FL curriculum in our schools has remained extremely limited. Serious dissatisfaction with it is being expressed at all levels by teachers, students, and parents despite the fact that strong social forces remain in this country for the maintenance of an interest in FL's and foreign cultures. Being bombarded by criticisms from both external and internal sources, the FL teaching field now finds itself on the defensive after enjoying two decades of unparalleled expansion and support.

This then is the sobering assessment with which the field is confronted today and the situation from which it must recover Corrective measures are clearly in order, but what are they to be and which direction are they to take? There is a danger here which must be avoided and which lies in the fact that redressive activities that stem from a reaction to the inadequacies of existing conditions tend to overshoot the mark whether it be in the area of politics, legislation, or education. The present shortcomings of the not-so-new audiolingualism may be viewed in part as attributable to the unchecked swing of the pendulum away from the earlier traditionalist emphasis on prescriptive grammar, translation, and the reading of belletristic literature. The danger, now that audiolingualism is on the defensive and students are increasingly demanding "reading" courses is that the pendulum might be allowed to swing back too far so that we lose sight of the vastly superior instructional technology which we now have at our disposal but was non-existent in the earlier dark ages of FL teaching.

We must strive to reach a correct balance between what our educational technology gives us the potential to achieve and what the students are interested in attaining. The key to this balance (the Newer Key, one might say in jest), lies in individuated FL instruction that is sufficiently flexible to adjust to the particularised characteristics of the individual learner and the learning context. Let us review here the arguments that are presented in this chapter concerning the psychology of second language learning and teaching. These might perhaps serve as guidelines to the corrective measures that are needed.

- There is no one single proper goal for FL study which can logically be demonstrated. There is no proof that speaking is necessarily primary or more desirable to reading and, of course, vice versa. Neither can one rationally justify the claim that proficiency in all four skills should be the ultimate goal of FL study. We must recognise that students have different interests, needs, and aptitudes and to refuse to accept this fact has the simple and devastating consequence that they shall learn nothing of significance.
- The goals of a particular course in a FL programme must be clearly defined in specific terms that specify the terminal knowledge and skills to be reached. To purport to teach general language skills is a retreat from reality in that it ignores the facts of the matter which are that under such conditions a substantial proportion of students fail to derive any demonstrable value out of their FL study. The extent of specificity of goals to be defined for any particular course

would seem to depend on the conditions that hold for that situation: the specific needs, interests, and aptitude of the students involved, the time available for study, the age of the learners, the overall FL programme and its cumulative effect, the wider conditions of social support and maintenance interests, the particular language and culture involved, and so on. Some examples of such specific goals may be, "to be able to read German literature on chemistry" or, "to be able to obtain information for travel purposes" or, "to be able to understand radio broadcasts" or, "to be able to write business letters," etc. The assessment of FL attainment for degree and requirement purposes should not be in terms of course grades or number of years of study but rather in terms of tests that evaluate such terminal behaviours. In that case, a variety of such terminal behaviours and combinations thereof may be defined for different degree and curricular requirements.

- Not only must we recognise variable goals and interests in FL study but also variable abilities and FL aptitude. In the past differential aptitude was tacitly recognised by the expectation of a distribution of grades in standard FL courses as well as, more explicitly, by the placement of students in classes being taught at different rates. But what is needed is the recognition that different aptitudes permit the attainment of different terminal goals both in range and degree within the time requirements and opportunities to learn provided by the FL programme. Students should be counselled with respect to the specific terminal goals they may reasonably be expected to achieve taking into account their aptitude, the time available for study, and the amount of effort it may require within the context of their motivation and their other educational aspirations and requirements.
- The question of when FL's are to be taught within our educational system is a complex problem that involves political, social, philosophical, and psychological considerations and should not be reduced to a matter of neurophysiology-as it has become fashion able to do in recent years. Since the sociopolitical context varies from place to place, not only on the international plane but also within a

particular country, including, of course, the United States, the decision must be considered by each school district in the light of the conditions that prevail within its geographic boundary. The knowledge that has accumulated on this matter indicates that there are both advantages and disadvantages to FL study at any age compared to any other age. Generalisations about the optimum age that fail to take context into account are almost certainly to be false.

- More serious attention must be given to the social-psychological ramifications of FL study. The proposition that bilingualism entails biculturalism has serious implications for both the personal adjustment of the individual and the wider sociocultural character of a nation. There is evidence that it also relates to the type and degree of achievement in FL study, and thus, is an additional important variable which the FL teacher must contend with.

- Global comparisons between methods of instruction are unrealistic. In general studies that have attempted such comparisons were unproductive. There are two principal reasons for this. One is that what is usually defined as a method actually consists of a large variety of instructional activities most of which remain undefined and unobserved. The other reason is that the learner makes his own contribution to the learning situation and these learner strategies are to a greater or lesser extent independent of the teacher's activities. What is needed is a more detailed and explicit description of the specific activities of both the teacher and the student in the instructional situation. Once adequate observation techniques are developed, evaluation criteria of effectiveness can then suggest specific changes in instructional activities.

- It is necessary to take seriously the oft-quoted distinction between competence and performance, between knowledge and behaviour. Experience has indicated that there are no mysterious transfer effects across various language skills and competencies. Not only is it true that ability to read does not insure ability to speak, and vice versa, but also, ability to function in one communicative context is not necessarily matched in other contexts, and this means that the instructional Programme that produces school-made bilinguals must take into account the full "dominance configuration" of the natural bilingual. The question of what it is to know a language is not yet well understood and consequently the language proficiency tests now available and universally used are inadequate because they attempt to measure something that has not been well defined. The tendency to gear the instructional programme to enable the achievement of high scores on these tests is thus inappropriate, as is the evaluation of the success of the programme in terms of these tests. No doubt due to considerations such as these, some specialists in the language testing field are attempting to develop new kinds of tests that are not based on the notion of sampling the surface manifestations of linguistic items and units but rather the underlying potentialities of functionally significant aspects of utterances. These newer efforts take seriously what every FL teacher knows but often neglects in his teaching, namely that learning a FL cannot be separated from learning about the culture for which it is a vehicle.

- The instructional process involved in the teaching of a FL must take proper account of the existence of a "folk linguistics," a term used here to refer to assumptions which individuals hold about language and language acquisition. Students have definite ideas about what it is to "know" a language and use self-generated evaluation criteria to assess their progress. These notions are often unrealistic and tend to underestimate both the complexity of the knowledge to be acquired and the extent of their true achievement. The result is frequently discouragement and a consequent loss of motivation. Likewise parents may have inappropriate expectations about the rate of progress of their children, minimise their achievement and ultimately withdraw their support and encouragement for FL study. Teachers, too, may not sufficiently differentiate between essential and non-essential features of variations in their students' performance, may not be sufficiently aware of subcultural and idiolectal variations in codes in the language, and may use general standards of evaluating achievement neglecting in their demands to take account of individual capacities. To take proper account of the existence of folk linguistics would involve activities of the following sort: to determine what notions the student has about language and critically discuss their validity with him; to make the student aware of the true complexity of language so that he may appreciate the difficulty of the task he sets for himself; to justify in terms that are meaningful to the student the relevancy of the classroom activities and study assignments; to disabuse parents of their unrealistic expectations and make them aware of the cumulative long term impact of FL study; and finally, to make sure that the teacher himself is knowledgeable about recent sociolinguistic and ethnolinguistic advances.

It might be well to end this chapter by reminding the reader that teaching is an art and that there are no sure methods of extrapolating scientific knowledge to the classroom. This review represents the point of view of its author, which is one possible vantage point, and it is safe to say that for every argument presented here one can probably find one or more counterarguments. This is the nature of the beast. But some arguments are more convincing than others, not, hopefully, because of their authoritativeness, but because they may be more rational and their assumptions more likely correct in the light of existing knowledge. As long as decisions about educational matters must be made and ineffective practices corrected, it behooves us to be self-critical about our activities as teachers and researchers and to continually strive for the best possible solutions which available knowledge and logical reasoning can provide.

5 Curriculum Development and Syllabus Formation

(Programmed Instruction Course for English Language Teaching)

Curriculum Development

Curriculum development - what is it? It is the organised preparation of whatever is going to be taught in schools at a given time in a given year. They are made into official documents, as guides for teachers, and made obligatory by provincial and territorial departments. Teachers use curricula when trying to see what to teach to students and when, as well as what the rubrics should be, what kind of worksheets and teacher worksheets they should make, among other things.

It is actually up to the teachers themselves how these rubrics should be made, how these worksheets should be made and taught; it's all up to the teachers. In a practical understanding, though, there is no concrete way to say what methodology is right to use. But it is also true that the way in which a certain topic is taught habitually resolves what is actually taught. This is why it is required to make a distinction between the official or planned curriculum and the de facto curriculum; the one that is formal and the one that is actually taught in schools. That report which this was information was taken from, has also referenced another author who discussed curriculum development a decade earlier than Jerome Bruner, named Ralph Tyler, who did so in his model text on curriculum development. His work was centred on the following four ideas:

- To determine what educational principles must be reached by schools
- The best way of deciding what kinds of learning experiences are apt to be valuable in reaching these objectives
- The best way of putting in order familiarity of learning for effective instruction
- The best way of evaluating aforementioned familiarity of learning (learning experiences). Finally, to review, what is curriculum development? It is the idea of organised preparation of what should be taught to students at a given time in a given year. They are made into certified documents, as guides to teachers, and made mandatory.

Objectives of Language Curriculum

A national curriculum can aim for

- a cohesive curricular policy based on guiding principles for language teaching and acquisition, which allows for a variety of implementations suitable to local needs and resources, and which provides illustrative models for use.

A consideration of earlier efforts at curriculum renewal endowed some of our discussion with an uneasy sense of *déjà vu*. However, we hope that current insights from linguistics, psychology, and associated disciplines have provided a principled basis for some workable suggestions to inform and rejuvenate curricular practices.

English does not stand alone. It needs to find its place along with other Indian languages i. in regional-medium schools: how can children's other languages strengthen English teaching/learning? ii. in English-medium schools: how can other languages be learnt.

Shape of a Curriculum

Input-rich Environments: Input-rich communicational environments are a prerequisite for language learning. Languages are learned implicitly, by comprehending and communicating messages, either through listening or reading for meaning. We suggest a comprehensible input-rich curriculum that lays the foundation for spontaneous language growth, with the understanding of spoken and written language as precursors to language production (speech and writing). We also suggest how literacy may be meaningfully integrated into such a curriculum. We have already touched on the connection between literacy in English and in other school languages; in this section, the twin perspectives of multilingualism and language across the curriculum occur as recurrent themes.

A number of researchers (Prabhu 1987, Krashen 1985, Elley and Mangubhai 1983) have stressed that language is acquired when attention is focused not on language form, but on the meaning of messages. On this common ground stand such diverse innovations as the Bangalore Project or Communicational Teaching Project (Prabhu 1987), the Communicative Approach (Widdowson 1978), the Natural Approach (Krashen and Terrell 1983), and the Whole Language movement.

Moving specifically into the area of literacy acquisition, a number of researchers have stressed the need for a balance of explicit skills instruction and a strongly meaningful language-learning environment (Adams 1990; Snow, Burns and Griffin 1998; Stanovich 2000). The focus of literacy development needs to be both on skills and meaning.

The role of meaningful language exposure or "input" for the mind to work on is acknowledged by all cognitive theories of learning and language learning (as opposed to behaviourist theories of learning as habit formation). The "burden of languages" (as of all education) is the burden of incomprehension. This happens when language is taught for its own sake as a set of forms or rules, and not introduced as the carrier of coherent textual meaning; it becomes another "subject" to be passed.

The question is how the learner can receive meaningful language input that is appropriate to her or his age and knowledge of language or readiness for language skills, given the variety and range of English learning situations in India. Such input must be provided at least in the classroom, but can also be made available to learners at their own initiative, in a variety of ways; the class and its teacher need not be a limiting factor to learning. The language environment of disadvantaged learners needs to be enriched in particular ways. Many successful innovations in this regard exist in this country; their generalisability beyond their immediate locales needs exploration and encouragement, for example, Interactive Radio Instruction, the Task-based Communicational Approach, and the Whole Language narrative programmes. We describe such *success stories* below.

Curriculum Requirements

- A variety of materials should be available to provide an input-rich curriculum, which focuses on meaning.
- Multilinguality should be the aim in English medium as well as regional-medium schools. Similarly, language-across-curriculum perspectives should be adopted.

This has implications for textbook design and choice of appropriate methods (class libraries and media support).

Syllabus Creation

The syllabus—what students eagerly await on the first day; a record of the class; one of the only artifacts to remain after the students move on. Your syllabus represents both an end and a beginning—a final product of your course planning and a valuable way to introduce yourself and the course to your students. Because your syllabus is one of the few formal, tangible links between you and your students and because it will be referred to throughout the semester, time and energy should be spent on constructing your syllabus. Research indicates that outstanding instruction and a detailed syllabus are directly related (Grunert, 1997).

Students will appreciate and respond positively to a syllabus that bears the marks of being well planned. The information you will need to include in your syllabus will vary depending on the course or section you are teaching as well as your responsibilities in the class.

For example, GSIs teaching discussion sections will include different kinds and amounts of information than GSIs who are responsible for an entire course. Therefore, you will need to tailor the following description to your particular teaching duties. It is, however, a good idea in all courses and sections to hand out some form of syllabus on the first day.

The syllabus sets forth your responsibilities and those of your students. This does not mean that your calendar or your assignments are set in stone on the first day and that you have no flexibility. Those kinds of precautions can be written in (e.g., This calendar is subject to change.). What it does mean is that both you and your students are agreeing to a certain course of action, with specific expectations on both parts, and you are all accountable for maintaining the agreed upon route. Major changes—like changes in the grading policy or additions of assignments—are not fair to students and should be avoided. In the initial planning stages, you may find it helpful to look at others' syllabi, especially if you can find past examples from the course or section you are teaching.

This will give you a good idea of what has been expected in the past in terms of the average number of pages of reading assigned per week, the kinds of texts used, average page length of papers, and general policies for the course or section. It is also useful to read the department's course description that can often be found on the Web or in the departmental office. Additionally, there are many Internet resources on syllabus planning that can be helpful in designing your syllabus. Get a feel for what others' syllabi look like and don't be afraid to use others' structure or language.

Just remember that course material, like other academic writing, is intellectual property and the original source should be given credit. Usually the syllabus is the first document students receive from you and one which will be closely examined and continually revisited. Make sure to communicate the high expectations you have for your students. The tone you set throughout your syllabus should reflect your teaching style. For example, if you have an informal style of teaching you might wish to write your syllabus in a more familiar tone, maybe in the first person. If you would prefer to create a more formal atmosphere, a third person approach might be better.

Basic Information?

The syllabus should include the name of the course or section and the course or section number as well as the particular semester and year (e.g., Fall 2008). Include the meeting times and days of the class as well as the building name and room number where you will meet. You should also include your name, your *e*-mail address, the location of your office, your office phone number (or a university number where messages can be left), and the days and times of your office hours. If your syllabus or other course or section material is available on the Internet, you will want to include the URL address. Also, if you have created a group *e*-mail for the class, you may provide that *e*-mail address as well. Some instructors choose to give students their home phone numbers. You should not feel obligated to do this. If you decide to include your home phone number, emphasise to students that this is a privilege. Include times when it is acceptable to call you at home (e.g., Please call only between the hours of 9AM and 10PM.). Many instructors and students prefer the convenience and flexibility of *e*-mail communication, and you may consider encouraging your students to contact you this way.

Forming the Course Syllabus

At this stage of the tutorial, one has set overarching goals, organised content, developed a course plan, selected teaching and assessment strategies, and begun to develop some specific assignments and activities. A detailed syllabus gives students a sense of the nature of the course, what they will be expected to do in the course, and how their performance will be assessed. In many cases, the syllabus is viewed as a contract between you and the students. Whether considered a legal contract or not, a syllabus should be clear about policies and procedures related to the course. Some institutions have specific requirements regarding what should be included on the syllabus. Following there points are to be considered.

Goals: A syllabus should be more than the course schedule. You've worked hard to articulate the goals for the course and including them on the syllabus makes it clear to the students what they should be able to do when they have completed the course.

Expectations: While syllabi generally include something about your expectations of students (e.g., assignments, due dates, exams), it is helpful to be specific about other things you expect of students (e.g., your expectations for class participation, attendance, class preparation, their responsibility for learning) and why you have those expectations. It is also important to be clear about what students can expect of you (e.g., the time frame in which you will return assignments, how you will handle late work, that you will start and end class on time).

Tone: A syllabus helps to set the tone for the course. Consider your syllabus from the perspective of a student who is considering taking your class. Do you seem approachable? Welcoming? Organised? Excited about the course?

Syllabus Components

Information about the instructor (and TA) including name, office number, telephone number, *e*-mail, and office hours; Course title and other course information including meeting times, room number, credits, prerequisite courses or skills, co-requisite courses, course website; Titles and authors of required/recommended textbooks; Course goals; Statement of why students should want to take a course; Describe how the course relates to students' lives; Course description, which might include the "big questions" this course will address and/or how the course fits into the discipline and the curriculum; Some type of graphic or image that is related to the course content; Course schedule including dates of field trips and other scheduled meetings outside class time; this might convey the conceptual structure used to organise the course; Information about assignments and assessments including types of assignments and assessments, nature of exams (take home, open book, in-class) due dates, grading criteria and grading scale, rubrics, and so forth).

Other course requirements such as attending an office hour or forming study groups; Description of students' responsibilities in the learning process; How is hope the students will approach the readings, take responsibility for their learning, the amount of study time expected in the course; Statement that the syllabus is subject to change; Policies on attendance, academic integrity, late assignments, missed exams, cell phones; Important dates such as last day to withdraw from the course; Suggestions on how to succeed in the course such as strategies for studying, taking tests, and taking notes, information about campus resources; Statement regarding accommodation for students with disabilities.

6 Contents of English Language Teaching

Varieties of English

- England, the historical home of English, has significant regional language differences in pronunciation, accent, vocabulary and grammar.
- The thriving communities of English native speakers in countries all over the world also have some noticeable differences in pronunciation, vocabulary and grammar.
- English has no organisation that determines the most prestigious form of the language - unlike the French language which has the *Academie de la langue française*, Spanish language's *Real Academia Española*, the Brazilian Portuguese Academia Brasileira de Letras, or the Italian *Accademia della Crusca*.

Teaching English therefore involves not only helping the student to use the form of English most suitable for his purposes, but also exposure to regional forms and cultural styles so that the student will be able to discern meaning even when the words, grammar or pronunciation are different to the form of English he is being taught to speak.

Differences between Spoken and Written English

As with most languages, written language tends to use a more formal register than spoken language. The acquisition of literacy takes significant effort in English.

***Spelling*:** probably the biggest difficulty for non-native speakers since English spelling doesn't follow the alphabetic principle consistently. Because of the many changes in pronunciation which have occurred since a written standard developed, the retention of many historical idiosyncrasies in spelling, and the large influx of foreign words (mainly from Danish, Norman French, Classical Latin and Greek) with different and overlapping spelling patterns, English spelling is difficult even for native speakers to master. This difficulty is shown in such activities as spelling bees that generally require the memorisation of words. The generalisations that exist are quite complex and there are many exceptions leading to a considerable amount of rote learning. The spelling system causes problems in both directions - a learner may know a word by sound but not be able to write it correctly (or indeed find it in a dictionary), or they may see a word written but not know how to pronounce it or mislearn the pronunciation. However, despite the variety of spelling patterns in English, there are dozens of rules that are 75% or more reliable.

Vocabulary

A person's vocabulary is the set of words within a language that are familiar to that person. A vocabulary usually develops with age, and serves as a useful and fundamental tool for communication and acquiring knowledge. Acquiring an extensive vocabulary is one of the largest challenges in learning a second language.

Types of Vocabulary

(Listed in order of most ample to most limited)

***Reading Vocabulary*:** A literate person's reading vocabulary is all the words he or she can recognise when reading. This is generally the largest type of vocabulary simply because it includes the other three, though in some cases, notably Chinese characters, as in Chinese and

Japanese, where the pronunciation is not transparent, some words may be part of the oral vocabulary but not the written. For example, a Japanese speaker may not recognise that 'žŸž is pronounced *kirin.*

Listening Vocabulary: A person's listening vocabulary is all the words he or she can recognise when listening to speech. This vocabulary is aided in size by context and tone of voice.

Writing Vocabulary: A person's writing vocabulary is all the words he or she can employ in writing. Contrary to the previous two vocabulary types, the writing vocabulary is stimulated by its user.

Speaking Vocabulary: A person's speaking vocabulary is all the words he or she can use in speech. Due to the spontaneous nature of the speaking vocabulary, words are often misused. This misuse – though slight and unintentional – may be compensated by facial expressions, tone of voice, or hand gestures.

Focal Vocabulary: "Focal vocabulary" is a specialised set of terms and distinctions that is particularly important to a certain group; those with a particular focus of experience or activity. A lexicon, or vocabulary, is a language's dictionary, its set of names for things, events, and ideas. Some linguists believe that lexicon influences people's perception on things, the Sapir–Whorf hypothesis. For example, the Nuer of Sudan have an elaborate vocabulary to describe cattle. The Nuer have dozens of names for cattle because of the cattle's particular histories, economies, and environments. This kind of comparison has elicited some linguistic controversy, as with the number of "Eskimo words for snow". English speakers can also elaborate their snow and cattle vocabularies when the need arises.

English Vocabulary

Several word lists have been developed to provide people with a limited vocabulary either quick language proficiency or an effective means of communication. In 1930, Charles Kay Ogden created Basic English (850 words). Other lists include Simplified English (1000 words) and Special English (1500 words). The General Service List, 2000 high frequency words compiled by Michael West from a 5,000,000 word corpus, has been used to create a number of adapted reading texts for English language learners. The knowledge of 2,000 English words provides a comprehension of most of the English language, enough to render one literate.

Native and Foreign-language Vocabulary:

Native-language Vocabulary: Native speakers' vocabularies vary widely within a language, and are especially dependent on the level of the speaker's education. A 1995 study estimated the vocabulary size of college-educated speakers at about 17,000 word families, and that of first-year college students (high-school educated) at about 12,000.

Foreign-language Vocabulary:

The Effects of Vocabulary size on Language Comprehension: Francis and Kucera studied English texts totalling one million words and found that the learning of the most frequent words in an English text provides a comprehension of most of the words in that text:

Vocabulary Size	*Written Text Coverage*
1000 words	72.0%
2000	79.7
3000	84.0
4000	86.8
5000	88.7
6000	89.9
15,851	97.8

The knowledge of the 2000 most frequent English words provides a comprehension of 80% of English words. The figures look even better than this if we want to cover the words we come across in an informally spoken context. Then the 2000 most common words would cover 96% of the vocabulary. These numbers should be encouraging to beginning language learners, especially because the numbers in the table are for word lemmas and knowing that many word families would give even higher coverage. However, the number of words needed may differ substantially between different languages.

Vocabulary Growth

During his/her infancy, a child builds a vocabulary by instinct, with zero effort. Infants imitate words that they hear and then associate those words with objects and actions. This is the listening vocabulary. The speaking vocabulary follows, as a child's thoughts become more reliant on his/her ability to self-express in a gesture-free and babble-free manner. Once the reading and writing vocabularies are attained – through questions and education – the anomalies and irregularities of language can be discovered.

In first grade, an advantaged student (i.e. a literate student) learns about twice as many words as a disadvantaged student. Generally, this gap does not tighten. This translates into a wide range of vocabulary size by age five or six, at which time an English-speaking child will have learned about 2,500–5,000 words. An average student learns some 3,000 words per year, or approximately eight words per day.

After leaving school, vocabulary growth reaches a plateau. People usually then expand their vocabularies by engaging in activities such as reading, playing word games, and by participating in vocabulary-related programmes.

Importance of Vocabulary

- An extensive vocabulary aids expressions and communication.
- Vocabulary size has been directly linked to reading comprehension.
- Linguistic vocabulary is synonymous with thinking vocabulary.
- A person may be judged by others based on his or her vocabulary.

Second Language Vocabulary Acquisition

Learning vocabulary is one of the first steps of learning a second language, yet a learner never finishes vocabulary acquisition. Whether in one's native language or a second language, the acquisition of new vocabulary is a continual process. Many methods can help one acquire new vocabulary.

Knowing and Using a Word

Vocabulary is commonly defined as "all the words known and used by a particular person". Unfortunately, this definition does not take into account a range of issues involved in *knowing* a word.

Productive and Receptive Words

The first major distinction that must be made when evaluating word knowledge is whether the knowledge is productive (also called active) or receptive (also called passive) and even within those opposing categories, there is oftentimes no clear distinction. Words that are generally understood when heard or read or seen constitute a person's receptive vocabulary. These words may range from well-known to barely known.

In most cases, a person's receptive vocabulary is the larger of the two. For example, although a young child may not yet be able to speak, write, or sign, he or she may be able to follow simple commands and appear to understand a good portion of the language to which he or she is exposed. In this case, the child's receptive vocabulary is likely tens, if not hundreds of words but his or her active vocabulary is zero. When that child learns to speak or sign, however, the child's active vocabulary begins to increase. It is possible for the productive vocabulary to be larger than the receptive vocabulary, for example in a second-language learner who has learned words through study rather than exposure, and can produce them, but has difficulty recognising them in conversation.

Productive vocabulary, therefore, generally refers to words which can be produced within an appropriate context and match the intended meaning of the speaker or signer. As with receptive vocabulary, however, there are many degrees at which a particular word may be considered part of an active vocabulary. Knowing how to pronounce, sign, or write a word does not necessarily mean that the word has been used correctly or accurately reflect the intended message of the utterance, but it does reflect a minimal amount of productive knowledge.

Degree of Knowledge

Within the receptive/productive distinction lies a range of abilities which are often referred to as *degree of knowledge*. This simply indicates that a word gradually enters a person's vocabulary over a period of time as more aspects of word knowledge are learnt. Roughly, these stages could be described as:

- Never encountered the word.
- Heard the word, but cannot define it.
- Recognise the word due to context or tone of voice.
- Able to use the word but cannot clearly explain it.
- Fluent with the word – its use and definition.

Depth of Knowledge

The differing degrees of word knowledge imply a greater *depth of knowledge*, but the process is more complex than that. There are many facets to knowing a word, some of which are not hierarchical so their acquisition does not necessarily follow a linear progression suggested by *degree of knowledge*. Several frameworks of work knowledge have been proposed to better operationalise this concept. One such framework includes nine facets:

- orthography - written form
- phonology - spoken form
- reference - meaning
- semantics - concept and reference
- register - appropriacy of use
- collocation - lexical neighbours
- word associations
- syntax - grammatical function
- morphology - word parts

Memorisation

Although memorisation can be seen as tedious or boring, associating one word in the native language with the corresponding word in the second language until memorised is considered one of the best methods of vocabulary acquisition. By the time students reach adulthood, they generally have gathered a number of personalised memorisation methods. Although many argue that memorisation does not typically require the complex cognitive processing that increases retention (Sagarra & Alba, 2006), it does typically require a large amount of repetition, and spaced repetition with flashcards is an established method for memorisation, particularly used for vocabulary acquisition in computer-assisted language learning. Other methods typically require more time and longer to recall.

Some words cannot be easily linked through association or other methods. When a word in the second language is phonologically or visually similar to a word in the native language, one often assumes they also share similar meanings. Though this is frequently the case, it is not always true. When faced with a false cognate, memorisation and repetition are the keys to mastery.

If a second language learner relies solely on word associations to learn new vocabulary, that person will have a very difficult time mastering false cognates. When large amounts of vocabulary must be acquired in a limited amount of time, when the learner needs to recall information quickly, when words represent abstract concepts or are difficult to picture in a mental image, or when discriminating between false cognates, rote memorisation is the method to use. A neural network model of novel word learning across orthographies, accounting for L1-specific memorisation abilities of L2-learners has recently been introduced (Hadzibeganovic & Cannas, 2009).

Keyword Method

One useful method to build vocabulary in a second language is the keyword method. When additional time is available or one wants to emphasise a few key words, one can create mnemonic devices or word associations. Although these strategies tend to take longer to implement and may take longer in recollection, they create new or unusual connections that can increase retention. The keyword method requires deeper cognitive processing, thus increasing the likelihood of retention (Sagarra & Alba, 2006). This method uses fits within Paivio's (1986) dual coding theory because it uses both two verbal and image memory systems. However, this method should be used only with words that represent concrete and imageable things. Abstract concepts or words that do not bring a distinct image to mind are difficult to associate. In addition, studies have shown that associative vocabulary learning is more successful with younger aged students (Sagarra & Alba, 2006). As students advance and age, they tend to rely less on creating word associations to remember vocabulary.

Vocabulary Differences between Social Classes

James Flynn reports the remarkable differences in vocabulary exposure of pre-schoolers between different classes in the USA. Apparently, pre-schoolers of professional families are typically exposed to 2,150 different words, pre-schoolers from working class families to 1,250 words, while those from households on welfare just 620.

Phrase

In everyday speech, a phrase may refer to any group of words. In linguistics, a phrase is a group of words which form a constituent and so function as a single unit in the syntax of a sentence. A phrase is lower on the grammatical hierarchy than a clause.

For example, *the house at the end of the street* is a phrase. It acts like a noun. It can further be broken down into two shorter phrases functioning as adjectives: *at the end* and *of the street,* a shorter prepositional phrase within the longer pre-positional phrase. *At the end of the street* could be replaced by an adjective such as *nearby*: *the nearby house* or even *the house nearby. The end of the street* could also be replaced by another noun, such as *the crossroads* to produce *the house at the crossroads.*

Most phrases have an important word defining the type and linguistic features of the phrase. This word is the head of the phrase and gives its name to the phrase category. For example the phrase *the massive dinosaur* is a noun phrase because its head word (dinosaur) is a noun. The head can be distinguished from its dependents (the rest of the phrase other than the head) because the head of the phrase determines many of the grammatical features of the phrase as a whole.

Categories of Phrases

Phrases may be classified by the type of head taken by them:

- Prepositional phrase (PP) with a preposition as head (e.g. *in love, over the rainbow*). Languages using post-positions instead have post-positional phrases. The two types are sometimes commonly referred to as appositional phrases.
- Noun phrase (NP) with a noun as head (e.g. *the black cat, a cat on the mat*)
- Verb phrase (VP) with a verb as head (e.g. *eat cheese, jump up and down*)
- Appositive It renames noun as a pronoun and is always placed between commas (e.g. "Bob, my annoying neighbour, is short")
- Absolute Modifies the entire sentence and is linked with commas. (e.g. "Mike threw the book, his eyes are red")

Complexity

A complex phrase consists of several words, whereas a simple phrase consists of only one word. This terminology is especially often used with verb phrases:

- simple past and present are simple phrases, which require just one verb
- complex verbs have one or two aspects added and hence require additional two or three words

"Complex," which is phrase-level, is often confused with "compound", which is word-level. However, there are certain phenomena that formally seem to be phrases but semantically are more like compounds, such as "women's magazines," which has the form of a possessive noun phrase, but which refers (just like a compound) to one specific lexeme (i.e. a magazine for women and not a magazine owned by a woman). it described people, things, places, events, etc.

Semiotic Approaches to the Concept of Phrase

In more semiotic approaches to language, such as the more cognitivist versions of construction grammar, a phrasal structure is not only a certain formal combination of word types whose features are inherited from the head. Here each phrasal structure also expresses some type of conceptual content, be it specific or abstract.

Phrase Structure Grammar

Phrase structure grammar has several different common meanings. It was originally introduced by Noam Chomsky as the term for grammars as defined by phrase structure rules, i.e. rewrite rules of the type studied previously by Emil Post and Axel Thue. Some authors, however, reserve the term for more restricted grammars in the Chomsky hierarchy: context-sensitive grammars, or context-free grammars.

In linguistics, it refers to any one of several related theories for the parsing of natural language, developed from Chomsky's work, including the head-driven phrase structure grammar, the lexical functional grammar and the generalised phrase structure grammar. The subject divides clauses into two constituents, the noun phrase

(NP) and the verb phrase (VP), reminiscent of the more rudimentary linguistic syntactical analysis, that of subject and pre-dicate. From these the subject works down to the individual words within the sentence, parenthesising phrases according to the clauses' words' form classes in a way universally applicable to the English language.

Paragraph Structure

- Paragraphs are the basic structural unit of essays and other academic assignments.
- A paragraph is a short piece of writing in which all sentences are related.
- The first sentence expresses the point of the paragraph and all other sentences expand further on this point.
- The content of the paragraph therefore develops from a general statement to more specific statements.
- An academic paragraph is generally 4-7 sentences in length.
- The ability to write a well-structured paragraph will make a sound base for further academic writing.
- *Main Idea:* The point/issue of the paragraph is expressed in the first sentence of each paragraph
- *Explanation:* A further explanation/clarification of the point/ issue is provided in the next sentence or two
- *Illustration:* The point or issue is supported with indirect quotes/paraphrases in the remaining sentence or sentences

Writing Conclusions

Finally a good essay has a conclusion which restates the argument, reminds the reader of the two or three points which provide the most important support for the argument and then draws the essay to a gentle close.

Situation and Rhymes

Definition of Perfect Rhyme

Following the strict definition of rhyme, a perfect rhyme demands the exact match of all sounds from the last stressed vowel to the end of the word. Therefore, words with the stress far from the end are more likely to have no perfect rhymes. For instance, a perfect rhyme for *discomBOBulate* would have to rhyme three syllables, *-OBulate.* There are many words that match most of the sounds from the stressed vowel onwards and so are near rhymes, called slant rhymes.

Ovulate, copulate, and *populate,* for example, vary only slightly in one consonant, and thus provide very usable rhymes for most situations in which a rhyme for *discombobulate* is desired. However, no other English word has exactly these three final syllables with this stress pattern. And since in most traditions the stressed syllable should not be identical—the consonant before the stressed vowel should be different—adding a prefix to a word, as *be-elbow,* does not create a perfect rhyme for it.

Because rhymes reflect pronunciation, words that rhyme in some English dialects may not rhyme in others. A commonplace example of this is the word "of", which had no rhymes in British Received Pronunciation prior to the 19th century, but rhymed with "love" in General American. In the other direction, *iron* has no rhyme in General American, but many in RP. Words may also have more than one pronunciation, one with a rhyme, and one without.

Words with Obscure Perfect Rhymes

- *arugula,* rhymes with *Bugula,* a genus of bryozoan
- *chaos,* rhymes with *naos,* the inner chamber of a temple
- *circle,* rhymes with *hurkle,* to pull in all one's limbs
- *else,* rhymes with *wels,* the fish *Silurus glanis*
- *film, -s* rhymes with *pilm,* Scottish word for dust. The plural *films* rhymes with *Wilms,* a kidney tumour.
- *fugue, -s* rhymes with *jougs,* which is rarely found in the singular.
- *kiln* rhymes with the surname *Milne*
- *midst* rhymes with *didst,* archaic for did.
- *month* rhymes with *en-plus-oneth* (n + 1)th, a mathematical term; also *hundred-and-oneth* (= hundred-and-first)

- *music* rhymes with *anchusic,* as in *anchusic acid, dysgeusic,* having a disorder that causes alterations in one's sense of taste and *ageusic,* lacking a sense of taste
- *opus* (with a short *0),* rhymes with *Hoppus,* a method of measuring timber
- *orange* rhymes with *Blorenge,* a hill in Wales
- *pint* rhymes with *rynt,* a word milkmaids use to get a cow to move
- *plankton* rhymes with *Yankton* (Sioux)
- *plinth* rhymes with *synth,* colloquial for *synthesiser.*
- *purple* rhymes with *curple* (the hindquarters of a horse or donkey) and *hirple* (to walk with a limp)
- *rhythm* rhymes with *smitham,* fine malt or ore dust
- *silver* rhymes with *chilver,* a female lamb
- *siren* rhymes with *gyron,* a type of triangle in heraldry, and a few technical terms.
- *toilet* rhymes with *oillet,* an eyelet
- *wasp* rhymes with *knosp,* a decorative knob
- *width* rhymes with obsolete *sidth,* meaning length
- *woman* rhymes with *toman,* a Persian coin and military division
- *yttrium* rhymes with *liberum arbitrium,* a legal term

English Words without Rhymes

The following is a list of English words without rhymes, or refractory rhymes, *i.e.,* a list of words in the English language which rhyme with no other English words in the strict sense that they are pronounced in the same way from the vowel sound of the main stressed syllable onwards. They may not be considered rhymes if they are identical in those syllables—for instance, *bay* and *obey* often do not count as rhymes. The list was compiled from the point of view of Received Pronunciation and may differ from lists of words that do not rhyme in other accents or dialects. Multiple-word rhymes, self rhymes (adding a prefix to a word and counting it as a rhyme of itself), and compound words have not been considered.

Non-rhyming English Words

One-syllable Rhymes: *This list is incomplete; you can help by expanding it.*

Refractory one-syllable rhymes are uncommon; there may be fewer than a hundred in English. A great many end in a present or historical suffix *-th.* This list includes a few polysyllabic masculine rhymes such as *oblige,* which still has one syllable in its rhyming part.

angst, -s; breadth, -s; bulb, -s, -ed; cusp, -s, -ed; depth, -s; eighth, -s; eth, -s; fifth, -s, -ed; filmed; glimpsed; gulf, -s; heighth, -s; karsts; kirsch; mulcts; ninth, -s; oblige, -ed; sculpts; sowthed, southed; sixth, -s; twelfth; whilst; wolve, -s.

Nonce words ending in *-ed* ('provided with') may produce other rhymeless words, such as *be-fezzed* (wearing a fez) and *aitched* (full of H's). However, these are not always certain *(rached,* a horse with a white streak down its face?).

Two-syllable Rhymes

Once the stress shifts to the penultimate syllable, rhymeless words are quite common, perhaps even the norm: there may be more rhymeless words than words with rhymes. The following words are representative, but there are thousands of others.

angel; angry; anxious; aspirin (as two or three syllables); *chimney; citrus; comment; elbow; empty; engine; foible; hundred(th); husband; liquid; luggage; monster; neutron; nothing; olive; pedant; penguin; polka; problem; sanction; sandwich; secret; something; transfer* (noun); *vacuum* (as two or three syllables); *zigzag.*

Three-syllable Rhymes

Perhaps the majority of words with antepenultimate stress, such as *animal, citizen, comedy, dangerous,* and *obvious,* and with pre-antepenultimate stress, such as *necessary, logarithm, algorithm* and *sacrificing,* have no rhyme.

Rehearsal

Definition of Rehearsal: Rehearsal Definition: For other uses, see Rehearsal (disambiguation) or Dress rehearsal (disambiguation).

Rehearsal rhymes with 372 known words and/or phrases available has 9 letters, 5 are consonants with 4 vowels. When pronounced, rehearsal should have 3 syllables. An extensive rhyming dictionary for words that rhyme with rehearsal!

- How Many Letters In Rehearsal? 9 - Find words with 9 letters. Unique Letters: a, e, h, l, r, s
- How Many Consonants In Rehearsal? 5 - Find words with 5 consonants
- How Many Vowels In Rehearsal? 4 - Find words with 4 vowels
- How Many Syllables In Rehearsal? 3 - Find words with 3 syllables
- The word starts with re and ends in al.
- Find other words starting with reh or ending in sal.
- Find other words starting with rehe or ending in rsal.

Below you will find an extensive list of words that rhyme with rehearsal. Please keep in mind the organisation of these words is lacking and we are working on making sure we provide you the best on-line rhyming service. Please be patient and check back often. More to come such as what rhymes with rehearsal and has 9 letters, or find words with two letters or more, and find other words with the letters a, e, h, l, r, s. We are even working on providing nouns, verbs and adjectives, and other grammar options that rhyme with rehearsal and much more.

Language Teaching through Literature

Maintaining the Attention of Students

Is there any one who doesn't like to listen to or read stories? It is possible that many TESOL students may or may not have any interest at all in English literature. They may come to a TESOL class simply to learn the language to meet practical ends.

At the same time, many students are able to hold their attention and progress further in learning another language only if the materials they are exposed to are interesting, not just meet their practical ends. Literature plays a crucial part in maintaining the interest of the students. Use of short stories, short novels, and plays helps maintain the interest of the students in learning the language. Teaching a short poem or a nursery rhyme helps enliven the atmosphere. When a nursery rhyme is acted out, the entire class enjoys the performance, and learns some intonation patterns not easily mastered otherwise.

Introduction to Society and its Values

Through the short stories, plays, and novels, which often try to portray the society in some realistic way, students have a glimpse of the culture of the native speakers of English. The conversations give them the nuances used by the native speakers of English in performing various roles in the society. They learn the social etiquette and the words, sentences, tone, and tenor which go with the etiquette.

Through the study of literature, the second/foreign language learner of English is introduced to the historical as well as the current culture of the English speaking peoples. With the culture, they also come to study and understand the world view of the native speakers. No language makes sense to its learner without some understanding of the world view it represents.

English speaking peoples do have a unique history, even though aspects of this history may be shared by the Europeans in general. The industrial revolution in Britain inaugurated the industrial revolution throughout the world. The evolution and progress of modern democratic institutions owe a lot to British history and traditions. Anglo-Saxon jurisprudence plays its unique role all over the world. University and other professional institutions of education have been established in most of the Third World countries through the efforts of the English speaking peoples. The Anglo-American alliance continues to be a great blessing for peace and prosperity.

True, the British and American dominion have been criticised by many for their alleged self-serving interests. And yet the balance is in favour of English education in the Third World countries. Students in the Third World countries (some of which may have been closed for Christian missionary work) flock to the TESOL classes in large numbers fully knowing that English does represent a culture and a religion which may militate against their own.

The morals and ethics represented by the English diction owe their origin largely to Christian morals and ethics with universal appeal. These universally applicable moral and ethical concerns are easily conveyed, raised, and impressed in the minds of the learners through English literature, even as they enjoy reading and listening to the stories. Movies further accentuate these concerns.

Our goal is not the teaching of English literature, but teaching and improving English already acquired by the TESOL learners. Through a careful selection of literary pieces which match the learner's difficulty level, self-learning of English is greatly accelerated.

Diversity and Varied Use of Literary Material

It is important for us to recognise that "the English language is no longer the preserve of a few nations, but is now used globally" (Lazar 1993:5). This means that quality literary products by the non-native writers of English from other countries as well as the translation of masterpieces in the native literature of the TESOL learners may have to be included as part of our course materials.

Use of literature in language teaching helps improve the knowledge of English in many ways. Literary pieces are susceptible to multiple level of interpretation. In a literary work, content is communicated in many novel ways, with metaphors and multiple meanings, sarcasm, cynicism, etc. The intent of the message is hidden and needs to be unravelled by the individual readers. The writers use the words in some unique manner to create novel meanings and expressions.

These and many other characteristics of literary pieces help the TESOL learner to improve his skill in understanding and using English effectively, since they will be confronted with similar characteristics even in their day to day conversations. Students master new sentence and phrasal patterns through reading literary works. They learn to use familiar words in new contexts with new meanings.

Study vs Use of Literature

Whether literate or illiterate, sophisticated or not, all of us have an inherent ability to understand the basic story-telling conventions. This helps us enjoy literature and appreciate the meaning it conveys. It is this implicit competence that we try to take advantage of in using literature to teach language. Students get absorbed in the story, and the language (sentences, sentence and phrasal patterns, and words) is understood and mastered without much effort in the process. However, we need to distinguish between the study of literature per se and the use of literature as a resource for language teaching.

Our goal is not teaching literature. Our goal is teaching language. We intend to use literature to teach language. The most important function of using literature in a TESOL class is its motivating role for performance within the classroom. Study of literary pieces provides opportunities to the class to reflect on the events and characters, share the opinions of the readers, and get them involved in discussions. Introduction to the cultural background is another important function.

Substitute for Face to Face Communication

Study of literature helps language acquisition in another peculiar way: The students in Third World countries have only a limited access to spoken English. Face to face communication with the native speakers is a rarity. Under this circumstance, students can have continued touch with English mostly through the written English. If this written English is motivating, interesting and instructive, students will come back to use English day after day.

Selection of Material

We need to select materials which match the interests of our students. Often the textbooks used to teach English as a second or foreign language in the Third World countries contain stories, dramas and poems. Some of these, especially stories and dramas, may be from the same cultural and literary background of the learners. These texts may not pose cultural problems for students. They are certain to pose problems for the TESOL teacher! Classical British and American texts (novels, plays, etc.) abridged and re-told would be an excellent addition to TESOL textbooks.

English is an international language. Many talented creative writers from the former colonies of Britain and the countries which have been traditionally close to the United States, have chosen to express themselves in English. In addition, there is an excellent body of literature from other languages in English translation. It is possible to supplement our TESOL textbook with materials taken from all the above four categories.

Lazar (1993:62) points out that "although students may find it easier to respond personally to a text from within their own culture, there is a strong argument for saying that exposing students to literature from other cultures is an enriching and exciting way of increasing their awareness of different values, beliefs, social structures and so on." You may have to edit these pieces to bring some native-English naturalness to the texts. You may have to edit the material for its difficulty level and length as well. In general, the following factors are always recommended for consideration while selecting the text (Lazar 1993):

> "The students' cultural background, linguistic proficiency, literary background, availability of texts (kinds and ease with which these are available), length of text (Do you have enough time available to work on the text in class? How much time do students have to work on the text at home? Could you use only part of a text, or an abridged version of it? If so, how much background information will you need to give students to make the text intelligible?), exploitability (What kinds of tasks and activities can you devise to exploit the text? Are there resources available to help you exploit the text, for example, a film or a particular novel the students are studying, recordings of a play or poem, library materials giving information about the life of an author, etc.), fit with syllabus (How do the texts link with the rest of the syllabus? Thematically? In terms of vocabulary, grammar or discourse? Can you devise tasks and activities for exploiting the text which link with the methodology you have used elsewhere in the syllabus?)."

Remember that our goal is not teaching literature. Our goal is to use literature to teach language. Literary pieces can be easily integrated with the syllabus for the course. At the lower level, stories are part of the textbook.

The story lesson may be "taught" following the usual steps, with focus on vocabulary and sentence structure. Students may be given tasks to paraphrase the story in their own words and manner. They can "listen" to the story, they can tell the story orally, they can "read" it aloud to others, or read it silently, they can rewrite the story in their own words, they can play with the words and find the meanings for the crucial words and use them in their own sentences.

They may try to identify the technique of narration, and adopt the same to write their own stories. They can identify the conversational strategies the characters in the story have employed, and try to use the same in conversations with their fellow students in the class. They can enact the story as a team and learn to behave like the characters. There is no limit to the kinds of activities which could be developed based on the story in the textbook. All language skills are covered in teaching the story in the class.

There is no better material than literary pieces for reading assignments outside the class. Quite a few abridged and re-told materials are available which could be assigned for reading outside the class. Short story collections and short novels are more useful than full length fiction. Ask the students to pencil those words, phrases, and idioms which are unfamiliar to them. Let them check with a second language learner's dictionary such as Oxford Advanced Learner's Dictionary of Current English not only for their meanings but also for their usage. Let them write a brief report or gist of the story to confirm that they have indeed read the book. Have a brief discussion in the class about the reading assignment. Lazar (1993) suggests three types of activities: Pre-reading activities, While-reading activities, and Post-reading activities.

Poetry

If you are good in reciting poetry with passion, then you should give your students a taste of what English poems are. If your students show great talents in appropriate recitation with passion, then have several poetry reading sessions.

Poems also help teaching language. Students need to make decisions about the correct order of the lines, decipher the metaphor and other poetic devices used by the poet, and convert them to the ordinary language syntax. Comprehension of meaning of a poem is more intricate than the comprehension of an ordinary text, either in story form or in business correspondence, etc.

As Lazar (1993) points out, poems are marked by unusual syntax, rich in words coined by the poet, reinforcing the students' knowledge of the norms of language use, and the manner in which they can be adapted to achieve different communicative purposes. Integrating poetry into the syllabus provides for an enjoyable way of reinforcing and revisiting contents, enabling students to make confident interpretations, understand figurative meanings, and nuances of creative literature in English.

Poems may have only a limited role to play in teaching language in a TESOL classroom. However, the textbooks prepared and used in the Third World countries correctly look at teaching languages as a means for comprehensive education. They always give an important place to poetry in their syllabus. So, some training in teaching poetry is not out of place for the TESOL teacher.

We would encourage you to be proficient in reciting and performing a number of nursery rhymes, as well as the poems written by poets such as Emily Dickinson and Robert Frost, and the reputed Indian poets.

Difficulties for Learners

Language teaching practice often assumes that most of the difficulties that learners face in the study of English are a consequence of the degree to which their native language differs from English (a contrastive analysis approach). A native speaker of Chinese, for example, may face many more difficulties than a native speaker of German, because German is closely related to English, whereas Chinese is not. Another example will be Spanish, because a lot of the words that come from this language are written in the same way though pronounced differently. This may be true for anyone of any mother tongue (also called first language, normally abbreviated L1) setting out to learn any other language (called a target language, second language or L2).

Language learners often produce errors of syntax and pronunciation thought to result from the influence of their L1, such as mapping its grammatical patterns inappropriately onto the L2, pronouncing certain sounds incorrectly or with difficulty, and confusing items of vocabulary known as false friends. This is known as L1 transfer or "language interference". However, these transfer effects are typically stronger for beginners' language production, and SLA research has highlighted many errors which cannot be attributed to the L1, as they are attested in learners of many language backgrounds (for example, failure to apply 3rd person present singular -s to verbs, as in 'he make').

Some students may have very different cultural perceptions in the classroom as far as learning a second language is concerned. Also, cultural differences in communication styles and preferences are significant. For example, a study looked at Chinese ESL students and British teachers and found that the Chinese learners did not see classroom discussion and interaction as important but placed a heavy emphasis on teacher-directed lectures.

Vocabulary

Phrasal Verbs: Phrasal verbs in English can cause difficulties for many learners because they have several meanings and different syntactic patterns. There are also a number of phrasal verb differences between American and British English.

Word Derivation: Word derivation in English requires a lot of rote learning. For example, an adjective can be negated by using the prefix *un-* (e.g. *unable*), *in-* (e.g. *inappropriate*), *dis-* (e.g. *dishonest*), or *a-* (e.g. *amoral*), or through the use of one of a myriad related but rarer prefixes, all modified versions of the first four.

Size of Lexicon: The history of English has resulted in a very large vocabulary, essentially one stream from Old English and one from the Norman infusion of Latin-derived terms. (Schmitt & Marsden claim that English has one of the largest vocabularies of any known language.) This inevitably requires more work for a learner to master the language.

Collocations: Collocations in English refer to the tendency for words to occur regularly with others. For example, nouns and verbs that go together (ride a bike/ drive a car). Native speakers tend to use chunks of collocations and the ESL learners make mistakes with collocations in their writing/speaking which sometimes results in awkwardness.

Slang and Colloquialisms: In most native English speaking countries, large numbers of slang and colloquial terms are used in everyday speech. Many learners may find that classroom based English is significantly different from how English is spoken in normal situations. This can often be difficult and confusing for learners with little experience of using English in Anglophone countries. Also, slang terms differ greatly between different regions and can change quickly in response to popular culture. Some phrases can become unintentionally rude if misused.

Pronunciation

Consonant Phonemes: English does not have more individual consonant sounds than most languages. However, the interdentals, /è/ and /ð/ (the sounds written with *th*), which are common in English (*thin, thing,* etc.; and *the, this, that,* etc.) are relatively rare in other languages, even others in the Germanic family (*e.g.,* English *thousand* = German *tausend*), and these sounds are missing even in some English dialects. Some learners substitute a [t] or [d] sound, while others shift to [s] or [z], [f] or [v] and even [ts] or [dz]. Speakers of Japanese, Korean, Chinese and Thai may have difficulty distinguishing [y] and [l]. Speakers of Xiang Chinese may have a similar difficulty distinguishing [n] and [l]. The distinction between [b] and [v] can cause difficulty for native speakers of Spanish, Arabic, Japanese and Korean.

Vowel Phonemes: The precise number of distinct vowel sounds depends on the variety of English: for example, Received Pronunciation has twelve monophthongs (single or "pure" vowels), eight diphthongs (double vowels) and two triphthongs (triple vowels); whereas General American has thirteen monophthongs and three diphthongs. Many learners, such as speakers of Spanish, Japanese or Arabic, have fewer vowels, or only pure ones, in their mother tongue and so may have problems both with hearing and with pronouncing these distinctions.

Syllable Structure: In its syllable structure, English allows for a cluster of up to three consonants before the vowel and four after it (*e.g., straw, desks, glimpsed*). The syllable structure causes problems for speakers of many other languages. Japanese, for example, broadly alternates consonant and vowel sounds so learners from Japan often try to force vowels in between the consonants (*e.g., desks* /desks/ becomes "desukusu" or *milk shake* /mjlk ƒejk/ becomes "mirukushçku").

Learners from languages where all words end in vowels sometimes tend to make all English words end in vowels, thus *make* /mejk/ can come out as [mejkY]. The learner's task is further complicated by the fact that native speakers may drop consonants in the more complex blends (*e.g.,* [mŒns] instead of [mŒnès] for *months*).

Unstressed Vowels: Native English speakers frequently replace almost any vowel in an unstressed syllable with an unstressed vowel, often schwa. For example, *from* has a distinctly pronounced short 'o' sound when it is stressed (*e.g., Where are you from?*), but when it is unstressed, the short 'o' reduces to a schwa (*e.g., I'm from London.*).

In some cases, unstressed vowels may disappear altogether, in words such as chocolate (which has four syllables in Spanish, but only two as pronounced by Americans: "*choc-lit*".)

Stress in English more strongly determines vowel quality than it does in most other world languages (although there are notable exceptions such as Russian). For example, in some varieties the syllables *an, en, in, on* and *un* are pronounced as homophones, that is, exactly alike. Native speakers can usually distinguish *an able, enable,* and *unable* because of their position in a sentence, but this is more difficult for inexperienced English speakers. Moreover, learners tend to overpronounce these unstressed vowels, giving their speech an unnatural rhythm.

Stress Timing: English tends to be a stress-timed language - this means that stressed syllables are roughly equidistant in time, no matter how many syllables come in between. Although some other languages, e.g., German and Russian, are also stress-timed, most of the world's other major languages are syllable-timed, with each syllable coming at an equal time after the previous one. Learners from these languages often have a staccato rhythm when speaking English that is disconcerting to a native speaker.

"Stress for emphasis" - students' own languages may not use stress for emphasis as English does.

"Stress for contrast" - stressing the right word or expression. This may not come easily to some non-native speakers.

"Emphatic apologies" - the normally unstressed auxiliary is stressed (I really *am* very sorry)

In English there are quite a number of words - about fifty - that have two different pronunciations, depending on whether they are stressed. They are "grammatical words": pronouns, prepositions, auxiliary verbs and conjunctions. Most students tend to overuse the strong form, which is pronounced with the written vowel.

Connected Speech: Phonological processes such as assimilation, elision and epenthesis together with indistinct word boundaries can confuse learners when listening to natural spoken English, as well as making their speech sound too formal if they do not use them. For example, in RP *eight beetles and three ants* /ejt biÐtYlz Ynd èriÐ ænts/ becomes.

Grammar

Tense, Aspect and Mood: English has a relatively large number of tense–aspect–mood forms with some quite subtle differences, such as the difference between the simple past "I ate" and the present perfect "I have eaten." Progressive and perfect progressive forms add complexity.

Functions of Auxiliaries: Learners of English tend to find it difficult to manipulate the various ways in which English uses auxiliary verbs. These include negation (e.g. *He hasn't been drinking.*), inversion with the subject to form a question (e.g. *Has he been drinking?*), short answers (e.g. *Yes, he has.*) and tag questions (*has he?*). A further complication is that the dummy auxiliary verb *do /does /did* is added to fulfil these functions in the simple present and simple past, but not for the verb *to be.*

Modal Verbs: English also has a significant number of modal auxiliary verbs which each have a number of uses. For example, the opposite of "You must be here at 8" (obligation) is usually "You don't have to be here at 8" (lack of obligation, choice), while "must" in "You must not drink the water" (prohibition) has a different meaning from "must" in "You must not be a native speaker" (deduction). This complexity takes considerable work for most English language learners to master.

Idiomatic Usage: English is reputed to have a relatively high degree of idiomatic usage. For example, the use of different main verb forms in such apparently parallel constructions as "try to learn", "help learn", and "avoid learning" pose difficulty for learners. Another example is the idiomatic distinction between "make" and "do": "make a mistake", not "do a mistake"; and "do a favour", not "make a favour".

Articles: English has an appreciable number of articles, including the "the" definite article and the "a, an" indefinite article. At times English nouns can or indeed must be used without an article; this is called the zero article. Some of the differences between definite, indefinite and zero article are fairly easy to learn, but others are not, particularly since a learner's native language may lack articles or use them in different ways than English does. Although the information conveyed by articles is rarely essential for communication, English uses them frequently (several times in the average sentence), so that they require some effort from the learner.

7 Role and Importance of Audio/Visual Teaching Learning Aids

The teaching profession is filled with countless opportunities to enrich the academic lives of students. While some concepts and educational objectives will be easy for students to grasp, others will require you to think creatively to ensure that important learning objectives are met. Using audio/visual aides in teaching is one way to enhance lesson plans and give students additional ways to process subject information.

Use of Audio-Visual Aids in Teaching

Audiovisual aids in the classroom can enhance teaching methods and improve student comprehension. Today's technology offers many choices to the informed educator who wishes to capitalise on a new generation's appetite for multimedia presentations. Lesson plans that incorporate the use of audiovisual aids should be consistent with curriculum objectives and not segued improperly.

Auditory Learners and Aids

- Auditory learners focus more on the spoken word rather than the written one. Taped recordings of lectures or movies are helpful to auditory learners because they pick up on speech nuances such as tone and pitch. Computers with speech-recognition devices will also help auditory learners to process and retain information better than just reading from a textbook. Students with hearing disabilities will also benefit from teachers who use microphones while lecturing.

Visual Learners and Aids

- Slide projectors have given way to Power Point presentations in the modern classroom, but the concept is the same. Visual learners understand meaning through graphic portrayals such as charts, illustrations and diagrams. Teachers that take the time to compose or find visual supplements to accompany their lectures help to greatly augment learning potential. The old adage that "a picture is worth a thousand words" still rings true, especially in today's image-submerged society.

Movie Clips

- Incorporating a YouTube moment or any other instructional video clip into a lesson plan can greatly increase understanding as well as enjoyment during the learning process. If an interactive white board with Internet capabilities is not available, many video clips from the web can be downloaded and embedded in a Power Point presentation for classroom purposes. Be sure to prepare students before watching the clip by telling them what to expect or what to look for and then following up with discussion questions that tie in to the lesson plan.

Special Education Students

- Students with special needs often require information to be presented to them in several different formats before they can adequately understand a concept or process information. Playing a book on tape while simultaneously reading together in class is a good way to reinforce material. Videos that deal with the targeted subject matter can be shown afterwards to further augment learning.

Don't Overdo it:

- Audiovisual technology has an important role to play in the modern classroom, but teachers who rely too much on technology may actually inhibit learning. It's the law of diminishing returns: you can only get so much useful enjoyment and assistance from a machine. The personal relationship between teacher and student is ultimately more valuable and rewarding in a brick and mortar classroom environment. This is not to say that there aren't some students who are quite capable of learning by themselves through interactive technology, but if that were true in all cases, then schools wouldn't need teachers, would they?

Audiolingual Method

The audiolingual method in some sense represents a return to the direct method, as its main goal is to develop native-like speaking ability in its learners. It is an extension as well as a refinement of the Direct Method. Translation and reference to L1 are not permitted. Underlying this approach, however, is the notion that "L2 learning should be regarded as a mechanistic process of habit formation . . . Audiolingual learning comprises dialogue memorisation and pattern drills, thus ensuring careful control of responses. None of the drills or patterns are to be explained, since knowledge of grammatical rules would only obstruct the mechanical formation of habits."

"Just as the Direct Method was an extension of the Natural Method, so Audiolingualism had its theoretical roots in the Direct Method." The Audiolingual method used exhaustively the linguistic structures identified in the descriptive analysis of the target language. It resulted in carefully prepared materials. It was skill oriented, with a practical emphasis on oracy. "It provided contextualised language practice in true-to-life situations including dialogue. It provided a wide variety of activities to help maintain interest, and it made extensive use of visuals. It arranged for abundant practice, although "the grammar-based Audiolingual approach moved cautiously from supposedly simple to more and more linguistically complex features, often without adequate consideration for what might be needed in everyday situations."

Some of the things which led to the spread and success of this method in this century include: Greater allotment of time, smaller classes, greater emphasis on oral-aural practice which led to automatic production of sentences repeated or in the internalisation of sentence structures through repetition and inductive generalisation, the structural description and gradation of sentence and other linguistic utterances presented to the students for drill, contrastive analysis between the structures of the native and target languages, and careful preparation and presentation of learning materials based on all these.

Need for an Eclectic Approach

At present, teachers of English around the world prefer some form of communicative teaching and learning, rather than the audiolingual method and its derivatives. However, we must remember that a successful TESOL teacher is not necessarily biased in favour of one method or another. She should be first of all competent in and comfortable with the methods she wants to use. She tends to select different teaching strategies from different methods, and blends them to suit the needs of her materials and students.

It is important that the students are given ample opportunities to practice English in the class as well as outside the classroom, even as it is important for them to have time and freedom to digest, reflect and analyse what has been exposed to them. Internalisation of the linguistic structures and their ready and easy retrieval for communication are achieved in many ways.

A diligent TESOL teacher continually learns new techniques from her peers and her students, as she interacts with them. She needs to know the new directions in teaching of English to speakers of other languages which are debated in the journals and demonstrated in new textbooks. Her own English speech, pronunciation, and writing should be as close to the "standard" as possible, or native-like, if she is not a native speaker of English. She may use regional characteristics of English to inform and entertain, but she should be able to switch to the "standard" for presenting her lessons.

Her writing in English should be simple, straightforward and plain. She should have a good command and conscious knowledge of the grammatical structures of the language and should be at home with the grammatical terms used to describe the structures. She should be sensitive to the background and the needs of her class.

She should have a clear voice, and should be energetic and enthusiastic so that the class will come alive in her presence. It is important for her to get all her students involved in the drills and exercises conducted in the class. A good actor she should be!

Visual and Audio-Visual Aids

The terms visual and audiovisual aid refer to anything that an extension agent uses to help facilitate communication when interacting with farmers. The spoken word is the agent's main communication tool, but whether the agent is speaking to a large village meeting or discussing a problem in a field with a farmer, the impact and effectiveness can be greatly increased by the use of suitable visual and audiovisual aids. When selected and used properly, these aids can help in presenting the message in a number of different ways.

Types of Visual and Audiovisual Aids

Extension agents often use sophisticated extension aids which require electricity and complex equipment such as projectors or video players. There are also many simple aids which the agent can make or acquire locally and which have several advantages. They do not require a power source or heavy equipment, they are cheap and they can be made to suit the precise needs of the agent. Between these two extremes lies a wide range of more or less sophisticated aids. All the mass media described earlier can be used as visual or audiovisual aids: the distinction lies only in the way the medium is used. A video that is copied and widely distributed is a mass medium, because it is can be shown to audiences in many different places; but for an individual extension agent who uses it to introduce a discussion or to increase the impact of a talk, it is an audiovisual aid. Many of the principles of media use discussed earlier, therefore, also apply to visual and audiovisual aids. In these days of rapidly advancing communication technology, agents should not forget that there are many extension aids, visual aids in particular, which they can prepare without needing any great expense or technical skill. Some of the more common aids are discussed briefly below.

Audiovisual Aids

Audiovisual aids are defined as any device used to aid in the communication of an idea. From this definition, virtually anything can be used as an aid, providing it successfully communicates the idea or information for which it is designed. In this chapter, we not only use the term "Audiovisual Aids" but "Instructional Aids," "Teaching Aids," "Audio Aids," and "Visual Aids" as well. An audiovisual product is any audiovisual (AV) item such as still photography, motion picture, audio or video tape, slide or filmstrip, that is prepared singly or in combination to communicate information or to elicit a desired audience response. Even though early aids, such as maps and drawings, are still in use, advances in the audiovisual field have opened up new methods of presenting these aids, such as video-tapes and multimedia equipment which allow more professional and entertaining presentations to be presented. Most of the visual aids covered in this chapter can be grouped into the following categories—non-projected aids and projected aids.

Use of Visual and Audiovisual Aids

Visual and other aids are only effective if they are appropriate to the situation and are used properly by the presenter. Unsuitable aids or ones that are not used properly can at best distract and at worst mislead the audience. When selecting suitable aids, the agent will be limited to what is readily available or that can be made locally. Within these constraints, some aids are more suited to a particular objective than others. For an accurate visual representation, photographs, slides or a detailed drawing may be needed. If the presenter only wants to highlight the structure of a talk, and then list the main conclusions of a discussion, a chalkboard or flipchart will be suitable. The presenter must also consider where the aids will be used: indoors or outdoors, with or without electricity, in a large meeting or as part of a small group. All these factors will influence the choice of visual and audiovisual aids. One cannot learn how to use extension aids skilfully from a book. This only comes through practice. However, the following principles may be useful to consider with any visual or audiovisual aids.

- Select the aids most suited to the communication objective, the location, and the composition and size of the audience.
- Use the aids to reinforce the message or to support the activity that is going on. They are there to assist, to complement and supplement what the presenter is doing. In a talk to a group of farmers, for example, refer to the aids, explain them and

ask questions about them to check whether the audience has understood the key points.

- Make sure that the audience will be able to see and hear clearly. Audio cassettes that cannot be heard or words on a board that are too small to be seen can make the audience restless and inattentive, and even start talking amongst themselves.
- Practice using the aids beforehand. Where projectors aids are used, it is important that the presenter is fully accustomed to using the equipment.

Using Visuals

As a teacher of TESOL, you should familiarise yourself with a range of simple visual aids which would help you to teach the structures and words smoothly. You should develop some skills to prepare your own visual aids. You should know how to use the visual aids effectively. Doff (1988:81-92) presents some interesting information on the use of visual aids in TESOL classroom:

> Visual aids include pictures, objects, and things for the students to look at and talk about. Visual aids are important because showing visuals focuses attention on meaning, and helps to make the language in the class more real and alive; having something to look at keeps the students' attention, and makes the class more interesting; visuals can be used at any stage of the lesson, to help in presenting new language or introducing a topic, as part of language practice, and when reviewing language that has been presented earlier; good visual aids can be used again and again and shared by different teachers.

You can use the following as visual aids in your class: yourself, the blackboard, real objects, flashcards, pictures, and charts. The teacher can use gestures, facial expressions, and actions to help show the meaning of words and to illustrate situations. You can use the blackboard to draw pictures, diagrams, maps, etc. You can use real objects in the classroom and bring other things into the class – food, clothes, containers, household objects, vegetables, etc.

Flashcards with single pictures can be held up by the teacher in the class. These can be used for presenting and practising new words and structures, and for revision. The teacher can draw a picture on the flashcard, or stick on a picture from magazine. Flashcards can also be used to show words or numbers. Charts are large sheets of card or paper with writing, pictures or diagrams, used for more extended presentation or practice. These may be displayed on the wall or blackboard.

Instructions

- Bridge the gap between the different types of learners by adding audio/visual aides to your teaching techniques. Since most people are visual learners, it's important to go beyond "spoken words" when educating students. Students are also more likely to learn material is they're exposed to it in a variety of ways. Always look over your lesson plans to find ways to inject different teaching styles.
- Implement "show and tell" sessions to promote student involvement. This will also help you assess each student's overall understanding of the desired learning objectives. There are many ways to use show and tell sessions such as asking students to bring in modern items that still demonstrate colonial values.
- Provide audio/visual aides to demonstrate mathematical concepts to students. This will help students learn to think of complicated material in a practical way. For example, concepts like fractions and proportions can be better visualised through the use of audio/visual aides such as marble representations and pizza models.
- Watch videos and movies that reinforce lesson plans. Authors such as Shakespeare may be easier to understand when the material is seen as well as read. Use film clips to highlight historical events and to provide expert analysis of current situations.
- Invite guest speakers to help students learn concepts. The use of real people can make subjects such as social studies seem more relevant to daily life. The visual and auditory information conveyed to the students can make a lasting impression. Ask

guest speakers to bring in items for the class to pass around or to tell stories in their native languages.

Objects of Audio-Visual Aids

A real object is often the most effective aid. It enables the audience to understand exactly what the extension agent is talking about. Equipment and tools can be shown, samples of diseased plants and insect pests inspected and different seed varieties and fertilizers handled by farmers. Where an object is too large to be shown or is not available, a model or photograph can be used as a substitute.

Models: These can be particularly helpful in the case of buildings and other fixed structures. The construction of a poultry shed or grain store, for example, or the layout and dimensions of a fish pond, can be shown using a model, which can be assembled and taken to pieces in front of the audience.

Photographs: These can be passed around an audience or displayed by the agent. If a photograph is being taken to use as a visual aid, just the right amount of detail should be included for the audience to recognise it and see what the agent wants them to see. Too much detail confuses and distracts, making it difficult for the audience to focus on the main point of the photograph, while too little detail prevents recognition. Photographs of people doing things are more likely to interest the audience than photographs of objects alone.

Drawing: A good alternative to photographs is a drawing, particularly since a drawing can show detail and draw attention to specific items that need to be emphasised.

8 Use of Language Lab

The language laboratory is an audio or audiovisual installation used as an aid in modern language teaching. They can be found, amongst other places, in schools, universities and academies. Perhaps the first lab was at the University of Grenoble. In the 1950s up until the 1990s, they were tape based systems using reel to reel or (latterly) cassette. Current installations are generally multimedia PCs. The original language labs are now very outdated. They allowed a teacher to listen to and manage student audio via a hard-wired analogue tape deck based systems with 'sound booths' in fixed locations.

Role of Language Lab in English Language Learning and Teaching

Introduction of Technology in Language Teaching and Learning

Emerging technologies make it practical to approach learning in ways that have been advocated by scientists, theorists, and educational psychologists for years. Advanced information technologies such as virtual reality, visualisation, digital modelling, digitisation, simulation, games, virtual worlds and intelligent one-on-one tutoring systems dramatically enhance teaching and learning of elusive concepts by translating abstractions into real-world contexts and providing customised instruction and individualised assessments. To realise the full potential of this technology and to ensure its pervasiveness in all institutions of learning and training, we must undertake a long-term, large-scale effort to research, develop, test and disseminate tools for building advanced learning systems.

Pedagogy of Learning through Technology

- *Assimilating What has been Learned:* These are generally guided exercises. They are used to help students assimilate grammatical and lexical structures, as well as phonetics. They consist of the following:
  - Repetition Exercises (Word Pronunciation, Sentence Pronunciation).
  - Substitution / Transformation Exercises (Sentence Practice, Grammar Practice).
- *Putting the Rules into Practice:* These are guided exercises. Their objective is to highlight specific functional components within a language:
  - Reflection on the organisation of sentence components (Word Order).
  - The use of vocabulary and grammar in fill-in-the-blanks exercises, which require students to analyse a sentence in its entirety in order to place the correct word (The Right Word, Fill-in-the-Blanks).
  - Vocabulary practice with association exercises, which consist of matching a word with its synonym, antonym or a related image (Word Association, Picture / Word Association).
  - Reflection on vocabulary or grammar using texts or lexical groups, in which students must identify words belonging to a specific grammatical or lexical group (Words and Functions, Words and Topics).
- Mastering the language The objective of these types of exercises is to put the acquired knowledge into practice through written expression. The exercises consist of:

— Guided expression, consisting of the transformation of context (Text Transformation).

— Semi-guided expression, in which it is necessary to write texts based on an image or video, or to write a summary of a longer text (Written Expression).

Strategies of Teaching and Learning

Learner can respond at ease for communicative mode of teaching. Communicative method for learning languages combines extensive, high-quality content with flexible and interactive multimedia technology. This comprehensive language-learning method can act as a total solution for self-teaching, as well as a teaching support to formal courses. Through a wide range of activities, a variety of skills are aimed to develop in a learner. A learner needs to communicate: oral and written comprehension, as well as oral and written expression. It also addresses the concepts of grammar, lexicon, phonetics and conjugation. In order to achieve this objective, there are three possible Learning Modes:

> The Guided Mode offers a step-by-step study course. Organised into Learning Paths, this mode focuses on the acquisition of functional language patterns across a broad spectrum of themes. In this mode a learner at lower intermediate level can learn pronunciation, grammar, functions of words and vocabulary by applying and practising the rules.

The Free-to-Roam Mode gives a student the option of learning by topic or by linguistic skill. This mode is particularly useful for students who are at intermediate level of learning and also for teachers who want to familiarise themselves with the content available to them.

The Dynamic Mode takes a student under its wing. By analysing a student's results, this mode adapts the course of study to ensure that it corresponds to the student's needs and abilities. The activities offered evolve in relation to the student's results and original objectives. Advanced learners can immediately be immersed in an authentic learning context through:

- The various dialogues and videos, which illustrate everyday and professional life.

- In line with current pedagogical trends, familiarising students with the voicing of the language using recordings made by native speakers.
- Subsequently, students will address concepts of grammar, lexicon, phonetics and conjugation they have previously met in context, allowing them to understand and retain these notions.
- Finally, in order to reinforce the knowledge they have acquired, students will be asked to apply it in a practical context.

All the modes can be applied for the learners of the same class according to their abilities and capabilities. Thus individualised learning can be encouraged, through using the cultural texts, images, maps and corresponding activities.

Methodology of Instruction

It is followed in the Communicative and integrated approach. It keeps the ability to use language to communicate as central goal, to make meaning-focused activity which simulates real life transactions; crucially activity is on the learner's part, with the teacher being more of a facilitator and guide. The type of Syllabus framed is Analytic. It equips the learner with language to use it in a variety of situations (real or simulated) covering the varied purposes for which they have to communicate in corporate world. The learner analyses these wholes and develops a sense of the patterns of usage. Thus they learn language naturally by being immersed in its communicative use. In these activities, learners move from controlled practice of a conditional form presented in an Audio or Video form or Reading text or the combination of both to the activity in which they have to produce in Spoken or Written mode. This Presentation-Practice-Production (PPP) model is followed in the lesson plans.

Use of Language Lab with Teacher's Console

Language Lab can be used for teaching/learning through teacher's Console and Language Learning Software. It acts as a platform for learning, practising and producing language skills through interactive lessons and communicative mode of teaching. Learners can act and respond in a variety of ways at their own pace. Language lab may have the following objectives, purposes, functions to work upon.

Objectives:

- To maintain good linguistic competence- through accuracy in grammar, Pronunciation & Vocabulary.
- To develop pragmatic competence, to understand the grammatical form & function & scale of formality.
- To enrich the discourse competence, to prepare the learner to be able to produce contextualise written text and speech.
- To acquire strategic competence to use both spoken & written language to use in a wide range of communication strategies.

Purposes of Teacher's Console:

- Stay in control- Monitoring the students from the teacher's PC when they are on self learning.
- Reinforce learning- Facilitating broadcast and sharing files from Teacher's PC to the other student workstations through audio, video, text and image.
- Teaching with software that is approachable- Pairing and grouping the students to facilitate group discussions. Content authoring to create course material, and tests.
- To ensure the best learning results

Staying in Control

New ways of learning and interacting in the classroom demand new ways of managing student activity. Many software language learning solutions keep teachers and learners firmly at the centre of learning activity with a suite of classroom management tools: control web browsing; manage chat sessions; monitor students' on-screen work and activities; black out screens; lock cursors and keyboards to focus attention on a given task; shut down, log off or restart student computers etc.

Reinforce Learning

Teachers can use communication tools that are familiar to their students, such as text massaging or chat, to communicate with them in an engaging way and by creating more opportunities to interact in the target language. Learners can reinforce their language in various activities. They can revise pronunciation, grammar, vocabulary, sentence structure and conversations

Teaching with Software that is Approachable

Teachers will be perfectly at ease by using teaching software, as the interfaces are user-friendly and activity-driven, so that activities that are not in use cannot be accidentally selected to confuse the teacher and disrupt the lesson. No specialised IT skills are needed in the comfortable teaching and learning environment provided by the interface.

Ensuring the Best Learning Results

Language Learning Software gives learners access to resources for independent or supplemental learning and study. This unique learning-on-demand feature creates additional learning opportunities and reinforces classroom activity. It is possible to conduct & practice tests and get results in individualised manner.

Functions of Teacher's Console:

- Live Audio & Video broadcasting
  - To broadcast live Audio and Video from news and educational channels of TV or from internet
  - To broadcast the teacher's screen or a selected student's to other computers
  - To broadcast Audio and Video from any analogue source i.e. DVD, MP3 & CD etc.
- Monitoring the student's workstations
  - To Monitor students' screens as a whole and also on individual basis from the teacher's workstation
  - To take control or terminate applications on any student computer
- Speech drill exercises

  To practice voice based activities like speech drill exercises through model imitation, voice recording, voice graph and variable speed playback to neutralise accent & acquire fluency
- Group Discussions

- To bring the students into random or standard groups to conduct group discussions and role plays from their workstations.
- Live recording of discussion content for each group so that the teacher can provide feedback on their performance

• Content Authoring and Conducting on-line examination

- To combine text, video, images and audio to design customised course materials.
- To create, edit and score exams, quizzes and tests using text, graphics, audio and video.

Various Techniques

Techniques to Improve Macro Skills of Language through Language Lab

Among the four macro skills of language learning, listening and reading are receptive skills whereas speaking and writing are the productive skills. These skills can be improved effectively, when the learner learns at his own pace. With the help of the functional tool-Language Lab with Teacher's Console, language skills can be learnt, practised and evaluated through the techniques followed.

Techniques to Improve Listening

The primary form of linguistic communication is speech and so listening is the most important receptive (and learning) skill for foreign language students. An ability to listen and interpret many shades of meaning from what is heard, is a fundamental communicative ability.

Teaching listening involves training in some 'enabling skills' — perception of sounds, stress, intonation patterns, accents, attitudes and so on, as well as 'practice' in various styles of listening comprehension.

Techniques to Improve Speaking

Students' speech evaluation is possible through the digital recorder modules in language learning software. Students' audio recordings can be scored or saved for later evaluation. The Teachers can Record their own voice notes that students can hear later as they review their work.

Group Discussions & Role Plays: The students on different workstations can be grouped and put into random pairs or groups to participate in role plays and group discussions. Teachers can listen directly or intervene as when required to control, monitor and evaluate the process. It can also be recorded and saved for later evaluation.

Digital Recorder: This software module allows students to experience interactive multimedia programmes while simultaneously recording their own voices for practice. Using this, students feel like they are interacting with a live native speaker and they can increase their comprehension, vocabulary and speaking skills. By adding subtitles, reading skills are also increased. Quizzes and tests can be prepared by using text, graphics, video and audio materials. These quizzes are graded automatically

Voice Recognition Technology: This technology is integrated into the Pronunciation module of the software. Using the built in microphone on your computer, the learner will be able to repeat words after they hear from a native speaker through computer speakers. The software will analyse their pronunciation and compare a waveform representation of the native speaker's pronunciation with a waveform of their pronunciation. An accuracy scale on the screen with display their voice match to the native speaker on a scale of "Bad", "Acceptable", and "Good".

Techniques to Improve Reading and Writing

The key to learning a language is the frequent exposure and use of vocabulary and grammar. The average person must be exposed to a word or phrase 100s of times before integrating it into fluent conversation. The major thresholds of gaining language fluency are the learner's ability to:

> Learn a base vocabulary of approximately 2000 words for day–to–day use; Learn the rules of grammar; Vocabulary Lessons; Grammar Exercises; Interactive Stories/ situations.

Perception of Pronunciation

Accurate perception of the sounds of the language is the first stage which leads to interpretation and comprehension. When listening to a foreign language, we need to know the sounds, rhythms, tunes and stress patterns of that language. All the pronunciation work which we do will benefit the students' listening ability.

Phonetics: The sounds of the English language can be written down using the International Phonetic Alphabet (IPA) which is used in all Longman dictionaries. Use of minimal pair perception exercises (ship/sheep, ten /then) helps students learn the sounds of English. It can be well practised on pronunciation exercises with the help of software or by using CDs in language lab.

Interpretation: We listen to interpret meaning. Most of the exercises which students will do focus on listening comprehension, which is, interpreting meaning from spoken language.

Listening to Words: In written language, there are convenient white spaces between words. Whereas spoken language is a continuous stream of sound. The learner has to pay attention to understand the meaning of words spoken.

Tools for Listening

Acoustics: Our ability to hear is essential to our ability to listen. The first set of ideas concerns the production, corruption, transmission and reception of spoken language.

Usage of Language Laboratory: Earphones and headphones deliver undistorted sound directly to the ears. It is better practised in a language laboratory with the help of head phones and earphones; this provides ideal conditions for intensive listening.

Organising Listening Comprehension Activities

As in reading comprehension, there should always be a 'purpose' in listening. In most cases, this will be some form of comprehension. We should establish regular 'procedures' for listening activities in which students will develop from general (gist) to specific comprehension through repeated listening and a specific activity at each stage.

Understanding the Setting: After the first listening, students should be able to understand the setting of the recording — where the speakers are from, how many speakers there are, the ages, roles, professions, moods of the speakers, etc., and what they are talking about. This encourages students to think about the setting so that they can go on to speculate about the content of what the speakers will say. This first listening allows the students to get accustomed to the voices.

Pre-teach Difficult Vocabulary: Teaching isolated and meaningless lists of words and phrases is probably not a good idea. Teachers may choose to introduce the setting before the students listen. This provides an opportunity to elicit or introduce and explain the sort of language we might hear in that setting. This language is listed on the board and students listen and mark what they actually heard.

Focused Listening: Listening tasks should give the students a reason for listening and focus their attention. These listening tasks should be set before the students listen. This intense listening requires intense concentration. Therefore the listening task can be limited for ten to fifteen minutes.

Comprehending: In large classes we will probably have different levels of competence. There is no reason why all the students need to work on the same task. Equally, if we have more than 6 questions, groups of students can be given questions 1-5, questions 6-10 and so on. After listening students share their answers.

Analysis: After students have understood the gist and some important details of a recording, it can be analysed in more detail and investigate the way in which the speakers have expressed the ideas. How much have they revealed their mood, their opinions and so on? Analysis of the speed and style of speech, the use of hesitation, repetition, false starts, paraphrasing and so on can also be practised.

Graded Listening Tasks: We teach listening by building up comprehension from general understanding to identifying specific information. We can also grade the listening tasks from easy to more difficult by the form of questions we use and it can be evaluated based on the kind of out put by the learners in the form of writing or speaking.

Grammar Exercises – Reading, Writing, Comprehension

The goal of these exercises is to build the knowledge of how the words fit together to make sense. Some of the exercises may be translations; others can be designed to teach the learner to think in English by asking them to change a phrase in a specific way. This feature requires to type responses within the exercises, providing a practical and effective form of writing instruction.

Reading Comprehensions can be given in the form of stories, case lets, cases, descriptions and narrations. The learners can be encouraged by allowing them to follow the different methods of reading such as, skimming and scanning. They can be followed by activities in groups through exercises on word meanings, vocabulary, fill in the missing information, writing summary / gist. Note taking, thought provoking questions for group discussions, brainstorming sessions etc.

Writing Exercises: Writing can be practised through typing on gap fill exercises and model format for E-mail, letter, memo, reports and resume. They can also prepare the paper for presentations. These can be observed and edited by the instructor through the Teacher's Console.

Written Assistance: The teacher can send messages to guide learners with their work and learner can reply. The teacher can also initiate a text chat session with single & multiple learners. In this feed back can be given on the spot.

Track Learning Progress through Language Learning Software

Language learning software provides teachers with a number of methods for evaluating students' performance and tracking their progress. By using writing, listening, recorded and Web-based activities to stimulate learners to make use of their growing oral and written language skills, store results for comparison over time, so the teacher/ learner can measure progress.

Exam module under the Teacher's Console provides a complete interactive and automatic quiz module. They can contain text, graphics, audio, video in the quiz. This allows teacher to use virtually any media available to create tests and evaluate the learners. Ex. Question types may include multiple choices, true/false, fill in the blanks and essay. Speaking can also be evaluated through digital recorder module. Students' working on assignments or conversations in groups can be evaluated. Their audio recordings can be scored in and saved for evaluations.

Reports and statistics for tests are immediately available at the end of the each session, giving the important details of the class, individual student and individual question in tabular, graphical representation or pie diagram model.

Appearance and Configuration

The 'traditional' system generally comprises a master console (teacher position) which is electrically connected to a number of rows of student booths (US: carrels), typically containing a student tape recorder and headset with a boom arm microphone. The teacher console is usually fitted with master playback source equipment (tape recorder), some means of monitoring of each booth in the class via the teacher headset and an intercom facility offering 2-way communication between teacher and student.

All but the most simple or first generation laboratories allow the teacher to remotely control the tape transport controls of the student booths (record, stop, rewind etc.) from the master desk. This allows for easy distribution of the master programme material, which is often copied at high speed onto the student positions for later use by the students at their own pace.

Better tape laboratories housed the tape machine behind a protective plate (leaving only a control panel accessible to the students) or locked the cassette door. This kept the expensive and sensitive decks free from student misuse and dust etc.

Operation

Once the master programme had been transferred onto the student recorders, the teacher would then hand over control of the decks to the students. By pressing the record key in the booth, the student would simultaneously hear the playback of the programme whilst being able to record his or her voice in the pauses, using the microphone. This is known as an audio active-comparative system. From a technological point of view, this overdubbing was made possible by use of a two-channel tape recorder.

Problems

Language laboratories in the 1970s and 1980s received a bad reputation due to breakdowns. Common problems stem from the limitations and relative complexity of the reel to reel tape system in use at that time. Design played a part too; the simplest language laboratories had no electronic systems in place for the teacher to remotely control the tape decks, relying on the students to operate the decks correctly. Many had no way to stop the tape running off the reel in fast rewind or forward wind, which meant time wasting and greater chances of failure through misuse.

The tape recorders in use after the early 1970s in the language laboratory were more complex than those in the home, being capable of multitracking and electronic remote control. As a result, they often had several motors and relays, complex transistorised circuitry and needed a variety of voltages to run. They had lots of rubber parts such as idlers and drive belts which would perish and wear out. Bulbs in the control panels were also in continual need of replacement. Since the student booth tapes were not normally changed from one class to the next but were recorded over each time, these would eventually wear, and shed their oxide on the tape heads leading to poor sound and tangling.

The installations were usually maintained under contract by service engineers, but these often served a county or similar wide area, and would only call at 3-monthly intervals. This meant that if several booths malfunctioned, then for much of that time the laboratory was out of action.

Functionality of the Lab

The levels of functionality of current language labs vary from manufacturer to manufacturer. All labs will have a level of teacher control to manage student licenses / desktops. The more sophisticated 'software only' labs have a higher level of teacher management and control over the student desktop.

One of the key differences with the 'high end' 'software only' products is their ability to work 'live' with the students as they record and work with media. So instead of waiting to correct student recordings after they have been recorded and collected back it is now possible for a teacher to work synchronously and 'live' with students on their own, in pairs and in groups, thus enhancing the immediacy of the teaching and learning experience.

The next generation digital language labs allow teachers to monitor, control, deliver, group, display, review and collect, audio, video and web based multimedia content. The student player is linked to the teacher console and can play audio, video and web based formats.

Students can rewind, stop, start, go back to last silence, record, fast forward, repeat phrase and bookmark.

Digital Language Lab

The principle of a language lab essentially has not changed. It's still a teacher control connected to a number of student booths, containing a student control and headset with a microphone. Digital language labs have the same principle. A software only language lab changes the concept of where and what a language lab is. Software can be installed & accessed on any networked PC anywhere on a school, college or university campus. Software only systems can be located in one room, from room to room or campus to campus.

Change of Media

The demise of the traditional language laboratory came in the 1980s, with the falling out of favour of the audiolingual method commonly in place in 1960s teaching methodology, and the expensive repairs needed to the open reel tape machines due to student misuse, neglect, or wear and tear. Many schools transformed their old language labs into computer suites. However, the advent of affordable multimedia capable PCs in the late 1990s led to a resurgence and transformation of the language laboratory with software and hard drives in place of reels of analogue tape. In the 1990s new digital, hybrid PC based systems allowed extended functionality, in terms of better "management' of student / teacher audio with some levels of internet and video formats.

Media is 'managed' on these hybrid systems by language lab providers creating a supplementary network over and above the existing PC network for audio connections and communications in fixed locations. These hybrid systems are not without problems, mainly associated with hardware issues as the manufacturers of these hybrid systems have to replace parts and separate cabling. This both adds to the complexity of the product and has a cost implication via manufacturer annual 'service' fees.

Present Day Situation (2011)

Today all the major manufacturers say they have a 'digital' or a 'just software' solution. However in many cases they still rely on proprietary networks or expensive sound cards to successfully deliver their media. There are very few truly software only solutions that just rely on installing designated language lab software onto a network and then directing just the original network to manage the media between teacher and student, student and student or student back to teacher. In the past the quality of school, or university networks may have meant that the speed that the media could be delivered on 'software only' labs would have meant a 'lag' in the audio feed. These days all professionally run networks are able to work with these 'software only' language lab solutions and deliver media synchronously.

Software only systems can be easily installed onto an existing PC based network, making them both multi locational in their access and much more feature rich in how and what media they manage.

The content that is now used in the new language labs is much richer and self authored or free: now not just audio, but video, flash based games, internet etc. and the speed and variety of the delivery of media from teacher to student, student to teacher, is much quicker and therefore much more engaging for both teacher and student.

Conclusion

There is always scope for improvement and advancement in any field and for any subject. It has to be accomplished with commitment and enthusiasm. We are habituated to the traditional teaching methods. It is high time that our teaching methods have to undergo a change. Unless the new technology is adopted in English language teaching, we can not impart language skills in our learners at the rate of growing competition. According to my view, these are a few of the whole lot of techniques those can be used to improve language skills through technology in the present generation. It can be implemented for a learner of any age at any stage. It will be more effective if technology is introduced from the elementary level. According to my view comprehensive language learning (language along with skills) is possible through both classroom and language lab teaching, as applied for science subjects.

9

Role of Computers in English Language Teaching

Computers have made a triumphal entry into education in the past decade, and only a dyed-in-the wool Luddite would deny that they have brought significant benefits to teachers and students alike. However, an uncritical use of computers can be just as disadvantageous to students as a refusal to have anything to do with them. In this article I discuss some of the ways that computers can be used in English language teaching, with a view to helping colleagues make the most of the opportunities they offer to ESL students.

It is helpful to think of the computer as having the following main roles in the language classroom:

- teacher — the computer teaches students new language
- tester — the computer tests students on language already learned
- tool — the computer assists students to do certain tasks

- data source — the computer provides students with the information they need to perform a particular task
- communication facilitator — the computer allows students to communicate with others in different locations

Computer as Teacher: In the early days of computers and programmed learning, some students sat at a terminal for extended periods following an individualised learning programme. Although we have come a long way from the rather naïve thought, held by some at that time, that the computer could eventually come to replace the teacher, there has been a return to a much more sophisticated kind of computerised teaching using multimedia CD ROMS. In such programmes, students can listen to dialogues or watch video clips. They can click on pictures to call up the names of the objects they see. They can speak into the microphone and immediately hear a recording of what they have said. The programme can keep a record of their progress, e.g. the vocabulary learned, and offer remedial help if necessary. Many of these CD ROM programmes are offered as complete language courses. They require students to spend hours on their own in front of the computer screen, usually attached to a microphone headset. For this reason alone I prefer not to use them in my language teaching. Another of their serious drawbacks, in my view, is the fact that in many cases the course content and sequence is fixed. The teacher has no chance to include materials that are of interest and importance to the particular students in his or her class.

As an alternative to large CD ROM packages, there is an increasing number of useful sites on the World Wide Web, where students can get instruction and practice in language skills such as reading, listening and writing. Some examples.

Computer as a Tester: The computer is very good at what is known as *drill and practice*; it will tirelessly present the learner with questions and announce if the answer is right or wrong. In its primitive manifestations in this particular role in language teaching, it has been rightly criticised. The main reason for the criticism is simple: many early drill and practice programmes were very unsophisticated; either multiple-choice or demanding a single word answer. They were not programmed to accept varying input and the only feedback they gave was *Right* or *Wrong*. So for example, if the computer expected the answer "*does not*" and the student typed "*doesn't*" or " *doesnot*" or " *does not* ", she would have been told she was wrong without any further comment. It is not surprising that such programmes gave computers a bad name with many language teachers. Unfortunately, there are now very many of these primitive *drill and kill* programmes flooding the Internet.

Despite their obvious disadvantages, such programmes are nevertheless popular with many students. This is probably because the student is in full control, the computer is extremely patient and gives private, unthreatening feedback. Most programmes also keep the score and have cute animations and sounds, which many students like. There are some programmes which do offer more useful feedback than right or wrong, or that can accept varying input. Such programmes blur the role of the computer as teacher or tester and can be recommended to students who enjoy learning grammar or vocabulary in this way. If two or more students sit at the same computer, then they can generate a fair amount of authentic communication while discussing the answers together.

Computer as a Tool: It is in this area that I think the computer has been an unequivocal success in language teaching. Spreadsheets, databases, presentation slide generators, concordancers and web page producers all have their place in the language classroom, particularly in one where the main curricular focus is task-based or project-work. But in my opinion, by far the most important role of the computer in the language classroom is its use as a writing tool. It has played a significant part in the introduction of the writing process, by allowing students easily to produce multiple drafts of the same piece of work.. Students with messy handwriting can now do a piece of work to be proud of, and those with poor spelling skills can, after sufficient training in using the spell check, produce a piece of writing largely free of spelling mistakes.

Computer as a Data Source: I'm sure I don't need to say much about the Internet as a provider of information. Anyone who has done a search on the World Wide Web will know that there is already more information out there than an individual could process in hundred lifetimes, and the amount is growing by the second. This huge source of information is an indispensable resource for much project work, but there are serious negative implications. I shudder to think of how much time has been wasted and will continue to be wasted by students who aimlessly wander the Web with no particular aim in mind and with little or no guidance. I generally do not turn my students free to search the web for information. Instead, I find a few useful sites beforehand and tell the students to start there; anyone who finishes the task in hand can then be let loose! As an alternative to the Web, there are very many CD ROMs, e.g. encyclopaedias, that present information in a more compact, reliable and easily accessible form.

Computer as Communication Facilitator: The Internet is the principal medium by which students can communicate with others at a distance, (e.g. by *e*-mail or by participating in discussion forums). In fact at Frankfurt International School the single most popular use of computers by students in their free time is to write *e*-mails to their friends. Some teachers have set up joint projects with a school in another location and others encourage students to take part in discussion groups. There is no doubt that such activities are motivating for students and allow them to participate in many authentic language tasks. However, cautious teachers may wish to closely supervise their students' messages. Recent research has shown up the extremely primitive quality of much of the language used in electronic exchanges!

Development of English Language Teaching

English Language Teaching (ELT) has been with us for many years and its significance continues to grow, fuelled, partially at least, by the Internet. Graddol's study (2000) suggests that in the year 2000 there were about a billion English learners - but a decade later, the numbers will have doubled. The forecast points to a surge in English learning, which could peak in 2010. The same study indicates that over 80% of information stored on the Internet is in English. For the first time in history there are more non-native than native users of the language and diversity of context in terms of learners' age, nationality, learning background etcetera has become a defining characteristic of ELT today. What are the implications of this? (Jarvis, forthcoming).

Technological innovations have gone hand-in-hand with the growth of English and are changing the way in which we communicate, work, trade, entertain and learn and it is non-native users of English, frequently from Asian countries, who are arguably, at the heart of this. It is fair to assert that the growth of the Internet has facilitated the growth of the English language and that this has occurred at a time when computers are no longer the exclusive domain of the dedicated few, but rather widely available to many. Warchauer (2002) has discussed this change in terms of conflicts between local identities and the globalisation of the English language; whilst Jarvis and Atsilarat (2004), in this journal, have suggested that the Internet may be a contributory factor in shifting away from a communicative towards a context-based approach to language teaching pedagogy.

The notion of widespread availability requires some qualification as there are clearly important issues of a 'digital divide' and 'electronic literacy'. This issue is frequently presented as being between nations and it is clearly the case that the most powerful economies dominate Internet activity; but such a perspective explains unequal power relations purely from the influence of external factors and the picture is surely more complex than this. The same type of economic power relations also exist within nations, and divisions of social classes within are equally important here. In short, it is the middle and upper classes in virtually every country who have much greater access to computers and, significantly for this paper, it is the Asian countries which are experiencing massive growth as their economies develop and change.

Change of this magnitude clearly raises a number of issues for ELT and, it is argued, necessitates a revision of traditional definitions of what constitutes the English language as well as a move away from the established EFL\ESL classifications and towards a less culturally loaded view of English as a global or international language (EIL/EIL). This in turn has implications for language pedagogy and approaches to syllabus design.

Computers in English Language Teaching

To fully understand the impact that computers are currently having on ELT it is firstly necessary to step back and consider their how their role has developed.

Pre-internet Era

In pre-Internet days computers in ELT could be viewed from one of two perspectives. Firstly, computer assisted language learning (CALL) developed and concerned itself with the pedagogical applications of the technology. Students used the computer to develop and practise their English. CALL is, of course, still with us today but in pre-Internet times rather limited text-based provisions were something of a novelty for both students and enthusiastic practitioners; this novelty factor has, of course, long since gone for many who use computers as part of their day-to-day life. A second perspective was in the use of computers for assisting and understanding of what constitutes the English language and how it works. Corpus linguistics and the arrival of lexis as an item to be included within the syllabus began in the 1980s with Sinclair (1987) and others, and work of this type continues today.

This statistical analysis of language, initially analysis of written language, but more recently spoken language, has allowed us to examine the frequency of words and this has informed the profession from several perspectives. It has given us insights into the most useful vocabulary to teach and facilitated the emergence of the lexical syllabus. It has also allowed us to look at form-based words and this has given us insights into the grammar that we teach. One positive outcome from all this has been the arrival of a range of publications for teachers and students - such material can now be based on how the language is actually used rather than what the traditional grammar book prescribes. The work of Biber et al. (1999) is particularly useful; they found, for example that the modal verb 'may' is hardly ever used in spoken language for permission! For students, resource publications such as McCarthy and O'Dell (1994) provide good practice of such real language.

We can see that computers have had a role in pedagogical practice and in analysing language - both these aspects have further developed with the arrival of the Internet but the point here is that in pre-Internet days the role of the computer did not fundamentally influence the language itself and it is only with the arrival of the Internet (and related technologies such as text-massaging on mobile phones) that computers began to significantly change language.

Internet and a Changing Language

The Internet (of which CMC forms a major aspect) is changing the language partly because it gives rise to new vocabulary, but more importantly because the medium and its users drive the language in certain directions (Crystal, 2001). The following verbs are just one illustration of the influences on vocabulary, they all either meant different things, or did not exist, only a few year ago; to ... *e*-mail, text, boot, chat, surf, bookmark, e-shop, google, etcetera. More fundamentally, the Internet is changing language, a 'Netspeak' and a 'Netiquette' is emerging, the former refers to a language variant, the latter to the conventions which surround its use. This changing language is rapidly evolving and does not have a long history to inform syllabus designers and ELT practitioners. E-mails do not have, and arguably do not need, to follow punctuation conventions. Typos and spelling mistakes are also, depending on context, more acceptable with this medium.

To what extent should we allow this to influence the language content of *e*-mails in our teaching? Furthermore, synchronous *e*-mails, those in real time chat forums (e.g. MSN), are a kind of unique text version of spoken English and the language generated from this, along with text massaging on mobile phones, is at times completely different to anything else that we have hitherto known. I had the fortune, or perhaps misfortune, of picking up my daughter's mobile the other day and I read some of the messages which seem to occupy so much of her time. That the content of these messages were of little substance came as no surprise, but the ways in which English was being used was revealing. As my daughter explained these incomprehensible texts and smileys to me (e.g. "c u l8r m8" for "see you later mate" and o-:) for the user being an angel), I felt as though I needed to go back to a foreign language classroom again. Except of course on this occasion it wasn't a foreign language, it was a variety of English, a 'Netspeak', from which I had previously been excluded. On a different occasion I was chatting to a Thai colleague on MSN and "555" was typed to mean "ha ha ha" (laughter) - the word five translates as "ha" in Thai!

The Internet, as these simple examples show, is clearly impacting upon the ways in which we use language and what constitutes language. And this rapid and largely uncharted evolution of language is surely set to continue unabated - like it or loathe it we all, especially as language teachers, have to come to terms with it. Should we include Netspeak and Netiquette in our classroom practice? Can we avoid not including it? (Jarvis, forthcoming).

Within a traditional approach to syllabus design we arguably need to plot these new items of language and include them in our programmes, but as we will see later, I shall argue here this in a sense futile and it will be more useful to specify a series of tasks for our learners and allow them to generate whatever appropriate language is required in order to successfully complete such tasks. But before we come to these implications for pedagogical practice, let us firstly explore the potential impact of change on our well-established notions of EFL and ESL.

Implications

From EFL/ESL to EIL/GL: A few years ago the long-established UK-based newspaper of the profession the EFL Gazette changed its name to the EL Gazette. In due course I would fully expect this journal to follow suit and drop the F in EFL! Why is this and in what ways might the Internet be contributing to such changes? To answer this question it would be helpful to firstly clarify what is meant by EFL and ESL. Jarvis (forthcoming) notes that, "These terms are used to describe learners and users whose native language is not English. It is a foreign language if used by non-native speakers in a non-native English-speaking country which has not adopted it as the "official" language of that country." By official I refer here to the language of government and commerce. Asian countries here would include Japan, Korea, Thailand, China and many more. Jarvis continues, "It is also a foreign language when used by a non-native speaker who is a temporary visitor to a native English-speaking country." Asian students studying in the UK, Australia or the USA would fall into this category. "It is a second language if used by a non-native speaker who migrates to a native English-speaking country." The Chinese community who have settled in the UK, Australia or the USA would be an example of this group. "It is also a second language if used by a non-native speaker where it has been adopted as the official language in their country." In Asia, Indian or Pakistani users of English would fall into such a category.

These definitions have been with the language teaching profession for half a century. However, they carry with them connotations that the language does not actually belong to the users; it is foreign (alien), or it is second (not first) - this despite the fact that today these users are now a majority. A case can be made (Phillipson, 1992) that these connotations are contributory factors in the manifestation of a linguistic imperialism. Certainly there is an implied uneven power relationship which centres on ownership. Furthermore, and of critical importance for the arguments presented here, these definitions tend to be based around the notion of learners and users in physical spaces, a notion which is very much undermined by the virtual world of the Internet. The work of Crystal (2003), McKay (2002), Burns and Coffin (2001) and others, echo a view that today it is more useful to think in terms of English as an international or global language. This new majority being non-native users has, as we have seen, been considerably facilitated by the Internet, and, it is argued, the English language today belongs just as much to this new majority as it does to the now minority native users. (Jarvis, forthcoming).

It is in this sense that it is not a foreign or second language because it is their language too - it "belongs" to all users. Every minute, hour, day, week, month and year there are millions of users of English across the Asian region and beyond; more often than not the medium for such users is the Internet. When somebody from Korea, China, or Thailand communicates with A.N. Other from Japan, Malaysia or Indonesia they are likely to do so in English and they are likely to do so primarily via the Internet.

These people may well meet in person but a great deal of any communication is computer-mediated and they will use a variety of language appropriate to the medium. Given this situation, our challenge, it seems to me, is to promote a pedagogy which reflects what users are actually doing with language, rather than prescribing items to be taught. I would echo Phan Le Ha's (2005) call in this journal for a pedagogy "... in which the teaching and learning of EIL should involve valuing and nurturing the expression of other cultural voices in English... and helping learners to construct identities as owners, users, meaning makers and authorised users...". I would suggest a task-based approach is the most appropriate framework from which to address such challenges and it is to this which we now turn.

Towards a Task-based Approach

Typically, a traditional ELT syllabus lists learning items in terms of structures, functions, notions and vocabulary which are then set in situations and which usually integrate a variety of skills (reading, writing, listening and speaking). This dominant approach has been characterised as product-orientated because it focuses on what is to be learnt or on products (White, 1988). The problem with this approach, as Nunan (1988) has pointed out, is that input cannot be equated with output and that teaching cannot be equated with learning. In short, what the teacher teaches is not what the learner learns. It is a problem which is compounded within our proposed EIL framework.

Nunn (2005) has argued that linguistic, communicative and other kinds of competences have not been adequately addressed in relation to EIL and goes on to argue that "... international communication seems to require the ability to adjust to almost infinitely diverse intercultural communication situations" (pp. 61-62). An alternative approach can be characterised as process-orientated because it focuses not on items to be taught and learned, but on what the learner does with the language.

A task-based approach is very much process-orientated because it focuses on "learning through doing" i.e. on tasks. Tasks mean different things to different people and the work of Ellis (2003) has been particularly helpful in documenting and discussing these issues. For our purposes it is useful to distinguish between pedagogic and authentic tasks. In the case of the former, students are asked to do things which are unlikely to occur outside the classroom, information gap activities or ordering scrambled sentences are examples of these.

With authentic tasks students are asked to complete activities which are likely to be carried out in real life once the student has left the classroom. Working with a map to ask a classmate for directions, or listening for a departure time and gate number for a specific flight, would be examples of this. The example discussed below can be viewed as authentic, given certain assumptions about the learners. But let us firstly address a reservation by some to adopting a task-based approach.

A primary objection to task-based approaches is that they are considered unworkable and removed from everyday teaching and learning contexts. It is an argument which I have never really accepted because the approach can be implemented at various levels - it is really about encouraging learners to do useful, interesting and meaningful activities with language and this can be applied in a range of contexts. Indeed, the various levels at which task-based approaches can be delivered (even within a traditional structural syllabus) and a variety of case studies exploring how to do so is discussed in an excellent edited publication by Breen and Littlejohn (2000). This work goes a considerable way to addressing these objections. However, once computers are introduced into the ELT curriculum, and our discussion to date touches upon the case for doing so, then task-based approaches become arguably the only way to effectively take into account the changes in language that we have identified and to shift to an EIL/EGL perspective.

We have already noted the issue of the digital divide and I am addressing the discussion here at those practitioners who, along with their students, have regular access to networked computers in their teaching context. It would be undesirable and arguably quite impossible to list the variety of language generated by CMC and/or posted on web pages. It is, as we have noted, rapidly changing, subject to trend and fashion and varies in different contexts.

This makes product-based approaches virtually impossible; in contrast, as we will see, task-based approaches represent a perfect match! It is very easy to devise simple, achievable tasks which encourage students to use *e*-mail to communicate with each other, their tutors and the wider world; likewise it is not difficult to find useful meaningful ways in which students access and even post-information on the web. The needs of the learners and the contexts in which they work will ultimately determine the most appropriate tasks.

Jarvis (2004, 2003, 2001) for example provides extensive accounts of how such ideas can be realised with English for Academic Purposes students. Similar ideas can be utilised with general English students, they might for example be asked to prepare a travel itinerary for a visitor to their country, province or city. This could involve accessing websites to note and decide upon the best places to visit, using the web and *e*-mail to arrange flight bookings to and from the city, negotiating amongst themselves (via *e*-mail) on the best options etcetera. There must be literally hundreds of task-based activities of this type across the globe which involve students using computers to access information and to communicate with others.

The task is specified and students generate appropriate language, with help as required. Success is measured by the extent to which the task is successfully completed and the language is viewed as the tool to achieve the ends; it is not prescribed. The learners are viewed as working with tools which belong to them as much as to anyone else.

Conclusion

Several key threads emerge from our discussions. Computers are, on the one hand, impacting on the way in which we define our subject matter (EFL/ESL vs. EIL/EGL) and, on the other hand, are also impacting upon the English language, upon the subject matter itself. This new age would seem to go hand in hand with task-based approaches and represents challenges for everyone involved in ELT. For practitioners, applied linguists and educators there is a changed dynamic in which computers have now become much more than a tool or a tutor for developing language skills. This traditional distinction (Levy, 1997) would no longer seem adequate. Warschauer and Healey (1998) have observed that it is now less a question of the role of computers in the language classroom and more a question of the role of the language classroom in an information technology society.

Language teaching education is clearly entering a new and largely uncharted phase and we would seem to be at a crossroads. Warchauer and Kern (2000) have identified this as a "sociocognitive phase" where, unlike in previous phases, students interact with each other and the world via the computer. A great deal of work has focused on the value of computers in learning or second language acquisition but rather less, beyond resource publications (Dudeney, 2000; Sperling, 1998; Teeler, 2000; Windeatt et. al. 2000), on the implications of the content of teaching itself, i.e. the syllabus. Even less consideration seems to have been given to how we see, define or classify our learners.

A task-based syllabus offers a way forward and practitioners will need to reflect upon what is achievable within their own contexts. In addressing these challenges we will clearly need to develop a sense in which English belongs to the students and their fellow countrymen and women just as much as anyone else and to do this we will need to avoid classifying the vast majority of users as "foreign" or "second" language learners. ELT would seem to be at a crossroads and it is heartening to see that much of the momentum for change is coming from, and driven by, practitioners and students from the Asian nations and from journals such as this one. We live in interesting times and colleagues are invited to contact me if they are interested in setting up joint-research projects to investigate and further explore such issues.

10 English Language Teaching in India

India with a population of around one billion people is often regarded as a model of harmonious linguistic co-existence within a single state. It has two official languages, Hindi and English, other than 18 major languages scheduled in the Indian Constitution Art. 418 'listed' languages each spoken by 10,000 people or more. Today in the official domain there is a strict hierarchy of Indian languages and at the top are Hindi and English. English was used in India and elsewhere in the colonies as a tool of power to cultivate a group of people who identify with the cultural and other norms of the political elite. European values were considered inherently better whereas the indigenous culture was often considered barbaric. English was considered as 'a road to the light,' a tool of civilization. In India, English gradually acquired, socially and administratively, the most dominant roles. By the 1920s English had become the language of political discourse, intranational administration and law. Even after the colonial period ended English maintained its power over local languages. Ultimately the legal system, the national media and important professions were conducted in English.

English has been progressively gaining ground over the years. Regarded as a 'neutral' language for wider communication and the language of technology, modernity and development English is also a social status symbol. Parents see English medium schools as a way of pushing their children up the social scale. It is however ironical that even though English enjoys a high status in the wake of globalisation, its teaching and learning in the educational institutes is rather inadequate and unproductive. Current methods of treating the learning of English in the classroom however 'communicatively' they may be oriented are no longer sustainable.

Children need to be given the opportunity to acquire English through play activities at kindergarten age. Only in this way will they develop the kind of native speaker competence that they are going to need in the modern world to deal with the extensive range of varieties and styles of spoken and written English that they will be called upon to handle.

An Overview

Traditionally, English was taught by the grammar translation method. In the late 1950s, structurally graded syllabi were introduced as a major innovation into the state systems for teaching English (Prabhu 1987: 10). The idea was that the teaching of language could be systematised by planning its inputs, just as the teaching of a subject such as arithmetic or physics could be. (The structural approach was sometimes implemented as the direct method, with an insistence on monolingual English classrooms.) By the late 1970s, however, the behavioural-psychological and philosophical foundations of the structural method had yielded to the cognitive claims of Chomsky for language as a "mental organ". There was also dissatisfaction within the English teaching profession with the structural method, which was seen as not giving the learners language that was "deployable" or usable in real situations, in spite of an ability to make correct sentences in classroom situations. In hindsight, the structural approach as practised in the classroom led to a fragmentation and trivialisation of thought by breaking up language in two ways: into structures, and into skills. The form-focused teaching of language aggravated the gap between the learner's "linguistic age" and "mental age" to the point where the mind could no longer be engaged.

The emphasis thus shifted to teaching language use in meaningful contexts. British linguists argued that something more than grammatical competence was involved in language use; the term "communicative competence" was introduced to signify this extra dimension. The attempt to achieve communicative competence assumes the availability of a grammatical competence to build on, and indeed the communicative method succeeds best in the first category of school described above, introducing variety and learner involvement into classrooms where teachers (and learners) have confidence in their knowledge of the language, acquired through exposure. However, for the majority of our learners, the issue is not so much communicative competence as the acquisition of a basic or fundamental competence in the language (Prabhu 1987: 13). Input-rich theoretical methodologies (such as the Whole Language, the task-based, and the comprehensible input and balanced approaches) aim at exposure to the language in meaning-focused situations so as to trigger the formation of a language system by the mind.

Variety and Range of English Teaching in India

The teaching and learning of English today is characterised by, on the one hand, a diversity of schools and linguistic environments supportive of English acquisition, and, on the other hand, by systemically pervasive classroom procedures of teaching a textbook for success in an examination, modulated by teacher beliefs influenced to varying degrees by inputs from the English-language teaching profession.

Situation Needs

General Aspects

ELT in India is vibrant and dynamic today. The context of the whole teaching paradigm has changed totally. Due to its association with the British coloniser, English started life in India as not just a foreign language, but as a much-hated language. From the despised instrument of oppression to the reluctantly adopted lingua franca to the status symbol of the upper classes to its position today as a second language, English has come a long way. In fact, it would not be an aberration to label it a first language for some echelons of Indian society. Just as the status of the language underwent constant reinvention, the whole ELT paradigm also travelled the complete gamut of modification. In the closing years of the Twentieth century when English began to emerge as the global language, the Indian classroom was transformed because of the change in the environment of the learner. Whereas the earlier surroundings had been acquisition poor with regard to English, suddenly every language user seemed to be jumping upon the learn- English- bandwagon.

The liberalisation of the Indian economy ushered in all kinds of reasons to learn the language. While earlier in the century students who had specialised in English joined either teaching or the civil services, now a whole new spectrum of job opportunities has opened up. There are now call centres that need trainers to equip their employees with communication skills, there are multinationals who have been recruiting marketing staff who needed to be taught spoken English, there are medical transcription centres which need efficient translators and reporters. Those desirous of immigration to the west needed professional help for clearing tests like the IELTS. Hence, the avenues where ELT came to be required in India are unlimited today.

The change was first observed at the social, political and economic levels. Suddenly, English ceased to be the badge of status for the upper crust. Earlier, only the upper classes and a few limited size groups were seen using English in everyday life. The middle class reserved it for official purposes or those social occasions where they wished to leave an impression. The lower classes thought the use of English was beyond them and since the government schools of India made no effort to teach any kind of spoken English, this category of people had no exposure to it. However, around the year 1995, the whole paradigm began to change. The liberalisation of the economy led to the advent of multinationals resulting in many developments like varied job opportunities that demanded a command of English, more English channels on the television, an increasing number of English publications and international lifestyles becoming a tempting option.

Fluctuating and Varied Institutional Developments

The developments that have taken place in ELT methodology in the West took some time to reach Indian classrooms. The evolution of ELT in India, as in any other EFL country is linked with factors that are not pedagogic alone. Today, English can not be termed a foreign language in the Indian context, but in times past, it was a foreign language and its teaching had to take cognisance of all factors, pedagogic or otherwise. The growth of ELT given here are different because ELT pedagogy developed primarily in the West where political and social realities were different and the status of English was fixed whereas, in India, ELT pedagogy depends upon the subtle and not-so-subtle ways in which the status of English keeps changing. No diagrammatic representation can be complete without taking into account the fluid nature of the position of English in Indian society.

The author's representation of the development of ELT as a discipline in countries where English is the first language and the development of ELT in India, it is obvious from developments in ELT take time to take root in India. The causes behind this gap are three:

- Only around the year 1980 did English achieve adequate attention from policy-makers, administrators and teachers. Due to its chequered history in the country, its complete importance was realised more than three decades after independence.
- Apart from a One-year course in teacher training for school teachers, no formal teacher training is given to new recruits or practising teachers. There are orientation courses and refresher courses for teachers in general, but no course deals with ELT. It is only recently that the British Council has introduced CELTA and other such programmes; these are quite expensive, teachers do not want to spend money on them and their institutions rarely sponsor them.
- The examination system is more achievement oriented rather than performance oriented, leading to an emphasis on grades and positions rather than issues of fluency or proficiency. Indirectly, the teacher remains in many classrooms even today, the facilitator of examinations rather than of linguistic or communicative proficiency.

In spite of the slower rate of evolution, English Language Teaching in India has been widening in its approach and methods. The result is that there is an increasing tendency, scope and intent of reaching the end of the ELT cone. At its own eccentric pace, ELT in India is today in step with the rest of the world today. Where the issue of methodology is concerned, ELT seems to be in three transient stages according to the different levels of the paradigm and its demands:

- The first level is that of the institutions run by the government, mainly primary, secondary and high schools. Since the primary goal of these institutions is to provide education at affordable and subsidised levels to the public, ELT teaching can not be placed at the widest end of the cone for the basic reason that the teachers there do not have much access to latest research and materials for reasons economic as well as geographic. Most of these institutions are the sole providers of education in rural and remote settings where they can fulfil adequately the basic requirements alone. In the urban locales the planning bodies are now moving towards up gradation through teacher training, syllabus modification and improved resources. In another decade or so, this level of ELT should be more communicative in nature with language and literature fully integrated.
- At the second level are those institutions that are semi-government or are run by private managing bodies, assisted through government funds. These also include undergraduate colleges and post-graduate universities. Growth and development can be seen here in spurts. In some classrooms, teachers have reached the widest end of the cone, are aware of learner needs and adjust methodology accordingly and use a judicious blend of interaction and communication in the class. In others, an observer feels caught in a time warp with pure talk-chalk lectures that are mostly teacher-centred. The positive observation is that there are practising teachers between these two poles, who are trying to change their teaching practice and are looking at alternate methodology. Just as there is a mixed bag of teaching practice, the institutions also range from indifferent to proactive. While there are places where even a small audio player is not accessible, there are administrators who have invested heavily in state of the art, perfectly equipped language laboratories.
- The third level comprises pure private sector academies that undertake to make learners proficient English users within a stipulated period, of course by charging a fixed amount of fee. Since time means money for them, they are equipped with the latest materials like interactive, multimedia software. Jobs in the academic area are few and far between, so an increasing

number of qualified teachers find their way to these places. The teacher profile gets younger and younger, resulting in increasing amounts of innovation and experimentation where methodology is concerned.

While teachers belonging to the first level are content to remain followers, the second level is being influenced by the third. When learners are in a rush as they need part-time employment or have an IELTS to clear, they often join academies in addition to their undergraduate classes. This creates a ripple effect and the ripples can be felt in three ways:

- Young teachers who work in undergraduate colleges work part-time at these academies. At the academy, they use the latest teaching aids and materials since the purpose is to achieve fluency at the earliest. At their regular place of work, their teaching methodology undergoes a transformation because they tend to use the interactive, task-based and communicative methods more than the usual lecture methods used there normally.
- On taking into account the roaring business the academies are doing, the administrative bodies of undergraduate colleges are coming to realise that a whole untapped market needs to be explored. Along with their regular degree classes, they are gearing up to introduce revenue-earning courses in the field of English proficiency, open to the public. This leads to a spill over effect in the undergraduate classes too as some teachers would be common to both courses and the same campus sees a lot of innovative teaching.
- Parents of learners form an important component of the teaching paradigm in India. Earlier, any kind of change in courseware or teaching methodology would result in stiff opposition from them and the administrative body would recommend the continuation of age-old practices. Observing the winds of change resulting from the acceptance of the global status of English, parents today encourage innovation and experimentation in the classroom.

After attending interactive classes at the academy, learners search such stimulation in their regular classes too. This is a radical change, especially if one looks into the past. When communicative language teaching was introduced in India in the 1980s, it was a dismal failure for the first few years because of the lack of the right context. This context stands established in India today, so learners are receptive and are actively encouraging more learner-centred classes.

The context of the whole teaching situation started changing around the year 2000. Socioeconomic factors played a major role in this change that is dynamic even today. The liberalisation of the Indian economy led to the entry of many international brands into the learners' mindset. Call centres, shopping malls and trade fairs, all need young personnel, fluent in English. There is a mushroom growth of institutes and academies of the third category above, offering the whole range of proficiency in English from clearing the IELTS to speaking fluently. The Internet has played a major role in creating a resource-rich environment by giving a wide range of exposure to English. Becoming web-savvy has emerged as the need of the day and this is possible only through English. These are just a few of the factors that have created a panacea for the deadlock that CLT had found itself in.

Today, in India, a whole new generation is coming up; a generation that travels a lot in countries where English is a first language, works in places where English is the lingua franca and as a result, carries home to other generations the same English as a medium of communication. Hence, the empowerment that Bax 2 looks forward to for teachers in times to come has come sooner due to changes in the context of the complete teaching paradigm. Unless the context is supportive of upgrading English performance of the teacher -which should be inclusive of communicative competence- no teacher training or upgrading of methodology can be productive and fruitful. This is a significant conclusion that can be drawn from the Indian situation.

The results of all the changes listed above stand reflected in the classrooms where CLT is still practised. The whole process of curriculum change is riddled with cumbersome and time-consuming procedures in India, so in spite of the limited success of CLT, it has not been removed from courses. This, in the long run, has been for the better because while on the one hand, the teachers have been able to familiarise themselves with its approach and methodology; on the other hand, the changed and changing context has encouraged its growing success today. Since learners are a part of the whole context, they are aware of the growing need for proficiency, both linguistic and communicative, in English. Today, more and more students take up part-time work (that requires fluency in English) along with their studies, this was earlier an aberration, now is the norm.

The Road Ahead

ELT in India has come a long way from year 1880 when only 60% primary schools used English as the medium for teaching. Up to 1940, the grammar-translation method flourished and the spread of English remained confined to education and office circles, yet again in a haphazard manner. By 1970, structural linguistics started making its presence felt in Indian classrooms in the shape of drills and exercises. Around this time, all professional courses began to be taught in English, which had also become established as a library language and a subject for independent study. As compared to its establishment as an autonomous subject in other English-as-first-language countries around 1940, ELT emerged as an autonomous subject in India as late as 1980.

Similarly, the language laboratory also became a part of the ELT paradigm around 1985 as compared to the 1940 of these countries. CALI or Computer Assisted Language Instruction reached most classrooms in 1960 but it came to the Indian classroom around 1985; at present, in some places it has evolved into CALL or Computer Assisted Language Learning. Both CALI and CALL have not been adopted widely due to the obvious constraints of finance and the typically Indian mindset that learning cannot take place without the presence of a human teacher. In the Indian context, Tickoo's distinction between CALI and CALL took on special significance. While it is true that multinationals, call centres and some private institutes are encouraging CALL, it is CALI that has gained wider acceptance.

Communicative Language Teaching reached both regions (India and the West) between the years 1970 - 1980, with the difference that the Indian context was not ready for CLT. Hence, it took around two decades to gain acceptance among learners and teachers. Language-literature integration gained recognition among teachers around the same time. India after 1995 has made up for the slow elephant years by broadening the apex of the ELT cone with a generous mix of so many methodologies that come under the generic category of CA or the Communicative Approach.

It is true that mostly this CA is practised in the institutes that belong to the third category above but the ripple effect created is gradually reaching the ELT classroom. Most institutes that target the language users who need proficiency in a hurry or who need to clear certain examinations invest heavily in teaching materials from publishing houses like the Cambridge University Press. Since all materials published in such places of repute are state-of-the-art in terms of methodology, teachers and learners are in a position of maximum benefit. Moreover, teachers at these centres are usually young post-graduates who are receptive to novelty and innovation.

They borrow heavily from their materials and often create a methodology of their own by using combinations of audio lingual or situational or functional or interactive or task-based or communicative -or even the direct method language teaching. All these approaches and methods could be spread through a course or could even be used in one class, depending upon learner response. This pedagogy is still CA (Communicative Approach) oriented even if not restricted to one approach. Again teachers -especially the younger ones- are increasingly moving towards increasing the extent to which lessons are centred around CA.

The most significant impact of this approach is its sensitivity to learner needs and response. This sensitivity is what has been lacking in the academic aspect of ELT in India. The whole academic process is so unwieldy that it fails to respond to learner needs; learner response is too often ignored. The ELT cone of India is broadening at the base today because of factors that have little to do with the ELT classroom in academic institutions. The irony of the situation is that while academicians label these learning centres 'shops' or 'commercial institutes' it is these establishments that are a major influence behind the changing face of the ELT paradigm in India.

Relevance of English

English is in India today a symbol of people's aspirations for quality in education and a fuller participation in national and international life. Its colonial origins now forgotten or irrelevant, its initial role in independent India, tailored to higher education (as a "library language", a "window on the world"), now felt to be insufficiently inclusive socially and linguistically, the current status of English stems from its overwhelming presence on the world stage and the reflection of thi in the national arena. It is predicted that by 2010, a surge in English language learning will include a third of the world's peopl (Graddo 1997). The opening up of the Indian economy in the 1990s has coincide with an explosion in the demand for English in our schools becaus English is perceived to open up opportunities (Das 2005).

English in our Schools

The Level of Introduction of English: The visible impact of this presence of English is that it is today being demanded by *everyone* at the very *initial* stage of schooling. The English teaching profession has consistently recommended a relatively late (Class IV, V, or VI) introduction of English, and this is reflected in spirit in policy documents. The dissatisfaction with this recommendation is evident in the mushrooming of private English-medium schools and the early introduction of English in state school systems. The popular response to systemic failure has been to extend downwards the very system that has failed to deliver. The level of introduction of English has now become a matter of political response to people's aspirations, rendering almost irrelevant an academic debate on the merits of a very early introduction. There are problems of systemic feasibility and preparedness, for example, finding the required number of competent teachers. But there is an expectation that the system should respond to popular needs rather than the other way round.

We address this question, therefore, in various ways. First, we hope through multilingualism to counter some possible ill-effects such as the loss of one's own language(s), or the burden of sheer incomprehension. Second, we describe what can realistically be achieved in given situations, supplemented with affirmative action interventions where necessary; the aim is to identify delivery systems for comprehensible input to the child, whether in the classroom or outside it. For a fuller understanding of the issues around the early introduction of English, we have included an assessment of the "critical period" or "sensitive window" hypothesis to show that this does not entail a very early introduction of English.

In Relation to other Subjects

A language across the curriculum perspective is perhaps of particular relevance to primary education. Language is best acquired through different meaning-making contexts, and hence all teaching is in a sense language teaching. This perspective also captures the centrality of language in abstract thought in secondary education; whereas in the initial stages contextual meaning supports language use, at later stages meaning may be arrived at solely through language.

The aim of English teaching is the creation of multi-linguals who can enrich all our languages; this has been an abiding national vision. The multilingual perspective also addresses concerns of language and culture, and the pedagogical principle of moving from the known to the unknown.

Language Acquisition inside and outside the Classroom

Second-language pedagogy, more than the teaching of any other curricular subject, must meet the most stringent criterion of universal success: the spontaneous and appropriate use of language for at least everyday purposes. This is a feat achieved in one's own language(s) by every pre-school child (Chomsky 1975). It is this "minimum level of proficiency" (which can, however, be shown to require a mental grammar of remarkable sophistication, which allows for the comprehension and production of language in "real time") that the person on the street aspires to: "speak English", as against merely passing examinations in it, or knowing its grammar.

- Can the English-language classroom replicate the universal success in the acquisition of basic spoken language proficiency that a child spontaneously achieves outside the classroom, for the languages in its environment? If so, how?
- Other spoken language skills in limited domains (for example, for the travel and tourism industry) would build on such a basic proficiency.

Common Cognitive Academic Linguistic Proficiency

Language in education would ideally and ordinarily build on such naturally acquired language ability, enriching it through the development of literacy into an instrument for abstract thought and the acquisition of academic knowledge. We can then speak of a "cognitive academic linguistic proficiency" (cf. Cummins 1979) as language and thinking skills that build on the basis of a child's spontaneous knowledge of language. This is a goal of language education, and education through language. (This discussion has most often been in the context of language education in the mother tongue.)

- Such cognitive and academic skills, moreover, are arguably transferable across languages, to a second language.

This transferability is one of the premises for recommending a relatively late introduction of English: that language-in-education proficiency, developed in the child's own languages, would then naturally extend to a new language.

Foreign Language Teaching Now

The following extended statement by Professor Alfred S. Hayes represents in his words, "a summary of the state of foreign language teaching in the United States today:"

> "Traditional foreign language instruction in the United States was dedicated to the teaching of reading, approached through the study of the rules of grammar. The basic approach, with only minor variations, was extensive translation. But recent years have witnessed a shift of emphasis, since it has become a matter of national self-interest to increase the number of American citizens who can understand and speak a foreign language. This shift of emphasis is paralleled by recent advances in linguistic science and allied fields, which have contributed to a new view of language and language learning. This view is best characterised as a view of language as spoken communication, as signalling behaviour, as a system of habits, which must be acquired to the point of automatic production of, and response to, the structure of the language as isolated by linguistic science, to the point where novel utterances acceptable to a native speaker are freely generated by the learner. Grammar is thus by no means discarded, as is sometimes supposed, but the emphasis is on internalising it through practice, rather than discussing it. Gaarder (1961, pp. 171-172) gives a striking point-by-point comparison of language learning with learning to play a musical instrument.

There is reasonably general agreement on the following points in first-level foreign language-instruction, although, in practice, procedures vary widely:

- Learning proceeds in this order: (a) hearing and understanding; (b) speaking; (c) usually much later-reading; (d) writing. The tendency is, therefore, away from book-centred materials, and towards extensive audiolingual practice designed to develop a new set of habits.
- Instruction proceeds in the initial stages without reference to the printed word.
- Teaching pronunciation requires extensive hearing of the new sounds, preferably contrasted with similar sounds both in the foreign language and the language of the learner, followed by careful drill in their production.
- Spoken language is initially presented and practised in what are called pattern sentences or model sentences. Each pattern sentence contains a productive structure, i.e., one which, when mastered, will permit the generation of new utterances by substituting new vocabulary; e.g., subject-verb-object in English. Pattern sentences are subsequently manipulated in drills designed to highlight changes in form or order which occur within the structures. Such drills are called pattern drills or structure drills.
- Pattern sentences may or may not be presented originally in dialogue form.
- Pattern sentences are practised to the point of "overlearning," i.e., until they become reflex-like habits.
- The amount of vocabulary which must be acquired is severely restricted until a large number of structures have been mastered.
- Translation back and forth between the foreign language and the native language is avoided

Controversy exists on these points:

- Ways and means of narrowing the gap between manipulation and communication.

- The teaching of meaning and the use of English in the classroom.
- The role of grammatical statements and summaries.
- The handling of extensive vocabulary acquisition in the later stages of instruction.

A basic tenet of the audiolingual approach has been the assumption that students so trained will not only be able to understand and speak the foreign language, but will eventually achieve skill in reading and writing at least comparable to and possibly superior to that of students trained by traditional methods. Until recently no experimental evidence existed to substantiate this claim. But now a small-scale experiment by Pimsleur and Bonkowski (1961) offers modest support, while a large-scale classroom experiment by Scherer and Wertheimer (1962) offers convincing confirmation of this view.

The language laboratory, an electromechanical installation generally consisting of multiple facilities for student listening and responding to recorded lesson materials, usually on tape, is coming into widespread use, supported in part by funds made available to the several states under Title 111 of the National Defence Education Act (NDEA). These facilities are intended to relieve the teacher of some of the drudgery of repetitive drill and to furnish authentic models for imitation and practice.

The principles of programmed instruction discussed above are being applied to the problems of foreign language learning. The resulting programmes, designed for presentation through the language laboratory, or through similar audio or audiovisual devices of varying complexity, are thus far only in limited experimental use, and show great promise. Some thirty-five to forty research projects are presently active in this field.

The teaching of foreign languages in the elementary school (FLES) is spreading rapidly but is severely hampered (as is the entire field) by lack of qualified teachers and by frequent failure to provide an adequate continuing programme for children so trained. For a survey and evaluation of results to date see Alkonis and Brophy (1961). The research evidence supporting the notion of FLES is extremely slender (Carroll, 1960).

Teaching foreign languages by television is receiving strong support but results have been dubious because of the questionable methodological soundness of certain programmes, the impossibility of getting feedback from the learner, and the implication that classroom work following the TV presentation can be handled by teachers with no foreign language training or experience.

To help cope with the problem of retraining high school teachers to understand and use audiolingual methods, Summer Institutes have been operated by many colleges and universities pursuant to contracts with the US. Office of Education under Title VI of the NDEA. By the end of 1962 some 10,000 such teachers will have attended a total of 216 Institutes. It is chiefly among the products of these institutes that the awakening Miss F's are to be found. Pre-service teacher training programmes in colleges and universities are barely in the beginning stages of revision. Two new series of tests designed to measure teacher proficiency and student achievement respectively, developed under NDEA Title VI auspices, will eventually help training institutions to evaluate their products.

A broadly based programme of research in problems of foreign language teaching, as well as the construction of teaching materials pre-dominantly in critical but seldom taught languages, Language and Area Centres offering advanced study in such languages, and fellowship awards to students entering upon such advanced study, are likewise supported by Title VI of the NDEA.

The large foundations are providing increasing support for projects involving the teaching of foreign languages or research therein. Serving as a respected neutral intermediary in language matters of interest to government, military, the academic world, the foundations, and industry alike, the Centre for Applied Linguistics in Washington, D.C., an arm of the MLA supported by the Ford Foundation, is having an impact which is rapidly becoming worldwide. One of its major interests is the teaching of English as a second language.

The implementation of audiolingual teaching has caused an upheaval in the publishing industry, which must now supply and is supplying completely new materials which provide the extensive pattern practice and drills required, plus tapes for the language laboratory and even phonograph records for home practice. It was inevitable that certain publishers should give the impression of conversion by offering tapes to accompany traditional texts, a confusing and ill-advised practice. A recent publication of the MLA provides criteria for the evaluation of materials *(Al Iman, 1962).*

Language teaching in the United States is in a state of transition. Audiolingual teaching in high schools, variously understood and administered by teachers, is widespread, but commonest in the large urban centres. Thinly disguised traditional teaching clings in many conservative colleges and universities, where the language laboratory tends to provide misleading superficial evidence of change. So radical is the nature of the change in progress that this situation must be regarded as expected and unavoidable. The pot, however, is boiling. But a more general understanding of language as signalling behaviour is a necessary precursor to further progress in cross-cultural communication." *(Hayes, 1964. 150152).*

11 Classroom Approaches, Methods and Techniques

Presently, educational reformers are seeking answers to two fundamental questions: (1) How well are students learning? and (2) How effectively are teachers teaching? Classroom Research and Classroom Assessment respond directly to concerns about better learning and more effective teaching. Classroom Research was developed to encourage college teachers to become more systematic and sensitive observers of learning as it takes place every day in their classrooms. Faculty have an exceptional opportunity to use their classrooms as laboratories for the study of learning and through such study to develop a better understanding of the learning process and the impact of their teaching upon it. Classroom Assessment, a major component of Classroom Research, involves student and teachers in the continuous monitoring of students' learning.

It provides faculty with feedback about their effectiveness as teachers, and it gives students a measure of their progress as learners. Most important, because Classroom Assessments are created, administered, and analysed by teachers themselves on questions of teaching and learning that are important to them, the likelihood that instructors will apply the results of the assessment to their own teaching is greatly enhances.

Through close observation of students in the process of learning, the collection of frequent feedback on students' learning, and the design of modest classroom experiments, teachers can learn much about how students learn and, more specifically, how students respond to particular teaching approaches. Classroom Assessment helps individual college teachers obtain useful feedback on what, how much, and how well their students are learning. Faculty can then use this information to refocus their teaching to help students make their learning more efficient and more effective.

College instructors who have assumed that their students were learning what they were trying to teach them are regularly faced with disappointing evidence to the contrary when they grade tests and term papers. Too often, students have not learned as much or as well as was expected. There are gaps, sometimes considerable ones, between what was taught and what has been learned. By the time faculty notice these gaps in knowledge or understanding, it is frequently too late to remedy the problems.

To avoid such unhappy surprises, faculty and students need better ways to monitor learning throughout the semester. Specifically, teachers need a continuous flow of accurate information on student learning. For example, if a teacher's goal is to help students learn points "A" through "Z" during the course, then that teacher needs first to know whether all students are really starting at point "A" and, as the course proceeds, whether they have reached intermediate points "B," "G," "L," "R," "W," and so on. To ensure high-quality learning, it is not enough to test students when the syllabus has arrived at points "M" and "Z." Classroom Assessment is particularly useful for checking how well students are learning at those initial and intermediate points, and for providing information for improvement when learning is less than satisfactory.

Through practice in Classroom Assessment, faculty become better able to understand and promote learning, and increase their ability to help the students themselves become more effective, self-assessing, self-directed learners. Simply put, the central purpose of Classroom Assessment is to empower both teachers and their students to improve the quality of learning in the classroom.

Classroom Assessment is an approach designed to help teachers find out what students are learning in the classroom and how well they are learning it. This approach has the following characteristics:

Learner-Centred: Classroom Assessment focuses the primary attention of teachers and students on observing and improving learning, rather than on observing and improving teaching. Classroom Assessment can provide information to guide teachers and students in making adjustments to improve learning.

Teacher-Directed: Classroom Assessment respects the autonomy, academic freedom, and professional judgement of college faculty. The individual teacher decides what to assess, how to assess, and how to respond to the information gained through the assessment. Also, the teacher is not obliged to share the result of Classroom Assessment with anyone outside the classroom.

Mutually Beneficial: Because it is focused on learning, Classroom Assessment requires the active participation of students. By cooperating in assessment, students reinforce their grasp of the course content and strengthen their own skills at self-assessment. Their motivation is increased when they realise that faculty are interested and invested in their success as learners. Faculty also sharpen their teaching focus by continually asking themselves three questions: "What are the essential skills and knowledge I am trying to Teach?" "How can I find out whether students are learning them?" "How can I help students learn better?" As teachers work closely with students to answer these questions, they improve their teaching skills and gain new insights.

Formative: Classroom Assessment's purpose is to improve the quality of student learning, not to provide evidence for evaluating or grading students. The assessment is almost never graded and are almost always anonymous.

Context-Specific: Classroom Assessments have to respond to the particular needs and characteristics of the teachers, students, and disciplines to which they are applied. What works well in one class will not necessary work in another.

Ongoing: Classroom Assessment is an ongoing process, best thought of as the creating and maintenance of a classroom "feedback loop." By using a number of simple Classroom Assessment Techniques that are quick and easy to use, teachers get feedback from students on their learning. Faculty then complete the loop by providing students with feedback on the results of the assessment and suggestions for improving learning. To check on the usefulness of their suggestions, faculty use Classroom Assessment again, continuing the "feedback loop." As the approach becomes integrated into everyday classroom activities, the communications loop connecting faculty and students — and teaching and learning — becomes more efficient and more effective.

Rooted in Good Teaching Practice: Classroom Assessment is an attempt to build on existing good practice by making feedback on students' learning more systematic, more flexible, and more effective. Teachers already ask questions, react to students' questions, monitor body language and facial expressions, read homework and tests, and so on. Classroom Assessment provides a way to integrate assessment systematically and seamlessly into the traditional classroom teaching and learning process.

As they are teaching, faculty monitor and react to student questions, comments, body language, and facial expressions in an almost automatic fashion. This "automatic" information gathering and impression formation is a subconscious and implicit process. Teachers depend heavily on their impressions of student learning and make important judgements based on them, but they rarely make those informal assessments explicit or check them against the students' own impressions or ability to perform. In the course of teaching, college faculty assume a great deal about their students' learning, but most of their assumptions remain untested.

Even when college teachers routinely gather potentially useful information on student learning through questions, quizzes, homework, and exams, it is often collected too late — at least from the students' perspective - to affect their learning. In practice, it is very difficult to "de-programme" students who are used to thinking of anything they have been tested and graded on as being "over and done with." Consequently, the most effective times to assess and provide feedback are before the chapter tests or the midterm an final examinations. Classroom Assessment aims at providing that early feedback.

Classroom Assessment is based on seven assumptions:

The quality of student learning is directly, although not exclusively, related to the quality of teaching. Therefore, one of the most promising ways to improve learning is to improve teaching.

- To improve their effectiveness, teachers need first to make their goals and objectives explicit and then to get specific, comprehensible feedback on the extent to which they are achieving those goals and objectives.
- To improve their learning, students need to receive appropriate and focused feedback early and often; they also need to learn how to assess their own learning.
- The type of assessment most likely to improve teaching and learning is that conducted by faculty to answer questions they themselves have formulated in response to issues or problems in their own teaching.
- Systematic enquiry and intellectual challenge are powerful sources of motivation, growth, and renewal for college teachers, and Classroom Assessment can provide such challenge.
- Classroom Assessment does not require specialised training; it can be carried out by dedicated teachers from all disciplines.
- By collaborating with colleagues and actively involving students in Classroom Assessment efforts, faculty (and students) enhance learning and personal satisfaction.

To begin Classroom Assessment it is recommended that only one or two of the simplest Classroom Assessment Techniques are tried in only one class. In this way very little planning or preparation time and energy of the teacher and students is risked. In most cases, trying out a simple Classroom Assessment Technique will require only five to ten minutes of class time and less than an hour of time out of class. After trying one or two quick assessments, the decision as to whether this approach is worth further investments of time and energy can be made. This process of starting small involves three steps:

Step 1: Planning: Select one, and only one, of your classes in which to try out the Classroom Assessment. Decide on the class meeting and select a Classroom Assessment Technique. Choose a simple and quick one.

Step 2: Implementing: Make sure the students know what you are doing and that they clearly understand the procedure. Collect the responses and analyse them as soon as possible.

Step 3: Responding: To capitalise on time spent assessing, and to motivate students to become actively involved, "close the feedback loop" by letting them know what you learned from the assessments and what difference that information will make.

Five suggestions for a successful start:

- If a Classroom Assessment Techniques does not appeal to your intuition and professional judgement as a teacher, don't use it.
- Don't make Classroom Assessment into a self-inflicted chore or burden.
- Don't ask your students to use any Classroom Assessment Technique you haven't previously tried on yourself.
- Allow for more time than you think you will need to carry out and respond to the assessment.
- Make sure to "close the loop." Let students know what you learn from their feedback and how you and they can use that information to improve learning.

Method of Teaching

A teaching method comprises the principles and methods used for instruction. Commonly used teaching methods may include class participation, demonstration, recitation, memorisation, or combinations of these. The choice of an appropriate teaching method depends largely on the information or skill that is being taught, and it may also be influenced by the aptitude and enthusiasm of the students.

Evolution of Teaching Methods

Ancient Education: About 3000 BC, with the advent of writing, education became more conscious or self-reflecting, with specialised occupations requiring particular skills and knowledge on how to be a scribe, an astronomer, etc.

Philosophy in ancient Greece led to questions of educational method entering national discourse. In his *Republic*, Plato describes a system of instruction that he felt would lead to an ideal state. In his *Dialogues*, Plato describes the Socratic method.

It has been the intent of many educators since then, such as the Roman educator Quintilian, to find specific, interesting ways to encourage students to use their intelligence and to help them learn.

Classroom Teaching

For effective teaching to take place, a good method must be adopted by a teacher. A teacher has many options when choosing a style by which to teach. The teacher may write lesson plans of their own, borrow plans from other teachers, or search on-line or within books for lesson plans. When deciding what teaching method to use, a teacher needs to consider students' background knowledge, environment, and learning goals. Teachers are aware that students learn in different ways, but almost all children will respond well to praise. Students have different ways of absorbing information and of demonstrating their knowledge. Teachers often use techniques which cater to multiple learning styles to help students retain information and strengthen understanding. A variety of strategies and methods are used to ensure that all students have equal opportunities to learn. A lesson plan may be carried out in several ways: Questioning, explaining, modelling, collaborating, and demonstrating.

A teaching method that includes questioning is similar to testing. A teacher may ask a series of questions to collect information of what students have learned and what needs to be taught. Testing is another application of questioning. A teacher tests the student on what was previously taught in order to identify if a student has learned the material. Standardised testing is in about every middle school (i.e. Ohio Graduation Test (OGT), Proficiency Test, College entrance Tests (ACT and SAT).

Learning can be done in three ways- Auditory, Visual, and Kinaesthetic. It is important to try and include all three as much as possible into your lessons.

Explanation

This form is similar to lecturing. Lecturing is teaching by giving a discourse on a specific subject that is open to the public, usually given in the classroom. This can also be associated with modelling. Modelling is used as a visual aid to learning. Students can visualise an object or problem, then use reasoning and hypothesising to determine an answer.

In your lecture you have the opportunity to tackle two types of learning. Not only can explaining (lecture) help the auditory learner through the speech of the teacher, but if the teacher is to include visuals in the form of overheads or slide shows, his/her lecture can have duality. Although a student might only profit substantially from one form of teaching, all students profit some from the different types of learning.

Demonstration

Demonstrations are done to provide an opportunity to learn new exploration and visual learning tasks from a different perspective. A teacher may use experimentation to demonstrate ideas in a science class. A demonstration may be used in the circumstance of proving conclusively a fact, as by reasoning or showing evidence.

The uses of storytelling and examples have long since become standard practice in the realm of textual explanation. But while a more narrative style of information presentation is clearly a preferred practice in writing, judging by its prolificacy, this practice sometimes becomes one of the more ignored aspects of lecture. Lectures, especially in a collegiate environment, often become a setting more geared towards factorial presentation than a setting for narrative and/or connective learning. The use of examples and storytelling likely allows for better understanding but also greater individual ability to relate to the information presented.

Learning a list of facts provides a detached and impersonal experience while the same list, containing examples and stories, becomes, potentially, personally relatable. Furthermore, storytelling in information presentation may also reinforce memory retention because it provides connections between factorial presentation and real-world examples/personable experience, thus, putting things into a clearer perspective and allowing for increased neural representation in the brain. Therefore, it is important to provide personable, supplementary, examples in all forms of information presentation because this practice likely allows for greater interest in the subject matter and better information-retention rates.

Often in lecture numbers or stats are used to explain a subject but often when many numbers are being used it is difficult to see the whole picture. Visuals that are bright in colour, etc. offer a way for the students to put into perspective the numbers or stats that are being used. If the student can not only hear but see what is being taught, it is more likely they will believe and fully grasp what is being taught. It allows another way for the student to relate to the material.

Collaboration

Having students work in groups is another way a teacher can direct a lesson. Collaborating allows students to talk with each other and listen to all points of view in the discussion. It helps students think in a less personally biased way. When this lesson plan is carried out, the teacher may be trying to assess the lesson by looking at the student's: ability to work as a team, leadership skills, or presentation abilities. It is one of the direct instructional methods.

A different kind of group work is the discussion. After some preparation and with clearly defined roles as well as interesting topics, discussions may well take up most of the lesson, with the teacher only giving short feedback at the end or even in the following lesson. Discussions can take a variety of forms, e.g. fishbowl discussions.

Collaborating (kinaesthetic) is great in that it allows to actively participate in the learning process. These students who learn best this way by being able to relate to the lesson in that they are physically taking part of it in some way. Group projects and discussions are a great way to welcome this type of learning.

Learning by Teaching

Learning by teaching (German:LdL) is a widespread method in Germany, developed by Jean-Pol Martin. The students take the teacher's role and teach their peers.

This method is very effective when done correctly. Having students teach sections of the class as a group or as individuals is a great way to get the students to really study out the topic and understand it so as to teach it to their peers. By having them participate in the teaching process it also builds self-confidence, self-efficacy, and strengthens students speaking and communication skills. Students will not only learn their given topic, but they will gain experience that could be very valuable for life.

Medieval Education

Comenius, in Bohemia, wanted all boys and girls to learn. In his *The World in Pictures,* he gave the first vivid, illustrated textbook which contained much that children would be familiar with in everyday life, and use it to teach the academic subjects they needed to know. Rabelais described how the student Gàrgantua learned about the world, and what is in it.

Much later, Jean-Jacques Rousseau in his *Emile,* presented methodology to teach children the elements of science and much more. In it, he famously eschewed books, saying the world is one's book. And so Emile was brought out into the woods without breakfast to learn the cardinal directions and the positions of the sun as he found his way home for something to eat.

There was also Johann Heinrich Pestalozzi of Switzerland, whose methodology during Napoleonic warfare enabled refugee children, of a class believed to be unteachable, to learn and love to learn. He describes this in his account of the educational experiment at Stanz. He felt the key to have children learn is for them to be loved, but his method, though transmitted later in the school for educators he founded, has been thought "too unclear to be taught today". One result was, when he would ask, "Children, do you want to learn more or go to sleep?" they would reply, "Learn more!"

Compulsory Education in 19th Century

The Prussian education system was a system of mandatory education dating to the early 19th century. Parts of the Prussian education system have served as models for the education systems in a number of other countries, including Japan and the United States. The Prussian model had a side effect of requiring additional classroom management skills to be incorporated into the teaching process.

Education in 20th Century

In the 20th century, the philosopher Eli Siegel posited that the purpose of education is to "like the world through knowing it." Teachers in New York found that student performance improved when this principle was employed in their teaching methods.

Many current teaching philosophies are aimed at fulfilling the precepts of a curriculum based on Specially Designed Academic Instruction in English (SDAIE). Arguably the qualities of a SDAIE curriculum are as effective if not more so for all 'regular' classrooms.

Some critical ideas in today's education environment include:

Instructional scaffolding; Graphic organisers; Standardised testing.

According to Dr. Shaikh Imran, the teaching methodology in education is a new concept in the teaching learning process. New methods involved in the teaching learning process are television, radio, computer, etc.

Other educators believe that the use of technology, while facilitating learning to some degree, is not a substitute for educational method that brings out critical thinking and a desire to learn. Another modern teaching method is enquiry learning and the related enquiry-based science.

Elvis H. Bostwick recently concluded Dr. Cherry's quantitative study "The Interdisciplinary Effect of Hands On Science", a three-year study of 3920 middle school students and their Tennessee State Achievement scores in Math, Science, Reading and Social Studies. Metropolitan Nashville Public School is considered urban demographically and can be compared to many of urban schools nationally and internationally. This study divided students on the basis of whether they had hands-on trained teachers over the three-year period addressed by the study.

Students who had a hands-on trained science teacher for one or more years had statistically higher standardised test scores in science, math and social studies. For each additional year of being taught by a hands-on trained teacher, the student's grades increased.

Assessment of Classroom Techniques

What is Classroom Assessment?

Classroom assessment is both a teaching approach and a set of techniques. The approach is that the more you know about what and how students are learning, the better you can plan learning activities to structure your teaching. The techniques are mostly simple, non-graded, anonymous, in-class activities that give both you and your students useful feedback on the teaching-learning process.

How is Classroom Assessment Different?

Classroom assessment differs from tests and other forms of student assessment in that it is aimed at course improvement, rather than at assigning grades. The primary goal is to better understand your students' learning and so to improve your teaching.

How to use Classroom Assessment Techniques?

- Decide what you want to learn from a classroom assessment.
- Choose a Classroom Assessment Technique (CAT) that provides this feedback, is consistent with your teaching style, and can be easily implemented in your class.
- Explain the purpose of the activity to students, then conduct it.
- After class, review the results and decide what changes, if any, to make.
- Let your students know what you learned from the CAT and how you will use this information.

Why Should the CATs be Used?

For faculty, more frequent use of CATs can:

- Provide short-term feedback about the day-to-day learning and teaching process at a time when it is still possible to make mid-course corrections.
- Provide useful information about student learning with a much lower investment of time compared to tests, papers, and other traditional means of learning assessment.
- Help to foster good rapport with students and increase the efficacy of teaching and learning.
- Encourage the view that teaching is a formative process that evolves over time with feedback.

For students, more frequent use of CATs can:

- Help them become better monitors of their own learning.
- Help break down feelings of anonymity, especially in larger courses.

- Point out the need to alter study skills.
- Provide concrete evidence that the instructor cares about learning.

Methods of Teaching a Language

Language education may take place as a general school subject or in a specialised language school. There are many methods of teaching languages. Some have fallen into relative obscurity and others are widely used; still others have a small following, but offer useful insights.

While sometimes confused, the terms "approach", "method" and "technique" are hierarchical concepts. An approach is a set of correlative assumptions about the nature of language and language learning, but does not involve procedure or provide any details about how such assumptions should translate into the classroom setting. Such can be related to second language acquisition theory.

There are three principal views at this level:

- The structural view treats language as a system of structurally related elements to code meaning (e.g. grammar).
- The functional view sees language as a vehicle to express or accomplish a certain function, such as requesting something.
- The interactive view sees language as a vehicle for the creation and maintenance of social relations, focusing on patterns of moves, acts, negotiation and interaction found in conversational exchanges. This view has been fairly dominant since the 1980s.

Examples of structural methods are grammar translation and the audiolingual method. Examples of functional methods include the oral approach / situational language teaching. Examples of interactive methods include the direct method, the series method, communicative language teaching, language immersion, the proprioceptive language learning method, the Silent Way, Suggestopedia, the Natural Approach, Total Physical Response, Teaching Proficiency through Reading and Storytelling and Dogme language teaching.

A method is a plan for presenting the language material to be learned and should be based upon a selected approach. In order for an approach to be translated into a method, an instructional system must be designed considering the objectives of the teaching/learning, how the content is to be selected and organised, the types of tasks to be performed, the roles of students and the roles of teachers. A technique is a very specific, concrete stratagem or trick designed to accomplish an immediate objective. Such are derived from the controlling method, and less-directly, with the approach.

Learning Strategies

Code Switching: Code switching, that is, changing between languages at some point in a sentence or utterance, is a commonly used communication strategy among language learners and bilinguals. While traditional methods of formal instruction often discourage code switching, students, especially those placed in a language immersion situation, often use it. If viewed as a learning strategy, wherein the student uses the target language as much as possible but reverts to their native language for any element of an utterance that they are unable to produce in the target language (as, e.g., in Wolfgang Butzkamm's concept of enlightened monolingualism), then it has the advantages that it encourages fluency development and motivation and a sense of accomplishment by enabling the student to discuss topics of interest to him or her early in the learning process—before requisite vocabulary has been memorised. It is particularly effective for students whose native language is English, due to the high probability of a simple English word or short phrase being understood by the conversational partner.

Teaching Strategies

Blended Learning: Blended learning combines face-to-face teaching with distance education, frequently electronic, either computer-based or web-based. It has been a major growth point in the ELT (English Language Teaching) industry over the last ten years.

Some people, though, use the phrase 'Blended Learning' to refer to learning taking place while the focus is on other activities. For example, playing a card game that requires calling for cards may allow blended learning of numbers (1 to 10).

Sandwich Technique

In foreign language teaching, the sandwich technique is the oral insertion of an idiomatic translation in the mother tongue between an unknown phrase in the learned language and its repetition, in order to convey meaning as rapidly and completely as possible. The mother tongue equivalent can be given almost as an aside, with a slight break in the flow of speech to mark it as an intruder.

When modelling a dialogue sentence for students to repeat, the teacher not only gives an oral mother tongue equivalent for unknown words or phrases, but repeats the foreign language phrase before students imitate it: L2 => L1 => L2. For example, a German teacher of English might engage in the following exchange with the students:

Teacher: "Let me try - lass mich mal versuchen - let me try."

Student: "Let me try."

Skill Teaching

When talking about language skills, the four basic ones are: listening, speaking, reading and writing. However, other, more socially-based skills have been identified more recently such as summarising, describing, narrating etc. In addition, more general learning skills such as study skills and knowing how one learns have been applied to language classrooms.

In the 1970s and 1980s, the four basic skills were generally taught in isolation in a very rigid order, such as listening before speaking. However, since then, it has been recognised that we generally use more than one skill at a time, leading to more integrated exercises. Speaking is a skill that often is under-represented in the traditional classroom. This could be due to the fact that it is considered a less-academic skill than writing, is transient and improvised (thus harder to assess and teach through rote imitation).

More recent textbooks stress the importance of students working with other students in pairs and groups, sometimes the entire class. Pair and group work give opportunities for more students to participate more actively. However, supervision of pairs and groups is important to make sure everyone participates as equally as possible. Such activities also provide opportunities for peer teaching, where weaker learners can find support from stronger classmates.

Mother Tongue Mirroring

Mother tongue mirroring is the adaptation of the time-honoured technique of literal translation or word-for word translation for pedagogical purposes. The aim is to make foreign constructions salient and transparent to learners and, in many cases, spare them the technical jargon of grammatical analysis.

It differs from literal translation and interlinear text as used in the past since it takes the progress learners have made into account and only focuses upon a specific structure at a time. As a didactic device, it can only be used to the extent that it remains intelligible to the learner, unless it is combined with a normal idiomatic translation.

Back-chaining

Back-chaining is a technique used in teaching oral language skills, especially with polysyllabic or difficult words. The teacher pronounces the last syllable, the student repeats, and then the teacher continues, working backwards from the end of the word to the beginning.

For example, to teach the name 'Mussorgsky' a teacher will pronounce the last syllable: *-sky,* and have the student repeat it. Then the teacher will repeat it with *-sorg-* attached before: *-sorg-sky,* and all that remains is the first syllable: *Mus-sorg-sky.*

12 Short Notes

Language Learning

Europe and Asia have had a long tradition of teaching and learning languages. Memorisation of vocabulary and translation of sentences often formed the major part of such learning processes in the past. Ancient languages such as Sanskrit and Pali were mastered in Asia through the process of memorisation of texts and vocabulary lists. Learning vocabulary lists indeed formed the core of language learning.

The progress of Reformation in Europe brought within its wake change in methods of learning foreign and classical languages. While writing paradigms for individual verbs continued to be emphasised, teachers began to focus more on oral aspects of language. Until then learning a language was synonymous with learning the written language.

Currently these types of exercises are not favoured in teaching and learning languages. These are good exercises, no doubt, but are more useful in teaching literature, or more appropriately, teaching writing of literary pieces.

Presently we do make a distinction between learning language and literature. We may learn a language in order to study the literature written in it. But learning a language need not be necessarily done through studying its literature.

Language Acquisition

Language acquisition is the process by which humans acquire the capacity to perceive, produce and use words to understand and communicate. This capacity involves the picking up of diverse capacities including syntax, phonetics, and an extensive vocabulary. This language might be vocal as with speech or manual as in sign. Language acquisition usually refers to first language acquisition, which studies infants' acquisition of their native language, rather than *second language acquisition*, which deals with acquisition (in both children and adults) of additional languages.

The capacity to acquire and use language is a key aspect that distinguishes humans from other organisms. While many forms of animal communication exist, they have a limited range of non-syntactically structured vocabulary tokens that lack cross cultural variation between groups.

A major concern in understanding language acquisition is how these capacities are picked up by infants from what appears to be very little input. A range of theories of language acquisition has been created in order to explain this apparent problem including innatism in which a child is born prepared in some manner with these capacities, as opposed to the other theories in which language is simply learned.

History

Plato felt that the word-meaning mapping in some form was innate. Sanskrit grammarians debated over twelve centuries whether meaning was god-given (possibly innate) or was learned from older convention—e.g. a child learning the word for cow by listening to trusted speakers talking about cows.

In modern times, empiricists like Hobbes and Locke argued that knowledge (and for Locke, language) emerge ultimately from abstracted sense impressions. This led to Carnap's Aufbau, an attempt to learn all knowledge from sense datum, using the notion of "remembered as similar" to bind these into clusters, which would eventually map to language.

Under Behaviourism, it was argued that language may be learned through a form of operant conditioning. In B.F. Skinner's *Verbal Behaviour* (1957), he suggested that the successful use of a sign such as a word or lexical unit, given a certain stimulus, reinforces its "momentary" or contextual probability. Empiricist theories of language acquisition include statistical learning theories of language acquisition, Relational Frame Theory, functionalist linguistics, social interactionist theory, and usage-based language acquisition.

This behaviourist idea was strongly attacked by Noam Chomsky in a review article in 1959, calling it "largely mythology" and a "serious delusion". Instead, Chomsky argued for a more theoretical approach, based on a study of syntax.

Language Skills

Teaching English to speakers of other languages can be looked at from many different angles. One useful way is to look at the teaching process as the teaching of various language skills. There are, in general, four language skills, each based upon the modality of emphasis. These are the Listening, Speaking, Reading, and Writing skills. Generally speaking, it is emphasised that we first teach listening, then speaking, then reading and writing. However, in real life situations of language communication, these skills are interdependent in many ways, even though they can be taught independently to some extent.

Listening Skills

Listening in English is attending to and interpreting oral English. Listening is necessary to develop the speaking skill. The student listens to oral speech in English, then separates into segments the stretch of utterances he hears, groups them into words, phrases, and sentences, and, finally, he understands the message these carry. Listening prepares the students to understand the speech of the native speakers of English as they speak naturally in a normal speed and normal manner.

There are three approaches to listening: interactive (listening to a message and doing something as a consequence) and one-way communication or non-interactive (just listening and retaining the message, in activities such as conversations overheard, public address announcements, recorded messages, etc.) and self-talk. Listening to radio and watching TV and films, public performances, lectures, religious services, etc., generally reflect non-interactive listening. Responding to the commands given reflects interactive listening, which, in fact, is equally widespread in communicative situations. Self-talk is also an important process by which internal thinking and reasoning is carried out. All these three modes or approaches to listening may be included in our TESOL listening comprehension training.

In the classroom, students listen in order to repeat and to understand. In listening to repeat, students imitate and memorise linguistic items such as words, idioms, and sentence patterns. This is an important beginning task and focus of listening exercises. However, it is listening to understand that is real listening in its own right.

Students listen to understand as part of using English for communication purposes. In listening to understand, students may be involved in the question-oriented response model of learning or in the task-oriented model of learning. In the question-oriented response model, students may be asked to listen to a sentence, a dialogue, a conversation, a passage, or a lecture and asked to answer questions which may be presented in the form of true/false statements, multiple choice questions, fill in blank, or short answers. In the task-oriented response model, students may be asked to listen to a passage and accomplish the task described in the passage through interaction with others or by themselves.

Remember that research indicates that most students have difficulty with listening skills, even when listening to their native language. Among other factors, because of the phenomenon of stress (some syllables of a word may by stressed while others may not be), most learners of English have difficulty in mastering the correct placement of the primary and other stresses in English. (This could lead to misunderstanding the meaning of a word, phrase or sentence.) As a consequence, listening proficiency in English is to be cultivated with great care.

First Language

A first language (also native language, mother tongue, arterial language, or L1) is the language(s) a person has learned from birth or within the critical period, or that a person speaks the best and so is often the basis for sociolinguistic identity. In some countries, the terms *native language* or *mother tongue* refer to the language of one's ethnic group rather than one's first language. Sometimes, there can be more than one mother tongue, when the child's parents speak different languages. Those children are usually called bilingual.

By contrast, a *second language* is any language that one speaks other than one's first language.

Terminology

Sometimes the term *native language* is used to indicate a language that a person is as proficient in as a native individual of that language's "base country", or as proficient as the average person who speaks no other language but that language.

Sometimes the term *mother tongue* or *mother language* is used for the language that a person learnt as a child at home (usually from their parents). Children growing up in bilingual homes can, according to this definition, have more than one mother tongue or native language.

In the context of population censuses conducted on the Canadian population, Statistics Canada defines *mother tongue* as "the first language learned at home in childhood and still understood by the individual at the time of the census." It is quite possible that the first language learned is no longer a speaker's dominant language. This includes young immigrant children, whose families have moved to a new linguistic environment, as well as people who learned their mother tongue as a young child at home (rather than the language of the majority of the community), who may have lost, in part or in totality, the language they first acquired.

Mother Tongue

The origin of the term "mother tongue" harks back to the fact that linguistic skills of a child are honed by the mother and therefore the language spoken by the mother would be the primary language that the child would learn.

In some countries such as Kenya, India, and various East Asian countries, "mother language" or "native language" is used to indicate the language of one's ethnic group, in both common and journalistic parlance (e.g. 'I have no apologies for not learning my mother tongue'), rather than one's first language. Also in Singapore, "mother tongue" refers to the language of one's ethnic group regardless of actual proficiency, while the "first language" refers to the English language that was established on the island through British colonisation, which is the lingua franca for most post-independence Singaporeans due to its use as the language of instruction in government schools and as a working language.

J. R. R. Tolkien in his 1955 lecture "English and Welsh" distinguishes the "native tongue" from the "cradle tongue," the latter being the language one happens to learn during early childhood, while one's true "native tongue" may be different, possibly determined by an inherited linguistic taste, and may later in life be discovered by a strong emotional affinity to a specific dialect (Tolkien personally confessed to such an affinity to the Middle English of the West Midlands in particular).

21 February has been proclaimed the International Mother Language Day by UNESCO on 17 November 1999.

Significance

The first language of a child is part of their personal, social and cultural identity. Another impact of the first language is that it brings about the reflection and learning of successful social patterns of acting and speaking. It is basically responsible for differentiating the linguistic competence of acting.

To a person his mother tongue is a "blessing in disguise". It is not merely a time-table subject in his education but is forced upon him from all sides. It is learnt by both the direct or conscious and the indirect or unconscious method. The direct method supplements and regulates the knowledge gained by hearing. The mother tongue is an indispensable instrument for the development of the intellectual, moral and physical aspects of education. It is a subject thought and by which other subjects can be tackled, understood and communicated. Clarity of thought and expression is only possible when one has a certain command over the mother tongue. Weakness in any other subject means weakness in that particular subject only, but weakness in the mother tongue means the paralysis of all thought and the power of expression. Deep insight, fresh discoveries, appreciation and expansion of ideas are only possible when one understands the subject through being able to assimilate and be stimulated by the ideas of the subject.

On Multilinguality

One can have two or more native languages, thus being a native *bilingual* or indeed *multilingual*. The order in which these languages are learned is not necessarily the order of proficiency. For instance, a French-speaking couple might have a daughter who learned French first, then English; but if she were to grow up in an English-speaking country, she would likely be proficient in English. Other examples are India, Malaysia and South Africa, where most people speak more than one language.

The Brazilian linguist Cleo Altenhofen considers the denomination "mother tongue" in its general usage to be imprecise and subject to various interpretations that are biased linguistically, especially with respect to bilingual children from ethnic minority groups. He cites his own experience as a bilingual speaker of Portuguese and Riograndenser Hunsrückisch, a German-rooted language brought to southern Brazil by the first German immigrants. In his case, like that of many children whose home language differs from the language of the environment (the 'official' language), it is debatable which language is one's 'mother tongue'. Many scholars have given definitions of 'mother tongue' through the years based on common usage, the emotional relation of the speaker towards the language, and even its dominance in relation to the environment. However, all of these criteria lack precision.

Defining Mother Tongue

- Based on origin: the language(s) one learned first (the language(s) in which one has established the first long-lasting verbal contacts).
- Based on internal identification: the language(s) one identifies with/as a speaker of;
- Based on external identification: the language(s) one is identified with/as a speaker of, by others.
- Based on competence: the language(s) one knows best.
- Based on function: the language(s) one uses most.

Second Language

A second language or L2 is any language learned after the first language or mother tongue. Some languages, often called auxiliary languages, are used primarily as second languages or lingua francas (such as Esperanto).

A person's first language may not be their dominant language, the one they use most or are most comfortable with. For example, the Canadian census defines *first language* for its purposes as "the first language learned in childhood and still spoken", recognising that for some, the earliest language may be lost, a process known as language attrition. This can happen when young children move, with or without their family (because of immigration or international adoption), to a new language environment.

Age: According to some researchers, the defining difference between a first language (L1) and a second language (L2) is the age the person learned the language. For example, linguist Eric Lenneberg used *second language* to mean a language consciously acquired or used by its speaker after puberty. In most cases, people never achieve the same level of fluency and comprehension in their second languages as in their first language. These views are closely associated with the Critical Period Hypothesis.

In acquiring an L2, Hyltenstam (1992) found that around the age of six or seven seemed to be a cut-off point for bilinguals to achieve native-like proficiency. After that age, L2 learners could get *near-native-like-ness* but their language would, while consisting of few actual errors, have enough errors to set them apart from the L1 group.

The inability of some subjects to achieve native-like proficiency must be seen in relation to the *age of onset* (AO). "The age of 6 or 8 does seem to be an important period in distinguishing between near-native and native-like ultimate attainment... More specifically, it may be suggested that AO interacts with frequency and intensity of language use" (Hyltenstam, 1992, p. 364).

Later, Hyltenstam & Abrahamsson (2003) modified their age cutoffs to argue that after childhood, in general, it becomes more and more difficult to acquire native-likeness, but that there is no cutoff point in particular. Furthermore, they discuss a number of cases where a native-like L2 was acquired during adulthood.

As we are learning more and more about the brain, there is a hypothesis that when a child is going through puberty, that is the time that accents *start.* Before a child goes through puberty, the chemical processes in the brain are more geared towards language and social communication. Whereas after puberty, the ability for learning a language without an accent has been rerouted to function in another area of the brain—most likely in the frontal lobe area promoting cognitive functions, or in the neural system of hormone allocated for reproduction and sexual organ growth.

Similarities and Differences between L1 and L2

Speed: Acquiring a second language can be a lifelong learning process for many. Despite persistent efforts, most learners of a second language will never become fully *native-like* in it, although with practice considerable fluency can be achieved. However, children by around the age of 5 have more or less mastered their first language, with the exception of vocabulary and a few grammatical structures.

Stages

Acquiring a second language occurs in systematic stages. Much evidence has been gathered to show that basic sounds, vocabulary, negating phrases, forming questions, using relative clauses, and so on are developed. This development is independent of input (we do not hear nor read language in this order) and learning situation (in the classroom or on the street). It is also generally applicable across a spectrum of learners (from different language backgrounds). This is similar to the learning stages that babies go through when acquiring the first language: babbling (*bababa*), vocabulary (*milk* then later *milk drink*), negation (*no play*), question forming (*where she go*), and so on.

Correction

Error correction does not seem to have a *direct* influence on learning a second language. Instruction may affect the *rate* of learning, but the *stages* remain the same. Adolescents and adults who *know the rule* are faster than those who do not. In the first language, children do not respond to systematic correction. Furthermore, children who have limited input still acquire the first language.

Depth of Knowledge

Learners in the first or second language have knowledge that goes beyond the input they received, in other words, the whole is greater than the parts. Learners of a language are able to construct correct utterances (e.g. phrases, sentences, and questions) that they have never seen or heard before.

Success

Success in language learning can be measured in two ways: likelihood and quality. First language learners *will* be successful in both measurements. It is inevitable that all first language learners will learn a first language and with few exceptions, they will be fully successful. For second language learners, success is not guaranteed. For one, learners may become fossilised or *stuck* as it were with ungrammatical items. (Fossilisation occurs when language errors become a permanent feature. See Canale & Swain (1980), Johnson (1992), Selinker (1972), and Selinker and Lamendella (1978)). The difference between learners may be significant. Finally, as already noted, L2 learners rarely achieve complete *native-like* control of the second language.

Theories of Second Language Acquisition

The distinction between acquiring and learning was made by Stephen Krashen (1982) as part of his Monitor Theory. According to Krashen, the *acquisition* of a language is a natural process; whereas *learning* a language is a conscious one. In the former, the student needs to partake in natural communicative situations. In the latter, error correction is present, as is the study of grammatical rules isolated from natural language. Not all educators in second language agree to this distinction; however, the study of how a second language is *learned/acquired* is referred to as *Second Language Acquisition* or SLA.

Research in SLA *focuses on the developing knowledge and use of a language by children and adults who already know at least one other language... and a knowledge of second language acquisition may help educational policy-makers set more realistic goals for programmes for both foreign language courses and the learning of the majority language by minority language children and adults* (Spada & Lightbown, p. 115).

SLA has been influenced by both linguistic and psychological theories. One of the dominant linguistic theories hypothesises that a *device* or *module* of sorts in the brain contains innate knowledge. Many psychological theories, on the other hand, hypothesise that cognitive mechanisms, responsible for much of human learning, process language.

Foreign Language

In pedagogy, a distinction is often made between 'second language' and foreign language, the latter being learned for use in an area where that language is not generally spoken. Arguably, English in countries such as India, Pakistan, Bangladesh, the Scandinavian countries and the Netherlands can be considered a second language for many of its speakers, because they learn it young, speak it fluently, and use it regularly, indeed in southern Asia it is the official language of the courts, government and business.

The same can be said for French in the Arab Maghreb Union, except for Libya, although—like for English in the Scandinavian countries and the Netherlands—French is not an official language in any of these Arabic-speaking countries. In the post-Soviet states such as Uzbekistan, Kyrgyzstan and Kazakhstan, Russian can be considered a second language, and there are large Russophone communities there.

In China (with the exception perhaps of Hong Kong), however, English would be considered a foreign language due to the lack of a number of characteristics, such as historical links, media, opportunities for use, similar vocabulary, and common script.

French would be considered a foreign language in Romania, Lebanon and Moldova as well. This is despite Romanian and French being Romance languages (unlike Chinese and English, which come from two different language families). This is also despite Romania and Moldova being the only two countries in the world where Romanian is an official language at the federal level, Romania's historical links to France, and both Romanian-speaking countries' membership in the Francophonie.

For Lebanon, French would be considered a foreign language, even though most of its universities operate in either that language or English, French is an administrative language and—like Romania—Lebanon has historical ties to France and is a Francophonie member state.

George H. J. Weber, a Swiss businessman and independent scholar, founder of the Andaman Association and creator of the encyclopedic andaman.org Website, made a report in December 1997 about the number of secondary speakers of the world's leading languages.

Weber used the Fischer Weltalmanach of 1986 as his only source for the L2-speakers data, in preparing the data in the next table. These numbers should be compared with those referred to by Ethnologue, an authoritative site in the linguistics field, however, the data for English as L2 has not been yet reported by Ethnologue.

Bilingualism and Multilingualism

Multilingualism is the act of using, or promoting the use of, multiple languages, either by an individual speaker or by a community of speakers. Multilingual speakers outnumber monolingual speakers in the world's population. Multilingualism is becoming a social phenomenon governed by the needs of globalisation and cultural openness. Thanks to the ease of access to information facilitated by the Internet, individuals' exposure to multiple languages is getting more and more frequent, and triggering therefore the need to acquire more and more languages.

People who speak more than one language are also called polyglots.

Bilingualism

Receptive Bilingualism: Receptive bilinguals are those who have the ability to understand a second language, but do not speak it. Receptive bilingualism may occur when a child thinks that the community language is more prestigious than the language spoken within the household and chooses to speak to their parents in the community language only. Families who adopt this mode of communication can be highly functional, although they may not be seen as bilingual. Receptive bilinguals may rapidly achieve oral fluency when placed in situations where they are required to speak the heritage language.

Receptive bilingualism is not the same as mutual intelligibility, which is the case of a native Spanish speaker who is able to understand Portuguese, or vice versa, due to the high lexical and grammatical similarities between Spanish and Portuguese.

Simultaneous Bilingualism: Simultaneous bilingualism is a form of bilingualism that takes place when a child becomes bilingual by learning two languages from birth. According to Annick De Houwer, in an article in *The Handbook of Child Language*, simultaneous bilingualism takes place in "children who are regularly addressed in two spoken languages from before the age of two and who continue to be regularly addressed in those languages up until the final stages" of language development.

Both languages are acquired as first languages. This is in contrast to sequential bilingualism, in which the second language is learned not as a native language but a foreign language.

Official Bilingualism: Official bilingualism refers to the policy adopted by some states of recognising two languages as official and producing all official documents, and handling all correspondence and official dealings, including Court procedure, in the two said languages. It is destinct from personal bilingualism, the capacity of a person to speak two languages.

Multilingualism

One group of academics argues for the maximal definition which means speakers are as proficient in one language as they are in others and have as much knowledge of and control over one language as they have of the others. Another group of academics argues for the minimal definition, based on use. Tourists who successfully communicate phrases and ideas while not fluent in a language may be seen as bilingual according to this group.

However, problems may arise with these definitions as they do not specify how much knowledge of a language is required for a person to be classified as bilingual. As a result, since most speakers do not achieve the maximal ideal, language learners may come to be seen as deficient and by extension, language teaching may come to be seen as a failure.

Since 1992, Vivian Cook has argued that most multilingual speakers fall somewhere between minimal and maximal definitions. Cook calls these people *multi-competent.*

Multilingual Individuals: A multilingual person, in a broad definition, is one who can communicate in more than one language, be it actively (through speaking, writing, or signing) or passively (through listening, reading, or perceiving). More specifically, the terms *bilingual* and *trilingual* are used to describe comparable situations in which two or three languages are involved. A multilingual person is generally referred to as a polyglot. *Poly* means "many", *glot* means "language".

Multilingual speakers have acquired and maintained at least one language during childhood, the so-called first language (L1). The first language (sometimes also referred to as the mother tongue) is acquired without formal education, by mechanisms heavily disputed. Children acquiring two languages in this way are called simultaneous bilinguals. Even in the case of simultaneous bilinguals one language usually dominates over the other.

A further possibility is that a child may become naturally trilingual by having a mother and father with separate languages being brought up in a third language environment. An example of this may be an English-speaking father married to a Mandarin Chinese speaking mother with the family living in Hong Kong, where the community language (and primary language of education) is Cantonese. If the child goes to a Cantonese medium school from a young age, then trilingualism will result.

In linguistics, first language acquisition is closely related to the concept of a "native speaker". According to a view widely held by linguists, a native speaker of a given language has in some respects a level of skill which a second (or subsequent) language learner can hardly reliably accomplish. Consequently, descriptive empirical studies of languages are usually carried out using only native speakers as informants. This view is, however, slightly problematic, particularly as many non-native speakers demonstrably not only successfully engage with and in their non-native language societies, but in fact may become culturally and even linguistically important contributors (as, for example, writers, politicians and performing artists) in their non-native language. In recent years, linguistic research has focused attention on the use of widely known world languages such as English as lingua franca, or the shared common language of professional and commercial communities. In lingua franca situations, most speakers of the common language are functionally multilingual.

Comparing Multilingual Speakers: Even if someone is highly proficient in two or more languages, his or her so-called *communicative competence* or ability may not be as balanced. Linguists have distinguished various types of multilingual competence, which can roughly be put into two categories:

- For *compound* bilinguals, words and phrases in different languages are the same concepts. That means that 'chien' and 'dog' are two words for the same concept for a French-English speaker of this type. These speakers are usually fluent in both languages.
- For *coordinate* bilinguals, words and phrases in the speaker's mind are all related to their own unique concepts. Thus a bilingual speaker of this type has different associations for 'chien' and for 'dog'. In these individuals, one language, usually

the first language, is more dominant than the other, and the first language may be used to *think through* the second language. These speakers are known to use very different intonation and pronunciation features, and sometimes to assert the feeling of having different personalities attached to each of their languages.

- A sub-group of the latter is the *subordinate* bilingual, which is typical of beginning second language learners.

The distinction between compound and coordinate bilingualism has come under scrutiny. When studies are done of multilinguals, most are found to show behaviour intermediate between compound and coordinate bilingualism.

Some authors have suggested that the distinction should only be made at the level of grammar rather than vocabulary, others use "coordinate bilingual" as a synonym for one who has learned two languages from birth, and others have proposed dropping the distinction altogether.

Many theorists are now beginning to view bilingualism as a "spectrum or continuum of bilingualism" that runs from the relatively monolingual language learner to highly proficient bilingual speakers who function at high levels in both languages (Garland, 2007).

Potential Multilingual Speakers:

- Natives under a state in which they do not share the predominant language, such as Welsh people within the United Kingdom.
- People with a strong interest in a foreign language.
- People who find it necessary to acquire a second language for practical purposes such as business, information gathering (Internet, mainly English) or entertainment (foreign language films, books or computer games).
- Language immersion children (or any adult who chooses to immerse in a foreign language).
- Immigrants and their descendants. Although the heritage language may be lost after one or two generations, particularly if the replacing language has greater opportunity.

- Children of expatriates. However, language loss of the L1 or L2 in younger children may be rapid when removed from a language community.
- Residents in border areas between two countries with different languages, where each language is seen as of equal prestige: efforts may be made by both language communities to acquire an L2. Yet, in areas where one language is more prestigious than the other, speakers of the less prestigious language may acquire the dominant language as an L2. In time, however, the different language communities may be reduced to one, as one language becomes extinct in that area.
- Children whose parents each speak a different language, in multilingual communities. In monolingual communities, when parents maintain a different-parent/different-language household, their children may become multilingual. On the other hand, in monolingual communities, where parents have different L1s, multilingualism in the child may be achieved when both parents maintain a one-language (not the community language) household.
- Children in language-rich communities where neither language is seen as more prestigious than the other and where interaction between people occurs in different languages on a frequent basis. An example of this would be the city of Montreal, Canada and some border towns in the Canadian Province of Québec.
- Children who have one or more parents who have learned a second language, either formally (in classes) or by living in the country. The parent chooses to speak only this second language to the child. One study suggests that during the teaching process, the parent also boosts his or her own language skills, learning to use the second language in new contexts as the child grows and develops linguistically.
- People who learn a different language for religious reasons.
- People who marry into families where their first language is not commonly spoken.

Learning the Language

One view is that of the linguist Noam Chomsky in what he calls the human *'language acquisition device'* — a mechanism which enables an individual to recreate correctly the rules (grammar) and certain other characteristics of language used by speakers around the learner. This device, according to Chomsky, wears out over time, and is not normally available by puberty, which he uses to explain the poor results some adolescents and adults have when learning aspects of a second language (L2).

If language learning is a cognitive process, rather than a language acquisition device, as the school led by Stephen Krashen suggests, there would only be relative, not categorical, differences between the two types of language learning.

Rod Ellis quotes research finding that the earlier children learn a second language, the better off they are, in terms of pronunciation. See Critical period hypothesis. Many European schools offer secondary language classes for their students, if for no other reason than the proximity of other countries with different languages.

Based on the research in Ann Fathman's The Relationship between age and second language productive ability, there is a difference in the rate of learning of English morphology, syntax and phonology based upon differences in age, but that the order of acquisition in second language learning does not change with age. People who have Multilanguage background will find out their native language would influence their second language in any other ages.

In second language class, students will commonly face the difficulties on thinking in the target language because they are influenced by their native language and culture patterns. Robert B. Kaplan thinks that in second language classes, the foreign-student paper is out of focus because the foreign student is employing rhetoric and a sequence of thought which violate the expectations of the native reader. Foreign students who have mastered syntactic structures have still demonstrated inability to compose adequate themes, term papers, theses, and dissertations. Robert B. Kaplan describes two key words that affect people when they learn a second language. Logic in the popular, rather than the logician's sense of the word, which is the basis of rhetoric, is evolved out of a culture; it is not universal. Rhetoric, then, is not universal either, but varies, from culture to culture and even from time to time within a given culture. Language teachers know how to predict the differences between pronunciations or constructions in different languages, but they might be less clear about the differences between rhetoric, that is, in the way they use language to accomplish various purposes, particularly in writing.

Cognitive Ability

Bilinguals who are highly proficient in two or more languages are reported to have enhanced executive function, different organisation in some cortical areas, and are better at some aspects of language learning compared to monolinguals.

There is also a phenomenon known as *distractive bilingualism* or *semi-lingualism.* When acquisition of the first language is interrupted and insufficient or unstructured language input follows from the second language, as sometimes happens with immigrant children, the speaker can end up with two languages both mastered below the monolingual standard. Literacy plays an important role in the development of language in these immigrant children. Those who were literate in their first language before arriving, and who have support to maintain that literacy, are at the very least able to maintain and master their first language.

Evaluation

The examination is universally felt to be the single or main obstacle to curriculum reform. How can evaluation be made an enabling factor for learning rather than an impediment? Language Evaluation need not be limited to "achievement" with respect to particular syllabi, but must be reoriented to measurement of *language proficiency.* We discuss some ways of conducting ongoing evaluation of language proficiency.

Ongoing Continuous Evaluation

Recommendations for ongoing, continuous, or formative evaluation contrast with ground realities and problems reported by teachers, suggesting that ongoing evaluation can become meaningful only when teachers and learners both take responsibility for their own progress, rather than performing to external benchmarks (real or imaginary, immediate or ultimate). Teachers and learners must be able to recognise the "occurrence of learning", a mental growth as imperceptible as physical growth. Imagine the absurdity of a nutritional programme (excluding crash diets or miracle growth foods) that requires the heights and weights of students to be measured at daily, weekly, or even monthly intervals. Yet continuous evaluation seems to work on the ground in precisely such an unintuitive way.

This malaise cannot be cured except through a deep understanding of the learning process, which is individual and self-regulatory. This deeper understanding is essential for teachers to then be able to perceive (and appreciate) subtle changes in children's language learning and proficiency. Perhaps all evaluation should ultimately aim at self-evaluation (a term fashionable in distance education, where its absence is deplored) if learners are to be able to exercise choices for learning and become "lifelong learners". A teacher who knows his pupils is then primarily a sympathetic facilitator of the learner's self-evaluation (in contrast to an anonymous evaluator, who measures achievement with respect to standardised benchmarks).

It is *how* one evaluates that will decide whether a child will *want* to be evaluated. While even the most child-centred methods of evaluation will be anxiety provoking for some, there is no question that a system of evaluation must be put in place. It is thus a question of both how and how much.

Learners participate in evaluations with more comfort when the experience is not always a failure and the outcomes can be seen as a legitimate and appropriate way towards the next step in learning. Unfortunately, for most children the immediate role played by current evaluation methods within the *learning* process is not clear. Continuous evaluation has to facilitate and guide teaching: by determining the learner's current stage of development or attainment, in order to identify her "zone of proximal development" (cf. Krashen's requirement that input should be at the $i+1$ stage if the learner's language is at the i stage). Learning attainments are results of language opportunities. Below we list a few pointers to such attainment.

Objects of Evolution

- Evaluation to be made an enabling factor for learning rather than an impediment. Ongoing assessment should document a learner's progress through the portfolio mode. Language evaluation need not be tied to "achievement" with respect to particular syllabi, but must be reoriented to the measurement of language proficiency.

- National benchmarks for language proficiency should be evolved as a preliminary to the preparation of a set of English-language tests.

Error Analysis

In second language acquisition, error analysis studies the types and causes of language errors. Errors are classified according to:

- modality (i.e., level of proficiency in speaking, writing, reading, listening)
- linguistic levels (i.e., pronunciation, grammar, vocabulary, style)
- form (e.g., omission, insertion, substitution)
- type (systematic errors/errors in competence vs. occasional errors/errors in performance)
- cause (e.g., interference, interlanguage)
- norm vs. system

Methodology

Error analysis in SLA was established in the 1960s by Stephen Pit Corder and colleagues. Error analysis was an alternative to contrastive analysis, an approach influenced by behaviourism through which applied linguists sought to use the formal distinctions between the learners' first and second languages to predict errors. Error analysis showed that contrastive analysis was unable to predict a great majority of errors, although its more valuable aspects have been incorporated into the study of language transfer. A key finding of error analysis has been that many learner errors are produced by learners making faulty inferences about the rules of the new language.

Error analysts distinguish between errors, which are systematic, and mistakes, which are not. They often seek to develop a typology of errors. Error can be classified according to basic type: omissive, additive, substitutive or related to word order. They can be classified by how apparent they are: *overt* errors such as "I angry" are obvious even out of context, whereas *covert* errors are evident only in context. Closely related to this is the classification according to *domain*, the breadth of context which the analyst must examine, and *extent*, the breadth of the utterance which must be changed in order to fix the error. Errors may also be classified according to the level of language: phonological errors, vocabulary or lexical errors, syntactic errors, and so on. They may be assessed according to the degree to which they interfere with communication: *global* errors make an utterance difficult to understand, while *local* errors do not. In the above example, "I angry" would be a local error, since the meaning is apparent.

From the beginning, error analysis was beset with methodological problems. In particular, the above typologies are problematic: from linguistic data alone, it is often impossible to reliably determine what kind of error a learner is making. Also, error analysis can deal effectively only with learner production (speaking and writing) and not with learner reception (listening and reading). Furthermore, it cannot account for learner use of communicative strategies such as avoidance, in which learners simply do not use a form with which they are uncomfortable. For these reasons, although error analysis is still used to investigate specific questions in SLA, the quest for an overarching theory of learner errors has largely been abandoned. In the mid-1970s, Corder and others moved on to a more wide-ranging approach to learner language, known as interlanguage.

Error analysis is closely related to the study of error treatment in language teaching. Today, the study of errors is particularly relevant for focus on form teaching methodology.

Contrastive Analysis

Contrastive analysis is the systematic study of a pair of languages with a view to identifying their structural differences and similarities. Historically it has been used to establish language genealogies.

Contrastive Analysis and Second Language Acquisition

Contrastive Analysis was used extensively in the field of Second Language Acquisition (SLA) in the 1960s and early 1970s, as a method of explaining why some features of a Target Language were more difficult to acquire than others. According to the behaviourist theories prevailing at the time, language learning was a question of habit formation, and this could be reinforced or impeded by existing habits. Therefore, the difficulty in mastering certain structures in a second language (L2) depended on the difference between the learners' mother language (L1) and the language they were trying to learn.

The Background

The theoretical foundations for what became known as the Contrastive Analysis Hypothesis were formulated in Lado's *Linguistics Across Cultures* (1957). In this book, Lado claimed that "*those elements which are similar to* [the learner's] *native language will be simple for him, and those elements that are different will be difficult*". While this was not a novel suggestion, Lado was the first to provide a comprehensive theoretical treatment and to suggest a systematic set of technical procedures for the contrastive study of languages. This involved describing the languages (using structuralist linguistics), comparing them and predicting learning difficulties.

During the 1960s, there was a widespread enthusiasm with this technique, manifested in the contrastive descriptions of several European languages, many of which were sponsored by the Centre of Applied Linguistics in Washington, DC. It was expected that once the areas of potential difficulty had been mapped out through Contrastive Analysis, it would be possible to design language courses more efficiently. Contrastive Analysis, along with Behaviourism and Structuralism exerted a profound effect on SLA curriculum design and language teacher education, and provided the theoretical pillars of Audio-Lingual Method.

Criticism

In its strongest formulation, the Contrastive Analysis Hypothesis claimed that all the errors made in learning the L2 could be attributed to 'interference' by the L1. However, this claim could not be sustained by empirical evidence that was accumulated in the mid- and late 1970s. It was soon pointed out that many errors predicted by Contrastive Analysis were inexplicably not observed in learners' language. Even more confusingly, some uniform errors were made by learners irrespective of their L1. It thus became clear that Contrastive Analysis could not predict all learning difficulties, but was certainly useful in the retrospective explanation of errors.

Bibliography

Allwright, Dick; Hanks, Judith: *The Developing Language Learning: An Introduction to Exploratory Practice,* Palgrave MacMillan, Basingstoke, 2009.

Belenky, M.F. Clinchy, B.M. Goldberger, N.R. and Tarule, J.M.: *Women's Ways of Knowing: The Development of Self, Voice and Mind,* Basic Books, New York, 1986.

Bernhardt, E.B.: *Life in Language Immersion Classrooms,* Multilingual Matters ,England, 1992.

Berns, M. and Matsuda, P.K.: *Applied Linguistics: Overview and History,* Elsevier, Oxford, 2006.

Bhatia, Tej; Ritchie, William, C.: *The Handbook of Bilingualism,* Blackwell Publishing, Oxford, 2004.

Bimal Krishna Matilal: *The Word and the World: India's Contribution to the Study of Language,* Oxford University Press, New York, 1990.

Bruner, J.: *Thought and Language,* MIT Press, Cambridge, 1962.

Burck, Charlotte: *Multilingual Living,* Palgrave Macmillan, Basingstoke, 2007.

Calkins, L.M.: *The Art of Teaching Writing,* Heinemann, Portsmouth, 1986.

Cazden, C.: *Contexts for Learning: Sociocultural Dynamics in Children's Development,* Oxford University Press, New York, 1993.

Chang-Wells, G.L.M. and Wells, G.: *Contexts for Learning: Sociocultural Dynamics in Children's Development,* Oxford University Press, New York, 1993.

Christian, Donna: *Language: the Socio-cultural Context,* Cambridge University Press, Cambridge, 1988.

Cobarrubius, Juan and Joshua Fishman: *Progress in Language Planning: International Perspective,* Mouton, The Hague, 1983.

Cook, G.: *Applied Linguistics: In the Series Oxford Introduction to Language Study,* Oxford University Press, Oxford, 2003.

Cook, Vivian: *Second Language Learning and Language Teaching,* Arnold, London, 2008.

Cooper, Robert, L.: *Language Planning and Social Change,* Cambridge University Press, New York, 1989.

Davies, A. and Elder, C.: *Handbook of Applied Linguistics,* Blackwell, Oxford, 2004.

DeKeyser, Robert: *Focus on Form in Classroom Second Language Acquisition,* Cambridge University Press, New York, 1998.

Di Pietro, R.J.: *Language Structures in Contrast,* Newbury House, 1971.

Doughty, Catherine; Williams, Jessica: *Focus on Form in Classroom Second Language Acquisition,* Cambridge University Press, Cambridge, 1998.

Edwards, John: *Language, Prestige and Stigma,* Hans Goebel, New York, 1996.

Ellis, Rod: *The Study of Second Language Acquisition,* Oxford University Press, Oxford Oxfordshire, 1994.

Ferguson, Charles, A.: *Sociolinguistic Perspectives: Papers on Language in Society, 1959-1994,* Oxford University Press, Oxford, 1968.

Genesee, F.: *Learning Through Two Languages: Studies of Immersion and Bilingual Education,* Newbury House Publishers, Cambridge, 1987.

Hall, C. J., Smith, P. H. and Wicaksono, R.: *Mapping Applied Linguistics. A Guide for Students and Practitioners,* Routledge, London, 2011.

Henry M. Hoenigswald: *Language Cange and Linguistic Reconstruction,* University of Chicago Press, Chicago, 1960.

John, E. Joseph, Nigel Love and Talbot Taylor, J.: *Landmarks in Linguistic Thought II: The Western Tradition in the Twentieth Century,* Routledge, London, 2001.

Johnson, Keith and Johnson, Helen: *Encyclopedic Dictionary of Applied Linguistics,* Blackwell, Oxford/Malden, 1999.

Kees Versteegh: *Landmarks in Linguistic Thought III: The Arabic Linguistic Tradition,* Routledge, London, 1997.

Keith Allan: *The Western Classical Tradition in Linguistics,* Equinox, London, 2007.

Konig, E. and Gast V.: *Understanding English-German Contrasts,* Erich Schmidt Verlag, Berlin, 2007.

Kozulin, A.: *Vygotsky's Psychology: A Biography of Ideas,* Harvester Wheatsheaf, Brighton, 1990.

Krashen, Stephen: *Second Language Acquisition and Second Language Learning,* Pergamon Press, New York, 1981.

Lado, R.: *Linguistics Across Cultures: Applied Linguistics for Language Teachers,* University of Michigan Press, Ann Arbor, 1957.

Lemke, J.L.: *Textual Politics, Discourse and Social Dynamics,* Taylor and Francis, London, 1995.

Lenneberg, Eric: *Biological Foundations of Language,* Wiley, New York, 1967.

Levy, M.: *CALL: Context and Conceptualisation,* Oxford University Press, Oxford, 1997.

Lightbown, P. and Spada, N.: *How Languages are Learned,* Oxford University Press, Oxford, 2006.

Lightbown, Patsy: *The Development of Second Language Proficiency,* Cambridge University Press, Cambridge, 1990.

Long, M.: *Handbook of Second Language Acquisition,* Academic Press, San Diego:, 1996.

McCarthy, Michael: *Issues in Applied Linguistics,* Cambridge University Press, Cambridge, 2001.

Mitchell, R. and Myles, F.: *Second Language Learning Theories,* Hodder Arnold, London, 2004.

Norris, J.M. and Ortega, L.: *Synthesizing Research on Language Learning and Teaching,* Amsterdam/Philadelphia, John Benjamins, 2006.

Ortega, L.: *Understanding Second Language Acquisition,* Hodder Arnold, London, 2009.

Paradis, M.: *Implicit and Explicit Learning of Languages,* Academic Press, London, 1994.

Prabhu, N.: *Second Language Pedagogy,* Oxford University Press, Oxford, 1987.

Robert Henry Robins: *A Short History of Linguistics,* Longman, London, 1997.

Schmidt, R.: *Cognition and Second Language Instruction,* Cambridge University Press, Cambridge, 2001.

Skehan, Peter: *A Cognitive Approach to Language Learning,* Oxford University Press, Oxford, 1998.

Stewart, William, A.: *Readings in the Sociology of Language,* Mouton Publishers, The Hague, 1968.

Swain, M. and Johnson, R.K.: *Immersion Education: International Perspectives,* Cambridge University Press, New York, 1997.

Tarone, E. and Swierzbin, B.: *Exploring Learner Language,* Oxford University Press, Oxford, 2009.

Tarone, Elaine; Bigelow, Martha; Hansen, Kit: *Literacy and Second Language Oracy,* Oxford University Press, Oxford, 2009.

Theodora Bynon: *Historical Linguistics,* Cambridge University Press, Cambridge, 1977.

VanPatten, Bill; Benati, Alessandro, G.: *Key Terms in Second Language Acquisition,* Continuum, London, 2010.

Vinay, J.P. and Darbelnet, J.: *Stylistique Comparée du Français et de l'Anglais,* Didier-Harrap, 1958.

Warschauer, H. and Kern, R.: *Network-based Language Teaching: Concepts and Practice,* Cambridge University Press, New York, 2000.

White, L.: *Second Language Acquisition and Universal Grammar,* Cambridge University Press, Cambridge, 2003.

Windeatt, S. Hardisty, D. and Eastment, D.: *The Internet,* Oxford University Press, Oxford, 2000.